D0937660

STRONG HELPERS' TEACHINGS

STRONG HELPERS' TEACHINGS
The Value of Indigenous Knowledges in the Helping Professions

Cyndy Baskin

Canadian Scholars' Press Inc.
Toronto

Strong Helpers' Teachings
By Cyndy Baskin

First published in 2011 by
Canadian Scholars' Press Inc.
180 Bloor Street West, Suite 801
Toronto, Ontario
M5S 2V6

www.cspi.org

Canadian Scholars' Press Inc. gratefully acknowledges financial support for our publishing activities from the Government of Canada through the Canada Book Fund (CBF).

Library and Archives Canada Cataloguing in Publication

Baskin, Cyndy, 1957–

Strong helpers' teachings : the value of Indigenous knowledges in the helping professions / Cyndy Baskin.

ISBN 978-1-55130-399-4

1. Social service. 2. Counseling. 3. Social values. 4. Native peoples—Canada—Social life and customs. I. Title.

HV40.B38 2011   361.3'208997071   C2011-904659-8

Text design by Aldo Fierro
Cover design by Aldo Fierro

The following photos were taken by Tania Anderson: Chapter 2 Girl with Trout, Chapter 3 Tundra and Sky, and Chapter 4 Hunting for Goose Eggs. All other chapter photos © Cyndy Baskin.

Cover photo © byphoto/Shutterstock

Printed and bound in Canada by UTP Print

TABLE OF CONTENTS

Author Biography

Cyndy Baskin, Ph.D., is of Mi'kmaq and Celtic descent. Originally from New Brunswick, she has been living in Toronto for many years. Her clan is the fish and her spirit name translates as something like "The Woman Who Passes on the Teachings."

Cyndy is currently an associate professor in the School of Social Work at Ryerson University in Toronto, Ontario. Her teaching and research interests centre on working with Aboriginal communities, especially on how Aboriginal world views can inform social work education, spirituality in social work practice, anti-racist inclusive schooling, post-colonial/anti-colonial theories and practices, and decolonizing research methodologies. She is a prolific writer with many publications including two novels, *The Invitation* (1992) and *Sage* (1999).

Cyndy is the chair of Ryerson University's Aboriginal Education Council, and the chair of the Toronto District School Board's Aboriginal Community Education Council.

Prior to joining Ryerson, Cyndy worked as a helper/social worker for many years within Aboriginal agencies in Toronto and assisted many First Nations communities to set up culture-based programs, the latter of which she continues to do today. She is also a consultant in the area of Aboriginal programming within various components of mainstream social services.

Cyndy enjoys spending time with her son and her friends, watching movies, reading, travelling, and listening to music. She is inspired by many strong Indigenous women, her spirituality, and the learners who engage with her in their efforts to make the world a better place for all.

Acknowledgements

First, chi meegwetch (a big thank you) to my son, Minadoo Makwa Baskin, for bringing joy into my world and for giving me a strong reason to do the work that I do. Thank you, my boy, for all those afternoons, evenings, and sometimes late-into-the-nights when we perched ourselves beside each other—me writing away on my computer and you playing video games on your 360—your patience was a gift of understanding. And I got to learn a little bit about video games even though I still suck at playing them. I love you best.

Next, wela'lin (thank you) to all the people who shared their stories with me for this book. Your generosity of time, knowledge, and sharing makes this book important.

Thank you to those who assisted me in researching and editing this work, especially to Tania Anderson—I could not have made it without your honest and helpful efforts. You helped to make this work worthwhile. And thank you to Marley Callow, Wesley Irwin, Bela McPherson, and Krystal Summers for all your work, which helped me to have a bit of a life while writing this book.

My thanks also go to the Faculty of Community Services and the Vice-Provost's Aboriginal Education Council at Ryerson University, which both assisted in funding, so I could hire research assistants. Not only did you help me, but you provided outstanding opportunities for Indigenous and non-Indigenous learners to build on their knowledge and skills.

Chapter 1
Starting at the Beginning

INTRODUCTION

Warm greetings! Welcome to *Strong Helpers' Teachings*! This book aims to encourage students, faculty, and practitioners in the helping professions, as well as anyone who has an interest in decolonization and healing the world, and learning and understanding fundamental aspects of Indigenous world views that can be applied to all peoples. It discourages attempts at teaching and taking up specific cultural practices that are not one's own. A way to gain from Indigenous knowledges—while not attempting to practise cultural specifics without the proper protocols, training, and respect—is to strive to embody Indigenous values that underpin and inform cultural practices. Indigenous world views can be learned and acted upon, whereas even though one may be aware of cultural practices, it does not mean that they should be taken up. I warmly invite readers to see that cultural practices need to remain in the hands and control of Indigenous peoples, but that there is much to be gained by welcoming Indigenous world views into one's life and work.

This introductory chapter will provide a background and a context to Indigenous approaches to helping that I believe can be valuable to all peoples of the world. But first it will provide some basic information about the history of colonization and its current impacts on Indigenous peoples; the historical role of social work with Indigenous peoples; and my concerns about the current appropriation of Indigenous cultural and spiritual practices.

WHO ARE INDIGENOUS PEOPLES?

Indigenous peoples are the original inhabitants of what the Haudenosaunee Nations call Turtle Island or what is also referred to as North America. According to the Canadian Constitution, there are three groups of Indigenous peoples—Indians, Métis, and Inuit. There is much diversity among us in languages, cultures, spirituality, political systems, and geographical territories. However, there is a foundational basis within Indigenous world views, values, and beliefs. This, along with a history of colonization, unites us. For the purposes of this book, the term "Indigenous peoples" will be used to include all three groups mentioned above, as well as those global peoples who are the original inhabitants of their territories. However, other terms, such as "Aboriginal" and "Native," are used by quoted authors and interviewees throughout the book.

In the 2006 Census, 1,172,790 Canadians (about 4 percent of the total population) reported some Indigenous ancestry (Statistics Canada, 2008). In this same Census, 54 percent of Indigenous peoples reported that they live in urban centres.

OVERVIEW OF THE HISTORY OF COLONIZATION

In order to understand the current struggles of Indigenous peoples today, one needs to understand the history and treatment of Indigenous peoples since the time of contact with those who came from European countries. I take the position that the near destruction of a land-based way of living, economic and social deprivation, substance abuse, the intergenerational cycle of violence, the breakdown of healthy family life, and the erosion of traditional values for many Indigenous peoples today are the direct result of colonization and ongoing systemic oppression. This is the history that has been deliberately left out of the Canadian consciousness.

According to Vern Morrissette (Anishnawbe Nation), Brad McKenzie, and Larry Morrissette (Anishnawbe Nation) (1993), colonization encompasses:

> ... cultural dimensions which involve efforts to achieve normative control over a minority group or culture. [With Indigenous peoples] these efforts included: displacement of traditional forms of governance with representative democracy and an authoritarian model of leadership; the devaluation of traditional spirituality, knowledge, and practices through the actions of missionaries, the residential school system, the health system, and the child welfare system; and the imposition of artificial legal distinctions among Indigenous peoples. (p. 94)

European peoples came to this continent with a world view based on Christianity and capitalism. Thus, the process of colonization grew in large part out of a belief that humankind was to "fill the earth and subdue it, rule over the fish in the sea, the birds of heaven, and every living thing that moves upon the earth" (Hamilton & Sinclair, 1991, p. 21). This world view was in direct contrast to that of the interconnected, holistic one of the original peoples of this land.

Historical events of systemic violence toward Indigenous peoples include:

- the brutality perpetrated upon Indigenous peoples by the French and English in securing pelts during the fur trade
- abuse against Indigenous peoples during the period of their slavery (early 1600s to 1833) in New France
- the use of women for the purpose of breeding as the direct result of a law passed in 1770 that sought to address the shortage of English and Scottish labourers
- the extermination of the entire Beothuck Nation on the east coast of Canada

- the wars waged against the original peoples of the Plains as a result of the British government's desire to "settle" the West
- the hanging of seven Indigenous men, including Louis Riel, in 1885 in western Canada
- the banning of political activity in Indigenous communities from the 1800s to the 1960s, which eliminated any challenges to colonial rule (Adams, 1999)

The Indian Act of 1876 was the vehicle by which the goal of assimilating Indigenous peoples was to be implemented, and it governed every facet of Indigenous life. This Act, along with the creation of the reserve system, imposed a White, capitalist, patriarchal governance structure on Indigenous communities. Through the Indian Act, the Canadian government sought to make Indigenous peoples into imitation Europeans, to eradicate Indigenous values through education and religion, and to establish new economic and political systems and new concepts of property. An oppressive, bureaucratic system of government has been imposed upon Indigenous peoples at the cost of many of our traditional governing practices and spiritual beliefs. A colonizing government, through the Indian Act, promoted hierarchical, male-dominated, political, economic, and social structures that led to the disintegration of traditional tribal structures, which were clan-oriented and based on the concepts of the extended family and collectivity. This Act, which continues to control the lives of Indigenous peoples today, created the reserve system, outlawed many spiritual practices, eliminated an egalitarian economic system, and ignored our inherent right to self-government. This, in turn, has created great social confusion within Indigenous communities and provided the environment from which the profound social and economic problems have taken root.

Specific practices of assimilation were the outlawing of traditional Indigenous ceremonies, the enforced training of men to become farmers and women to become domestics, and a systematic indoctrination of Christian theory and practice through the residential school system. The establishment of residential schools was rationalized by the assertion that these institutions would make Indigenous children competitive with their White counterparts—moral, industrious, and self-sufficient. These schools equated Euro-Canadian socio-economic standards and materialism with success, progress, and civilization. The schools taught Indigenous children to aspire to be like Euro-Canadians rather than who they were, and yet Euro-Canadians never accepted them as equals in Canadian society.

The residential school system is an example of Canada's shameful and paternalistic "Indian" policies used over a long period of time (Dion Stout & Kipling, 2003). These institutions disrupted and even destroyed many traditional ways of life for Indigenous peoples during their existence and for subsequent generations to come. These schools removed children at an early age from their homes and communities, and then forced them to reside within one of the institutions, where their languages and cultures were forbidden. In recent years, many Indigenous peoples have disclosed their experiences in these schools, which include painful stories of sexual and physical abuse by authorities who operated the schools and the death of many children at the hands of these same authorities (Annett & Lawless, 2007; Dion Stout & Kipling, 2003).

Residential schooling is a direct cause of the many struggles in Indigenous communities because, in addition to the widespread abuse of the children who attended these institutions, it led to the decline of parenting skills as children were denied their appropriate parental role models. This removal of Indigenous children from their parents, extended families, and communities continued with the child welfare system, which consistently placed children in White families and communities. Hence, generations of Indigenous children did not learn about the central role of family in their cultures (Fournier & Crey, 1997; Knockwood, 1992). The experiences of the residential school system were detrimental to the development of Indigenous peoples, as was the "sixties scoop," which followed when most of the residential schools were phased out in the 1960s (Royal Commission on Aboriginal Peoples [RCAP], 1996). The "sixties scoop" was a term used to describe the practice that emerged in the 1960s whereby large numbers of Indigenous children were removed from their families and placed in White homes, where many were treated in the same way as those who attended the residential schools (Johnston, 1983). The subsequent generations of the survivors of both the schools and the child welfare system continue to have poor overall health status, commonly referred to by Indigenous peoples as intergenerational effects. Ongoing effects of colonization produced various results that include poverty, high unemployment rates, lack of education, inadequate or lack of affordable housing, family violence, dependence on social services, and substance abuse (Shah, 2004). In view of this, many Indigenous peoples experience severe social and health inequalities as compared to other Canadians (Campaign 2000, 2005). In addition, in the 2001 Census, it was reported that 52.1 percent of all Indigenous children throughout Canada were identified as poor, and 46 percent of the

Indigenous population had an annual income of $10,000, which is considerably below the poverty line in Canada (Canadian Council on Social Development, 2003). The ongoing oppression of Indigenous peoples has been summarized in just a few words by federal Finance Minister Ralph Goodale, who declared during the 2005 federal budget release that: "for too long in too many ways, Canada's Indigenous peoples as first citizens—have been last in terms of opportunity for this country" (Fontaine, 2005).

It is also important to note that since the jurisdiction over "Indians" and land resources for "Indians" is assigned exclusively to the federal government, urban Indigenous peoples, organizations, and social services agencies are severely underfunded (RCAP, 1996). Generally, the federal government has a fiscal responsibility for "status Indians" living on reserves, and all other Indigenous peoples living off reserve are the responsibility of the provinces. This leaves the increasing population of many urban Indigenous people depending on municipal services and programming for survival.

In the effort to manage its fiscal position, the federal government has also limited the growth of expenditures related to a number of existing Indigenous programs by capping them (RCAP, 1996). It has also cut funding for some services, including those under health care, such as the Diabetes Prevention Program and the Prescription Drug Program, and has generally been reluctant to implement new programs, which has resulted in increasing pressure on provinces to assume responsibility for some essential services (Assembly of First Nations, 2005). Thus, Indigenous peoples perpetually find themselves caught between this jurisdictional volleying back and forth of the provincial and federal governments, which tends to leave them without services.

Everyone who lives in Canada today—both Indigenous peoples and Canadians—has inherited the Indian Act. Today's citizens did not write the Indian Act or send Indigenous children to residential schools, but we all need to deal with the injustice that has arisen because of these policies. We did not create the Industrial Revolution either, but nevertheless, we have to deal with the effects of it today, which include global warming and climate change. All people who live in Canada today are also all treaty people because these treaties do not only address Indigenous peoples and communities, but relationships between Indigenous peoples and Canadians. Even though Indigenous peoples did not get us to how things are today in the world, we are all in this together and everyone in Canada is here to stay. This reality means that we all need to work together for positive change for the future.

ROLE OF SOCIAL WORK IN COLONIZATION

Social work educator and activist, Akua Benjamin (2007), notes that the profession of social work has a long history of social justice-oriented activities, forms of resistance, and organizing against oppressive forces. She, like most social work academics, credits Jane Addams with the early formation of the profession in the 1890s, which centred on activism that began a long period of social action and reform. Then came a time when social work began to seek recognition from other helping professions, such as psychiatry and psychology, and moved into a period of what has been referred to as "scientific philanthropy," whereby the role of the social worker was to rationally and scientifically help the client to deal with whatever problems she or he had. Fortunately, as Benjamin (2007) writes, later on, during the 1960s, "social work again expressed methods of resistance, advocacy and transformation through social movements such as the feminist movement, civil rights movement and peace movement" (p. 199). Generous with her praise, Benjamin goes on to write:

> With the early settlement house movement, as well as these later phases, social work has a wonderful history of resistance and transformation. We need to thank these pioneers for their vision, their voices and their legacy. They provide examples of social work using radical strategy and tactics to address the major problems of society. These radical social workers were some of the main catalysts for change, laying the foundations of our current anti-oppressive approaches to social work and social transformation. (p. 199)

Is this view true of the profession of social work with *all* populations? Fortunately, Benjamin (2007) addresses this question as well in her work, stating, "However, let us not forget that while social movements were mobilizing in North America, whole populations were being decimated and systematically marginalized. Populations such as First Nations peoples faced genocide during Jane Addams's era and again with the continuation of the residential schools. . . . " (p. 199). In fact, Indigenous peoples were facing genocide long before Jane Addams began to form the profession of social work, and residential schools were operating while she was practising as they began in 1874, with the last one closing in 1996 (Indian and Northern Affairs Canada, 2004). Furthermore, during the 1960s, when social movements were flourishing, Indigenous children across North America were being removed from their families and communities by the thousands, not so much through residential schools, but through social work's most significant area—child welfare (Bennett, Blackstock & De La Ronde, 2005; Crichlow, 2002; Fournier & Crey, 1997; RCAP, 1996; Sinclair, 2009). Social workers were the people removing these children. Clearly, when it came to the feminist, civil rights, and peace movements, Indigenous peoples were not only excluded, they were still being targeted for assimilation and cultural genocide.

Cree social work practitioner and academic, Michael Hart (2002), takes up the topic of colonization by implicating social work as part of the continuing problem. He emphasizes that social work is not meant to challenge the colonial system since it hides behind its colonial altruism. Likewise, Morrissette, McKenzie, and Morrissette (1993) point out that "the ethnocentric nature of social work has received only inconsistent attention. Where cultural differences are recognized these have most often led to proposals for culturally sensitive practice and related guidelines for recognizing differences in cross-cultural work" (p. 92). Such practices and guidelines are insufficient as they divert attention from the current impacts of colonization upon Indigenous peoples while individualizing their struggles.

Lakota social work scholar, Hilary Weaver (2000), also implicates social workers in the colonization process as they have too often been an extension of it. She clearly and passionately provides a personal and political example of this implication by stating: "I have frequently heard Native people share stories from their childhoods of social workers who came and took them away or took away their relatives, in the midst of tears, screams, and much bewilderment. I cannot recollect ever hearing a story of a social worker who came in during a time of need and used advocacy or activism skills to make a positive difference" (p. 14).

FEARS OF APPROPRIATION

I have one fear about Indigenizing social work and other helping professions. This concern has to do with responsibility and appropriation. I have the responsibility to teach Indigenous ways of knowing and helping within the context of helping/social work, and I am accountable to students, communities, the Elders, and Traditional Teachers who have passed on their knowledge to me, and to the Creator for how this is done. I also have the responsibility to safeguard against the appropriation of Indigenous knowledges by students, colleagues, and educational institutions as explained by George J. Sefa Dei (2000):

> As we seek to integrate these knowledges into the conventional school systems, we must guard against appropriation and misappropriation. This is a contemporary challenge for educators. The process of validating Indigenous knowledges must not lead to Indigenous peoples losing control and ownership of knowledge. (p.47)

Indigenous teachings have so much to offer the world, but we need to figure out how to share their meanings and purposes without our practices being appropriated. It is disturbing to see that one can go on the Internet, find a "shaman," and pay her or him to participate in a "sweat lodge ceremony." In fact, some Traditional Teachers I know welcomed a non-Indigenous person into their lodge a few times, and this person went off, without their knowledge, and conducted these ceremonies for money with unsuspecting people. I also see countless posters in New Age shops and non-Indigenous healing centres advertising "women's full moon ceremonies," weekend retreats on finding one's "clan and animal guides," classes on how to become a "shaman," receiving a "spirit name," all led by non-Indigenous peoples who charge money. It disturbs me that some people believe it is all right to appropriate our practices while taking advantage of those who do not have the proper information to make informed decisions about their participation.

Jacqui Lavalley is an Anishnawbe Elder originally from Shawanaga First Nation, who worked for 23 years as a traditional cultural teacher at First Nations School of Toronto. She conducts ceremonies and shares teachings with many people throughout Toronto, recently completed a Master's of environmental studies, and intends to go on to a Ph.D. Jacqui succinctly states her position about how disrespectful and unethical appropriation is:

> Throughout Western history, Indigenous peoples have always been considered as being of no account. Many times over the course of any given day we are aware of the abuses of stealing and taking away our sacred languages and spiritualities. With respect to the value we place on all of creation, we believe that you cannot use indiscriminately our sacredness or our traditional practices. (J. Lavalley, personal communication, June 22, 2009)

Ruth Koleszar-Green, a Mohawk woman who is pursuing a Ph.D. and works as an academic adviser to Indigenous students, addressed the appropriation of Indigenous spirituality in an interview we did together. She spoke about this topic from the perspective of a student:

> In my classroom experiences, students wanted to know about Aboriginal spirituality. They wanted to know about ceremonies or traditions they had read about in a book and they expected me to explain these. They wanted to take part in ceremonies and thought that I could teach them how to do so. They wanted to use our sacred medicines like sweetgrass and sage as though it was incense.
>
> Damage was done to my spirit in the classroom by professors practicing Aboriginal spirituality. It was damaging as they didn't know what they were doing. They put students sitting in a circle without explaining why. When asked, they said it's just a way to set up a room; that it's not anything to do with spirituality or Aboriginal peoples; that sitting in a circle is a way for everyone to have eye contact. This isn't what a circle is all about. Aboriginal peoples are seen with disrespect, yet some of our practices can be appropriated to use whenever wanted, such as sitting in a circle. (K. Koleszar-Green, personal communication, November 26, 2008)

Appropriation is not only hurtful; it is also dangerous. Some non-Indigenous peoples include versions of our ceremonies and rituals, such as the sweat lodge and use of medicines and sacred objects, as part of their work with others (Matheson, 1996). Such helpers appear to believe that their participation in smudging or a spiritual ceremony authorizes them to imitate what they experienced in their own work with people. But consider what Lou Matheson (1996) has to say about this:

> In current American society, it is unacceptable and usually illegal for people to perform surgery or provide legal representation without proper credentials. There are set standards for mental health practitioners and academic degrees for theologians. It is nearly unheard of for a person to publicly practice that for which he or she is not prepared. The road to shamanistic practice is made of knowledge. This knowledge is accumulated through years (sometimes as many as 10 or 15 years) of direct, sometimes life-threatening experiences with the earth, the elements, and the spirit

world. These experiences are guided by centuries of shamans learning to understand the universe and our relation to it as kept by generations before. The shaman's gift is power, earned through years of extreme sacrifice and self-discipline. His or her "diploma" is the understanding of how to use instruments, and plants, and songs, and communication with spirits for the power to heal. These tribal specific practices have become integrated into the shaman's culture, but the concept is the same in nearly every Indian group. (p. 51)

When I refer to the appropriation of Indigenous spirituality as dangerous, I am not exaggerating. Consider the recent example of James A. Ray, the non-Indigenous president of a multimillion-dollar company in California, who is also viewed as a New Age self-help guru who promises his followers a path of "harmonic wealth in all areas of life" (Archibold, 2010). Ray, who had been organizing retreats for seven years at the Angel Valley Spiritual Retreat Center near Sedona, Arizona, conducted a "sweat lodge ceremony," which he referred to as a "warrior ceremony," in October 2009 (Archibold, 2010; Katz, 2009). The "sweat lodge" was part of a five-day spiritual retreat that is reported to have cost participants thousands of dollars to attend (Archibold, 2010). Apparently, the participants fasted for 36 hours prior to the ceremony, and between 55 to 65 of them were packed into a 415 square-foot "sweat lodge" for over two hours (Katz, 2009). Three people died and a further 18 people were hospitalized following this ceremony (Archibold, 2010, Katz, 2009). Ray has been charged with three counts of manslaughter for the deaths of the "sweat lodge" attendees (Archibold, 2010).

These are the devastating consequences that can happen when those who do not know what they are doing dabble in spiritual undertakings that they have not been diligently trained to conduct. The tragic deaths of these three people teach us all how cautious we need to be when and with whom we enter the spiritual realm through ceremonies and other practices.

How do non-Indigenous students, faculty, and practitioners in the helping professions take up Indigenous ways of helping, then? The answer lies in concentrating on Indigenous world views rather than on cultures and spiritual practices. A world view is a foundation that guides how one sees the environment/land, people, communities, challenges, causes of problems, and possible solutions. It provides principles, values, and ethics for social work research, teaching, and practice. The position of this book is that much of Indigenous world views—such as a holistic approach, connection to the land, a focus on the family and community rather than the individual, healing instead of punishment, and the inclusion of spirituality—can be considered universal for many peoples of the world. Cultures, on the other hand, grow out of world views. Cultures are expressed through languages, ceremonies, governance, clan systems, and, yes, food. Complex, ever evolving, and adapting to environments and circumstances, cultures make little sense out of context and, unless one lives that culture, can be easily misunderstood.

World views and knowledges can be learned as they are general. Cultures cannot be learned unless one is immersed in the particular culture by, for example, living and working in an Indigenous community or working for an Indigenous agency where specific practices are taught and one participates in them. This view is, of course, applicable to all peoples of the world. For example, there are African world views and African-centred approaches to social work. However, there is no one African culture. How can there be? Africa is a continent! Rather, there are many African cultures that differ from one territory to another.

Here is an example of a difference between a world view and a culture: Within Indigenous world views, a holistic approach means, in part, looking at a person as having four aspects—spiritual, physical, emotional, and psychological—that impact on each other and need to be addressed in the healing process. *All* people are believed to have these aspects. However, there are specific ways in which the healing of these aspects will occur according to each particular culture of each particular Indigenous Nation. The idea is not to attempt to learn the healing practices specific to every culture of every Nation, which is not possible anyway. Rather, the suggestion is to consider the belief that people have four aspects that need to be taken into account in healing. What practices to implement in this process will depend on the service user and the helper/social worker.

Jennifer Ajandi, Ph.D., is currently a part-time instructor in the School of Social Work at Ryerson University and in the Centre for Women's Studies and in sociology at Brock University. Jennifer has also taught a course in Child and Youth Studies at Brock University. She is not Indigenous. In an interview for this book, she spoke briefly about how she views appropriation:

There is a line between valuing Aboriginal knowledges and appropriating them. I would say that it's a never ending journey to learn where the balance lies between these. I do a lot of reflection through journaling and questioning, which usually helps me know what is appropriate through what feels right to me. Some people view Aboriginal peoples' spirituality as exotic, which is clearly in part where appropriation comes from. There are some things that I would never do, such as conduct a smudge or a sacred circle in the classroom, as these would clearly be appropriation. What I do is focus on anti-colonial theory and acknowledging Aboriginal perspectives as equivalent to all other perspectives, which I see as appropriate and helpful to my teaching. (J. Ajandi, personal communication, December 8, 2008)

Liz Arger is a non-Indigenous psychotherapist and visual artist with many years of experience in the helping profession with Indigenous peoples. Currently, Liz works at the Centre for Addiction and Mental Health (CAMH) Aboriginal Services and in a private practice in Toronto. When I asked Liz to talk about what is and is not appropriation of Indigenous ways of helping, she told me:

If a non-Aboriginal social work practitioner has an Aboriginal mentor to teach them and they are learning by living the particular teachings, then this is not appropriating. However, such a helper needs to keep in mind at all times that this learning is not about one's ego, nor is the helper to romanticize the situation.

Such fortunate helpers need to honour the generosity of Aboriginal people, especially Elders, who welcome them, appreciate their diversity, and share their teachings, all of which helps to expand the understandings of the helper and which can be transmitted to how they work with people. It's amazing how some Aboriginal people share a little of what they know with others, considering the history of colonization, appropriation, and lack of acknowledgement of what has come from Aboriginal world views and cultures and how this has shaped and influenced Canada. Learners must always be sure to name where, from whom, and in what context knowledge comes from as not doing so is appropriation. They also need to be respectful of what they do not know about Aboriginal people and their world views. This sets them up as ongoing students who are open to learning. I think those students and practitioners who connect with others on a spiritual level will likely be open to many tools for helping. They are the ones who will see how Aboriginal knowledges can inform their practice and help them to take care of themselves. (L. Arger, personal communication, April 3, 2009)

There is literature that supports what Jennifer and Liz communicate about appropriation. Both Indigenous and non-Indigenous writers caution that misunderstandings can occur when non-Indigenous peoples attempt to interpret or conduct Indigenous spiritual practices without a true understanding of the meaning or power of these practices (Garrett, Brubaker, Torres-Rivera, West-Olatunji & Cornwill, 2008). When writing about group counselling, for example, these authors emphasize that the choice to include Indigenous healing methods "should be based on the intent to use a technique that provides healing for group participants in very universal ways" (Garrett et al., 2008, p. 190). They also address what must not be done by non-Indigenous practitioners taking up Indigenous practices. They state that this "should not be based on the intent to represent themselves as 'healers' in a Native tradition, to conduct Native ceremonies, or to make Indians out of group participants. Thus, intention is the key to respectful implementation" (Garrett et al., 2008, p. 190).

In the winter of 2009, I taught a graduate course, "Indigenous Knowledges in Social Work," in the School of Social Work at Ryerson University. The students came from diverse backgrounds: a few were Indigenous, others identified as South Asian, Caribbean, and mixed blood; they differed in ages and sexual orientations; some were parents; others were working in the field of social work while they attended school. At the end of the course, I invited the students to participate in a Sharing Circle with me for this book. Most of them responded with excitement at this request. The following is a discussion they had about appropriation:

Eddy: Conscious awareness will help to make sure that one does not appropriate Indigenous knowledges.

Nathalie: Yep, in order not to appropriate, we need to know our own identities. And everyone needs to look at how knowledge is claimed to be known and be accountable for this.

Julia: There are some Indigenous peoples who will say no one else should be picking up our teachings. It is a form of resistance to be strict about sharing; we need to honour our teachings and hold them close.

Some of us are afraid to share much with non-Indigenous peoples as they know that the teachings can be taken and used inappropriately. I am talking about how teachings have been misconstrued, for instance, by taking a teaching and only using a piece of it to suit one's interest.

Here's an example: Recently at my placement, a well-intended colleague had a medicine mask from our society and was attempting to respect it and use it as a way of protecting himself/herself. However, this is seen as inappropriate because when one receives a mask, there is a ceremony about taking care of it and it must be continued to be taken care of forever through ceremonies. This person purchased a book written by a non-Native person who observed our teachings. S/he believed because it was written in a book, a mask could be used by anyone. Of course, I shared my teachings about this and now it is up to him/her to do what s/he wishes.

There are times when it is appropriate to share knowledge. Sometimes we need to advocate for the clientele we are working with or explain or educate other helpers about ceremonies or teachings which involve a person's well-being. For example, if a client belongs to a bear society and has dreams or visions of bears while awake, this may seem as a delusion or hallucination to the worker, especially if the dream or vision is directing the person toward some form of action. If this is not discussed, the worker may be focused on a mental health diagnosis. We would want to engage the worker in exploring a spiritual possibility for this behaviour first and then see what happens. (Eddy, Nathalie, and Julia, personal communication, April 6, 2009)

WHO IS THIS BOOK FOR?

It is my hope that this book will be taken up by both Indigenous and non-Indigenous students, practitioners, and faculty across the globe in the human services, particularly social work. For some who are Indigenous, the content of the book may confirm and reinforce what they already know. For others, perhaps it will offer new ideas, possibilities, and insights that can be implemented into their practice and lives. Still others may not have heard of some or all of the content. One area of diversity among Indigenous peoples is being on a continuum in terms of knowing about and practising our knowledges and world views. At one end of the continuum are those who have a deep understanding of our knowledges and live the practices every day. At the other end are those who have never had the opportunity to learn about their world views due to the effects of colonization, such as growing up in White adoptive homes, where their knowledges were not appreciated. Then, of course, there is a range of understanding and experiences between these two positions.

This book is also written for non-Indigenous peoples in the helping professions for several reasons. The first is that, especially for today's social work students, Indigenous peoples, their concerns, and perspectives must be central to any discussion about the discipline. This stance is significant because the descendants of the original peoples of this land need to be recognized, the descendants of the settler population can be assisted in acknowledging and appreciating whose land they are on, and the profession of social work would gain more respect by taking responsibility for its role in the past and ongoing oppression of Indigenous peoples and including our knowledges as a legitimate theory in the area of helping.

Second, another reason why this book is for non-Indigenous students and practitioners is because of its encouragement to those who are not White to consider that they may have much in common with us in terms of world views, such as how we view Elders, the family, and the community. If this book speaks to you in such a way, perhaps it will offer pathways to collaboration with Indigenous peoples and to the recognition of your knowledges within the profession of social work.

Third, since many social work policies and practices are clearly not helping the vast majority of service users, why do we continue to repeat what is not working? Why not open ourselves up to other ways of helping? This is particularly significant for practitioners who work in urban centres, where the populations are diverse in terms of world views and, of course, cultures. There is no doubt that we all have something to teach one another. If we want to have the finest helping approaches possible, does it not make sense to bring the best of the entire world's knowledges together?

Lastly, for faculty and other instructors of social work, this book may be useful as a teaching resource that does not problematize Indigenous peoples. This is a shift for students' learning as it provides an opportunity for them to see Indigenous peoples as strong and active contributors to ways of helping rather than as constant victims and mere recipients of social services. In addition, Indigenous faculty are expected to inform themselves about and then teach social work theories that do not arise from our knowledges and that are about many populations other than our own. It follows, then, that non-Indigenous faculty should be expected to learn and then teach something about Indigenous theories of helping and the historical and contemporary challenges facing Indigenous peoples to ensure equity within the discipline. This book, which includes the voices of many Indigenous helpers, could offer a comfortable beginning point for such teaching.

WHAT THIS BOOK IS AND IS NOT ABOUT

This book will focus on a general application of some aspects of Indigenous world views and how these can be implemented with all peoples involved in the helping professions within contemporary practice environments. It privileges Indigenous knowledges as having relevance for all. It offers a foundation of values and ethical principles that can be applied in social work practice with individuals, families, and communities. Centring Indigenous knowledges will be viewed as one area that can be a part of decolonization in Canada and elsewhere.

As this book is written by an Indigenous scholar and social worker, its standpoint does not come from an observer of Indigenous world views and helping practices, but rather from someone who is immersed in and connected to these experiences. The book privileges and, therefore, places at the forefront the scholarship of Indigenous academics and social workers with an experiential orientation, which is different from work written *about* Indigenous peoples. The approach to the book is consistent with Indigenous, critical, postmodern, and post-colonial approaches, although the latter three theories may be challenged at times.

What this book will not focus on is the history of colonization and its current impacts, although these will inevitably come up now and again. It will not focus on legislative, jurisdictional, and social welfare contexts or their analysis. Of course, these "bigger picture" issues are crucial in the teaching and learning of social work, and in fact need to be emphasized in all areas of education at every level. However, I and many other Indigenous scholars and community members have written extensively on this topic (Adams, 1999; Baskin, 2003, 2006; Crichlow, 2002; Fournier & Crey, 1997; Hamilton & Sinclair, 1991; Knockwood, 1992; Locust, 1988; Weaver, 2000), but few have emphasized the value of our world views for the betterment of all humanity and what this could look like in social work practice.

INDIGENOUS APPROACHES CAN ENRICH SOCIAL WORK

Indigenous peoples have been living according to a holistic approach, which includes spirituality, since the beginning of creation. It is only recently that some Western methods are making space for incorporating these practices as a result of their having been "proven" to be helpful in maintaining good holistic health. In addition, it is clear that the problems of the world are not being solved merely by professional expertise. There is an obvious interest in self and spiritual development, since books on this topic were the fastest-growing reading materials in non-fiction in both North America and Europe a decade ago (Jayanti, 1999). This interest has continued to grow as, according to a national survey conducted by the Higher Education Research Institute at UCLA in 2004, 80 percent of students have an interest in spirituality (Intervarsity, 2005). There is also fascinating information on the growth of the spiritual tours industry. According to Radigan (2007), one travel company called Globus in Littleton, Colorado, which has a religious travel division, has seen a 650 percent increase since it was launched in 2004. Furthermore, the market for spiritual and religious travel has grown into an $18 billion industry worldwide (Radigan, 2007). Clearly, many people of the world are seeking to incorporate spirituality into their lives. Indigenous peoples are leaders in including spirituality in our everyday lives and within helping processes. We have so much to offer in assisting in the healing of all humankind.

Most important, perhaps, is the concept of incorporating spirituality as power and knowledge throughout everyday life. In social work discourse, reminding service users of their inner power and knowledge is called "prevention." Incorporating a belief in spirituality as power involves reflexive knowledge, which is less preoccupied with outcome and more concerned with process. Spirituality encourages social workers not to construct an understanding of the client's reality through knowledge derived only empirically as this may block other ways of knowing. Alternative means to knowledge and power acquisition, such as those that arise from emotion and intuition, can be explored in social work discourse. Intuition, in particular, allows the social worker to have "direct, immediate knowledge of something without relying on the conscious use of reason or sense perception" (Percesepe, 1991, as cited in Damianakis, 2001, p. 5). With respect to spirituality, intuition is usually rooted in the collective unconscious. In its most valuable application, social workers' offerings of intuitive insights or hunches with their clients can affect those who experience them in integrative, powerful, and meaningful ways (Richards

& Bergin, 1997). To make this even more powerful, however, practitioners can assist their clients in learning how to access and implement their own intuitions and other spiritual gifts. In addition, social work practitioners can also help with service users' positive identity formation through a relationship with the collective unconscious that they share with other people.

No helping profession can be whole without including the spiritual dimension. If practitioners ignore it, then they are not fully responding to the needs of people who access services. Ideally, social work practice includes a focus on client strengths. Spirituality is the most powerful source of strength because everyone who chooses to go on in this world operates on some form of faith. A spiritual value or belief can be a powerful resource in a person's life that can be used in problem solving, coping, and trauma recovery. I advocate that spirituality be implemented within all aspects of social work. We must not relegate spirituality to only concerns about death and dying for it is just as much about life and living!

Spirituality, within Indigenous world views, also includes one's connection to the land. Throughout history, the place of learning has most often been within the community and on the land for Indigenous peoples. Watkins (2001) explains Indigenous peoples' relationship to the land as:

> . . . not one of ownership per se, for we are owned more by the land, tied to it by obligations and responsibilities established by our ancestors in times far back, and we pass those obligations on to our children and grandchildren. (p. 41)

Similarly, Hawaiian educator Meyer (2008) describes the relationship of space and knowing as:

> . . . place is the locus of all knowledge, its origin and function. We come from place and we grow in place. In developing relationship with place, one does not really learn about land, but one learns from land. Place is seen as fullness, as interactions, as thoughts planted . . . place is not merely physical; it engages knowledge and contextualizes knowing. (p. 21)

I see these elements of Indigenous world views as valuable to *all* peoples. If we see a person's concerns as inevitable life problems that everyone encounters from time to time, then we will see them as manifestations of an ongoing collective struggle instead of as individual deficits. This speaks to the impacts of colonization and other forms of oppression in society and moves away from judging, pathologizing, and blaming those who are struggling. Involving natural helpers could be valuable for all social workers as well as collaborating with these helpers is about community organizing and building on capacities, which leads to self-determination.

CONCLUSION

The messages in this introduction—the importance of understanding the current impacts of colonization for both Indigenous and non-Indigenous peoples; how current social work theories can work with Indigenous approaches to helping; and how these approaches have much to offer social work education, practice, and research—will all be explored in greater detail in the rest of this book. The next 13 chapters will discuss self-reflexivity and self-care; social work theories as seen through an Indigenous lens; centring *all* helping approaches; values, an emphasis on a holistic approach, the significance of community, spirituality, and justice that can be healing; caring for families and children; global connections, research, and pedagogy. There will be a final chapter that wonders "what if?" All of these topics will be viewed through a lens of how Indigenous approaches to helping can enrich the world for all peoples.

Just before proceeding, though, I would like to emphasize a fact that is rarely noted regarding Indigenous peoples. Despite the tremendous horrors of colonization and its ongoing implications for Indigenous peoples today, including the fact that our rates of youth suicide, incarceration, and addictions are higher than that of the non-Indigenous population, the majority of us are not in prison, addicted to alcohol and drugs, or violent. Rupert Ross (2008), a non-Indigenous assistant Crown attorney in northwestern Ontario, is one of the few writers who raises the possibilities about this fact:

> The logical question, then, involves asking where such families found the vision, strength and psychological wherewithal to maintain their health through decades living in this psychological war zone. If we can identify what has kept them healthy, we might then be closer to identifying what is needed to return health to others as well. (p. 12)

Shall we begin the journey then?

REFERENCES

Adams, H. (1999). *A tortured people: The politics of colonization*. Penticton: Theytus.

Annett, K.D. & Lawless, L. (Producers). (2007). *Unrepentant* [DVD]. Available from: http://www.hiddenfromhistory.org/

Archibold, R. C. (2010, February 3). Guru indicted in 3 deaths at Arizona sweat lodge. *The New York Times.*Retrieved from http://nytimes.com

Assembly of First Nations. (n.d.). Description of AFN. Retrieved from http://www.afn.ca/article.asp?id=58

Assembly of First Nations. (2005). Lack of federal funding threatens vital diabetes prevention program. *First Nations Health Bulletin* (Winter–Spring). Pp. 1–4. Ottawa: Assembly of First Nations Health and Social Secretariat.

Baskin, C. (2003). Structural social work as seen from an Aboriginal perspective. In W. Shera (Ed.), *Emerging perspectives on anti-oppressive practice* (pp. 65–79). Toronto: Canadian Scholars' Press Inc.

Baskin, C. (2007) Structural determinants as the cause of homelessness for Aboriginal youth. *Critical Social Work,* 8, 1. Retrieved from www.criticalsocialwork.com

Baskin, C. (2005). Storytelling circles: Reflections of Aboriginal protocols in research. *Social Work Review*, 22, 2, 171–187.

Benjamin, A. (2007). Doing anti-oppressive social work: The importance of resistance, history, and strategy. In D. Baines (Ed.), *Doing anti-oppressive practice: Building transformative politicized social work* (pp. 196–204). Halifax: Fernwood Publishing.

Bennett, M., Blackstock, C. & De La Ronde, R. (2005). *A literature review and annotated bibliography on aspects of Indigenous child welfare in Canada* (2nd ed.). Ottawa: First Nations Child and Family Caring Society of Canada. Retrieved from http://www.accel-capea.ca/pdf/childwelfarelitreview.pdf

Campaign 2000. (2005). *Decision time for Canada: Let's make poverty history: 2005 Report card on child poverty in Canada.* Retrieved from http://www.campaign2000.ca/reportCards/national/2005EngNationalReportCard.pdf

Canadian Council on Social Development. (2003). *Indigenous children in poverty in urban communities: Social exclusion and the growing racialization of poverty in Canada.* Notes for presentation to subcommittee on children and youth at risk of the standing committee on human resources development and the status of persons with disabilities. Retrieved from http://www.ccsd.ca/pr/2003/Indigenous.htm

Crichlow, W. (2002). Western colonization as disease: Native adoption and cultural genocide. *Critical Social Work,* 3(1). Retrieved from http://www.uwindsor.ca/criticalsocialwork

Damianakis, T. (2001). Postmodernism, spirituality, and the creative writing process: Implications for social work practice. *Families in Society, 82*(1), 23–34. doi: 10.1606/1044-3894.218

Davies, B. & Hare, R. (1990). Positioning: The discursive production of selves. *Journal for the Theory of Social Behaviour20* (1), 43–63.

Dei, G.J.S. (2000). Rethinking the role of Indigenous knowledges in the academy. *International Journal of Inclusive Education, 4*(2), 111–132. doi: 10.1080/136031100284849

Dion Stout, M. & Kipling, G. (2003). *Indigenous people, resilience, and the residential school legacy.* Ottawa: Aboriginal Healing Foundation.

Fontaine, P. (2005). Federal budget fails to offer solutions to First Nations poverty crisis. Assembly of First Nations news release, February 23. Retrieved from http://www.afn.ca.

Fournier, S. & Crey, E. (1997). *Stolen from our embrace: The abduction of First Nations children and the restoration of Indigenous communities.* Vancouver: Douglas & McIntyre.

Garrett, M.T., Brubaker, M., Torres-Rivera, E., West-Olatunji, C. & Cornwill, W.L. (2008). The medicine of coming to center: Use of the Native American centering technique—Ayeli—to promote wellness and healing in group work. *The Journal for Specialists in Group Work, 33*(2), 179–198. doi: 10.1080/01933920801977322.

Hamilton, A.C. & Sinclair, C.M. (1991). *Report of the Indigenous justice inquiry of Manitoba.* Winnipeg: Province of Manitoba.

Hart, M. (2002). *Seeking mino-pimatisiwin: An Aboriginal approach to helping.* Halifax: Fernwood Publishing.

Indian and Northern Affairs Canada (2004). Residential Schools. Retrieved from http://www.ainc-inac.gc.ca/ach/lr/ks/plhst/plhst_rsscl-eng.asp

Intervarsity. (2005). *Spiritual interest high among college students.* Retrieved from http://www.intervarsity.org/news/spiritual-interest-high-among-college-students

Jayanti, S. (1999). *Valuing the future: Education for spiritual development. Experiencing the difference: The role of experiential learning in youth development.* Conference report from the Brathay Youth Conference, Ambleside, England (pp. 43–50). (ED 444797) Ambleside, UK.

Johnston, P. (1983). *Native children and the child welfare system.* Toronto: Canadian Council on Social Development and James Lorimer & Company Publishers.

Katz, N. (2009, October 12). Sweat lodge death investigation turns to self-help guru James Arthur Ray. *CBS News.com.* Retrieved from http://cbsnews.com.

Knockwood, I. (1992). *Out of the depths.* Lockeport: Roseway Publishing.

Locust, C. (1988). Wounding the spirit: Discrimination and traditional American Indian belief systems. *Harvard Educational Review, 58*(3), 315–330.

Matheson, L. (1996). Valuing spirituality among Native American populations. *Counselling and Values, 41*(1), 51–59.

Meyer, M. (2008). Indigenous knowledge featured speakers. In M.P. Kumar (Ed.), *Seeing ourselves in the mirror: Giving life to learning: Executive summary and highlights* (pp. 30–33). University of Saskatchewan, Aboriginal Education Research Centre, Saskatoon, Saskatchewan, and First Nations and Adult Higher Education Consortium, Calgary, Alberta. Retrieved from http://aerc.usask.ca/projects/ablkcpublications.html

Morrissette, V., McKenzie, B. & Morrissette, L. (1993). Towards an Aboriginal model of social work practice. *Canadian Social Work Review, 10*(1), 91–108.

Percesepe, G. (1991). *Philosophy: An introduction to the labour of reason.* New York: Macmillan.

Radigan, M. (2007, February). *Companies see increased interest in spiritual tours.* Religion news service. Retrieved on from www.beliefnet.com

Richards, P. & Bergin, A. (1997). *A spiritual strategy for counseling and psychotherapy.* Washington, DC: American Psychological Association.

Ross, R. (2008). *Colonization, complex PTSD, and Aboriginal healing: Exploring diagnoses and strategies for recovery.* Adult Custody Division Health Care Conference. Vancouver: British Columbia Ministry of Public Safety and Solicitor General.

Royal Commission on Aboriginal Peoples. (1996). *Perspectives and realities: The search for belonging, perspectives of youth.* Ottawa: Indian and Northern Affairs Canada.

Shah, C. (2004). Indigenous health. In D. Raphael (Ed.), *Social determinants of health: Canadian perspectives* (pp. 267–280). Toronto: Canadian Scholars' Press Inc.

Sinclair, R. (2009). Identity or racism? Aboriginal transracial adoption. In R. Sinclair, M.A. Hart & G. Bruyere (Eds.), *Wicihitowin: Aboriginal social work in Canada* (pp. 89–113). Winnipeg: Fernwood Publishing.

Statistics Canada. (2008). *Aboriginal peoples highlight tables, 2006 census.* (97-558-XIE) Retrieved from http://www12.statcan.ca

Watkins, J. (2001). Place-Meant. *American Indian Quarterly, 25*(1), 41–45. doi: 10.1353/aiq.2001.0014

Weaver, H. (2000). Activism and American Indian issues: Opportunities and roles for social workers. *Journal of Progressive Human Services, 11*(1), 3–22. doi:10.1300/J059v11n01_02

Chapter 2
The Self Is Always First in the Circle

INTRODUCTION

There is an understanding within Indigenous world views that individuals locate themselves within their collective identity, which helps to identify the values they live by. This location of the self is somewhat like the concept of self-reflexivity within critical forms of social work theory and practice. I believe that the ability to engage in an ongoing exploration of our subjectivity in relation to how we teach and practise social work ought to include self-care. However, helpers are not solely responsible for taking care of themselves. The agencies, organizations, and institutions that employ social workers also need to take responsibility for the well-being of these helpers. In order to be effective in their work and healthy in mind, body, and spirit, social workers need strong institutional support from the places that employ them. Help for the helpers is one of the areas that is much emphasized within Indigenous world views, and can be of value to all who work in the helping professions.

LET'S BEGIN WITH ME

All Indigenous peoples I come into contact with always have an understanding about how we identify ourselves. We introduce ourselves geographically, politically, and genealogically. This is the first step in introducing and positioning myself.

My name is On-koo-khag-kno kwe, which roughly translates into the English language as "the woman who makes links or who links things," such as our teachings and people, together. I am a woman who makes links or who passes on our teachings, spirituality, understandings, and insights. I have come to see myself as "The Woman Who Passes on the Teachings," for that seems to be exactly what I do. I am a teacher. My Nations are Mi'kmaq and Celtic. I believe my name also connects to the fact that I am of mixed heritage. I see myself as a link between Indigenous and non-Indigenous peoples in a similar way to how Métis people are viewed as a bridge between these two peoples. I come from very small communities in northern New Brunswick. I say "communities" because I come from more than one; there's my mother's home community, my father's home community, the town where I was born, and another hamlet where we had our house. I lived in all of these places and they are all home to me.

My clan is the fish (salmon). My clan also tells something about me, for those who are a part of the fish clan are said to be the intellectuals, philosophers, mediators, and those who help others when they are struggling. I have lived in Toronto for most of my life now and, while here, I proudly follow the teachings of the Anishnawbe Nation whose territory I live in. These instructions were given to me by the Elders and Traditional Teachers who became my guides and mentors when I first came to Toronto. I was warmly welcomed into these Teachers' lodges and ceremonies, but explicitly told that while I was in their territory, I was to follow their specific teachings and practices. They added that when I was back home in Mi'kmaq territory, I would then follow my own ways. I am greatly privileged to carry the teachings of two Nations, which came about through the generosity and acceptance of the Anishnawbe people who took me under their wing.

I have four university degrees—one in English, two in social work, and one in sociology and equity studies in education. Although now separated, I was married (traditionally and civilly), and have one biological son, two stepchildren, a daughter-in-law, and two grandsons. I am committed to my family and to my community.

I was doing social work long before I got any academic degrees. I have worked in Indigenous communities, mostly in Toronto, for the past 25 years in community development, child welfare, family violence interventions, culture-based program development, healing initiatives, and training of other service providers. All of this work has taken place in Indigenous agencies and in communities striving to implement culture-based and community-controlled approaches. Most of what I learned that was valuable to me as a social worker came, not from school, but from other Indigenous helpers, service users, and experiences.

Two reasons led me to become an educator. The first was my social work education's failure to provide me with either theories or practice skills that enhanced or that were even related to the work I was doing in Aboriginal communities. Second, I came to believe that I must have something of value to share with others after all those years of social work practice. I am determined to make change within the system by making education more inclusive, especially for Indigenous students. Despite my critique of social work, I am honoured to be a part of a profession that grew out of the values of love, justice, community, and mutual responsibility. Each of these values encompasses my own spirituality. I believe that spirituality is the connection to all that is in existence. It comes from within and from outside the self. It is meant to assist us as individuals, families, and communities. Spirituality is also about resistance, and it connects us to the work of social change, which, I believe, must be the major focus of social work.

I have privilege in this society. I am able-bodied, heterosexual, light-skinned, highly educated, a university instructor, from the lower middle class, and in good physical health. I am oppressed because dominant society assigns me multiple marginalized identities as an Indigenous woman with two disabilities, which are clinical depression and an anxiety disorder. Some of my family members and I have also been the clients of social workers. Subsequently, part of locating myself is to state what Craig Womack (1997), of the Creek-Cherokee

Nations, does when he writes, "I'm not simply writing *about* Indians; I'm telling my family's story, and my story, which is at once Indian and poor and southern and white and a combination of all these things" (p. 48).

This brings me to some thoughts on being an insider/outsider person. I am, of course, an insider as I am an Indigenous person who is involved in many capacities with Indigenous communities. Yet, at the same time, I am an outsider because of the privileges that I have. Hence, I am an insider with many privileges, which make me an outsider. I am a combination of the two. I do not view myself as one who moves from one to the other and back again as some of my Indigenous colleagues do, meaning that they may be able to compartmentalize their identities depending on whether they are engaged in professional activities or personal activities. Rather, I am a complete, holistic package, such that, regardless of whether I am writing a paper or attending a sweat lodge ceremony, my privileges are with me.

I am quite conscious of the fact that I am viewed as a role model in Toronto's Indigenous community and in my home community as well. I am also a helper to the Elders who teach me. Therefore, I am closely watched. Thus, how I conduct myself both professionally and personally lives with me (and likely with my family) forevermore. It is personal as well as political for us insiders. Of course, having been a social worker for several years in Indigenous communities, I am used to this. Interestingly enough, this has benefited me in a way because it has always kept me on my toes. Accountability is important for all of us.

Maori scholar, Linda Tuhiwai Smith (2000), has good advice about being and staying accountable or keeping on one's toes. She writes about being an insider conducting research:

> The role of an "official insider voice" is also problematic. The comment "she or he lives in it therefore they know" certainly validates experiences but for a researcher to assume that their own experience is all that is required is arrogant. One of the difficult risks insider researchers take is to "test" their own taken-for-granted views about their community. It is a risk because it can unsettle beliefs, values, relationships and the knowledge of different histories. (p. 139)

The politics of representation is, of course, a contentious issue, so I will make my position as an educator, practitioner, and researcher explicit. This is in part why I sometimes write this book in the first person. The other major reason is that I intend to write from a place constructed from the values and principles of Indigenous traditions for gathering and passing on knowledge. These values privilege and respect a first-person voice. Hence, for me, there is a political project that connects to the intellectual agenda.

Until I attended the Ontario Institute for Studies in Education/University of Toronto (2001–2005) to get my doctorate, I always had teachers who were White, readings were always written by White authors, and fellow students were always White. I was always the only one who was "different." Being at school was painful. I was an isolated, persecuted, sad student. And yet, I learned how to read and write in these places, and this became my escape from the hurt. No matter what was done to me, it could not stifle my desire to learn. The harder schooling became for me, the more I delved into my studies. The more I heard that I would not make it to university, the more I grew determined to do exactly that. Great damage was done to me; some of it has been repaired, while some of the damage will never be repaired. It is a part of who I am. There were many times when I felt down, dropped out, and changed direction, but education is clearly my calling, and it has become a powerful symbol for me.

My story is, of course, a familiar one for many Indigenous peoples across North America, Australia, and New Zealand. Education, like social work, has more often than not been our enemy, a major arm of colonialism. For me, this is a lived reality. Being in the academy and becoming an educator, then, is one of my most powerful acts of resistance and anti-colonial activity.

SELF-REFLEXIVITY

It has always struck me as odd, especially from an anti-oppressive perspective, which has a strong focus on issues of power, that social workers expect service users to reveal incredibly personal information about themselves, usually right from the initial contact. These encounters occur without the social workers revealing anything about themselves other than their names, job descriptions, and credentials. Without any relationship-building, the service users are expected to share their stories of, for example, childhood sexual abuse, pain, homelessness, or reasons for drug abuse. Service users are supposed to trust such intimacies with these strangers, who ask questions and fill out forms, and who most likely have no idea what it is like to not have a place to live or to feel so utterly desperate that one must go through this humiliating experience in order to receive help. Should a service user refuse to answer some of the social worker's questions, she or he risks being viewed as "unco-operative," "resistant," or "not ready for help," which means that services may be denied. How many of us would feel comfortable walking into a stranger's office and disclosing that we are being physically abused by a partner or that we do not have enough food to feed our children today?

This power imbalance between social worker and service user is what I think of first when the notion of self-reflexivity comes to mind. However, even though social work education today refers to reflexivity as good practice, in that students and workers are encouraged to constructively critique their role and participation within their day-to-day activities, I do not see relationships included in this writing. Many social work authors (Baines, 2007; de Montigny, 2005; Kumsa, 2007; Massaquoi, 2007; Miehls & Moffatt, 2001) write about self-reflexivity. As Baines (2007) explains, reflexivity is a helpful process for our practice because without it, "we lose an invaluable source of information when we fail to use our own insights, frustrations, disappointments and successes as entry points into improving theory and practice" (p. 22).

It is also just as important to consider how one's social location impacts on the service users and the work that we are trying to do with them. Yet how are we ever going to know what the impact is if we do not acknowledge and share aspects about ourselves that are relevant to the helping process? When a young mother comes to a social worker, does she not have the right to know if the worker is a mother? Does an African-Canadian man need to know if the worker has experienced racism? Would it matter if the social worker grew up in Toronto or in rural India? Does the worker have any idea what it is like to live on the streets or spend time in jail? Has the worker ever lost a loved one to suicide or gang violence? Is it significant if the social worker grew up in an upper middle-class family and has never gone without the basics of survival, such as food, clothing, and shelter? Chances are that such questions will occur to service users as they sit in the social worker's office, answering all sorts of questions, but not being able to ask the social worker questions that might help build a stronger relationship.

When it comes to building good helping relationships with service users, it is the responsibility of social workers to look at which aspects of their subject positions will impact on service users and the specific situation each person is in. After all, every one of us has fluid and dynamic multiple selves or identities and certain aspects come to the forefront depending on the conversation or situation one is in. We all have a number of affiliations and highlight parts of ourselves while downplaying others within each of these (Davies & Harre, 1990). Thus, what is it about the social worker that may act as a challenge or as a route to connection with the service user? Is it age, race, class, sexual orientation, gender, skin colour, or religion or spirituality? Is it whether or not one is a parent, student, or experienced in social work practice? Is it the protocols the worker must follow, the amount of time allotted to a service user, the level of transparency, knowledge of resources, or willingness to bend rules?

In my work as a social work practitioner, educator, and researcher, I share information about myself, such as that in the first section of this chapter, with service users, students, and participants. I invite them to ask questions about me, adding that if they ask something I do not want to share, I will tell them, "That's none of your business!" People appreciate the humour! Relationship-building is one aspect of Indigenous approaches to helping that can be applied to all social work areas, taking into consideration the safety and comfort level of the worker and the policies of the agency. It is important to "walk your talk" should you strive to truly be an anti-oppressive social worker who is open to many ways of seeing the world and helping.

One of my dear friends and mentors, Charlene Avalos, who is currently the acting director of services at Native Child and Family Services of Toronto (NCFST), worked as a social work practitioner in two First Nations communities in British Columbia during the 1980s. She has been at NCFST since it opened in 1989. Charlene is not Indigenous. In talking about self-reflexivity, she shared this with me:

> It seems that when self-reflection is discussed within dominant social work, it's confined to what is known as "professionalism," meaning that, for example, what triggers us when we work with people, like in pushing our buttons or what makes us angry, and therefore leads to us not acting professionally. In Indigenous approaches, though, self-reflection is part of one's lifelong journey to knowing oneself on the physical, emotional, psychological, and spiritual realms. It's also about our own personal healing as taught to me by [Anishnawbe] Elder, Vera Martin, who always says "You can't take anyone any further than you yourself have gone." (C. Avalos, personal communication, December 20, 2008)

Charlene's thoughts about self-reflexivity, which she refers to as self-reflection, is echoed by many Indigenous social workers as well. Two Indigenous social work scholars, Jacquie Green, of the Haisla Nation, and Robina Thomas, of the Coast Salish Nation, (2007), conducted a research project with Indigenous social workers in the area of child welfare. They offer an example of how workers emphasized the importance of knowing oneself:

> One worker talked about always having to remember where she was from and why she was doing this work. It was the personal commitment to her community that kept her strong and wanting to do social work, but also remembering that she was, at the same time, a social worker and a First Nations person. She always had to remember the historical issues that have impacted our people while at the same time remember our traditional ways. (p. 37)

Here are some of the workers' suggestions to others that fall within the process of self-reflexivity, even though they do not call it this:

> I would recommend that they really try to deal with their own issues first before going out there. I mean, things are still going to happen that will trigger things for them, that will happen to everybody no matter how much you work out your own stuff.
>
> Why do you want to get into this line of work? How do you define success?
>
> You have to know yourself, who you are, work with yourself, be comfortable with your own self and always, always take care of yourself. Be balanced at all times.... You are never too old to learn.
>
> ... do a lot of things to develop yourself cognitively, spiritually, and all kinds of ways. (p. 18)

I will finish this part of the chapter on self-reflexivity with a few words from Buddhist nun Pema Chodron (2000), who gets across the message with both insight and humour:

> In all kinds of situations, we can find out what is true simply by studying ourselves in every nook and cranny, in every black hole and bright spot, whether it's murky, creepy, grisly, splendid, spooky, frightening, joyful, inspiring, peaceful, or wrathful. We can just look at the whole thing. (p. 74)

HELP FOR THE HELPERS/SELF-CARE

Social workers do a lot of caring about and helping others, whether they are doing one-to-one counselling or working with whole communities or presenting research findings to social policy developers. But who takes care of us? My own observations and conversations with many social workers over the years, unfortunately, indicate that often no one does. This reality includes social workers not taking care of themselves as well. We tend to be a busy group, working extra hours that we do not get paid for, digging for resources for service users that sometimes are not there, taking home our files so we can get our case notes completed, doing many tasks that are not included in our job descriptions, seeing service user after service user without a break, and eating lunch at our desks as we return telephone calls. Sound familiar?

Certainly there are many reasons for social work burnout, but I believe that not being cared for by our workplaces and not taking care of ourselves are major reasons for it. Much of the work we do entails listening to sad stories, witnessing people's pain and trauma, being frustrated because we live in a wealthy country in which so many people face poverty, and feeling helpless when we cannot achieve social justice goals fast enough. The sadness, fear, and anger that social workers experience on a daily basis do not simply disappear at the end of the day. Rather, these emotions are stored within our bodies, minds, and spirits, and if these emotions are not released, over time they will make us sick. This sickness may come in the form of physical ailments, such as headaches, or psychological struggles, such as depression, or spiritual illness, such as hopelessness. These impacts are not left at the office, but also affect our home lives and personal relationships.

My observations are backed up by other social work researchers. For example, in a recent research project, researchers found that 88.9 percent of social workers deal directly with service users' trauma; of these workers, 70.2 percent experienced at least one symptom of secondary traumatic stress, such as disturbing dreams; avoidance of people, places, and things; emotional numbing or hyper-vigilance; and 15.2 percent met the criteria for a diagnosis of post-traumatic stress disorder, which meant that they experienced six of the designated symptoms occasionally, often, or very often (Bride, 2007). Other research indicates that the costs of not dealing with secondary traumatic stress can lead to short- and long-term emotional and physical disorders, strains on interpersonal relationships, substance abuse, and burnout (Beaton & Murphy, 1995; Bride, 2007).

There is another aspect of trauma that social workers may face—their own. It is not uncommon for those of us who have suffered past trauma to enter a helping profession. This is understandable, but have personal traumas been dealt with? The question is: If social workers' past traumas resurface, are they supported? Charlene Avalos notes that: "mainstream social work does not address the fact that workers may be carrying unhealed trauma. In fact, I do not know anyone who has not suffered some form of trauma in their life. Yet due to this lack of support, many social workers feel embarrassed to disclose past trauma" (C. Avalos, personal communication, December 20, 2008).

The expectation that helpers who have not experienced trauma themselves are somehow experts on the impacts of these experiences is not realistic. Such a spiritual schism of bringing together one person who is "damaged" and one who is not can only promote inequality in helping relationships. The message is clear—social work needs to take care of its own!

Within Indigenous world views, a holistic approach to helping applies to everyone, including those who do the helping. Within Indigenous helping frameworks, we often refer to this notion as "help for the helpers." This means that it is in our best interests and, in the interests of our loved ones and those we help, that we take care of ourselves in order to be the best we can be. Since we are impacted on all levels—physically, psychologically, emotionally, and spiritually—by the work we do, we need to ensure that we are taking care of all aspects of self. Help for the helpers or self-care is another topic that is not discussed much in social work education or supported by many social services agencies, which is, I believe, irresponsible on the part of educators and managers. This lack of self-care may be one reason why some helpers or social workers leave the field prematurely (Bride, 2007; Figley, 1999).

What does self-care mean? In many Indigenous traditions, self-care involves taking care of all four aspects of a person, but there is no specific prescription for individual self-care. For Indigenous peoples, help for the helpers includes the kinds of cultural and spiritual activities that we offer to service users, including ceremonies such as the sweat lodge, fasting, praying, and smudging. Other ways of taking care of the self are:

- quieting the self through meditation, deep breathing, being with nature
- exercise like yoga, baseball, martial arts, or weight training
- relaxation such as warm, sea salt or bubble baths

- distractions via watching movies, reading fiction, and playing video games
- having fun
- resting
- being with people other than social workers
- seeing the rewards for all the hard work one does
- setting limits as to what you can and cannot do
- not being overly responsible by learning how to say "no" or "I'll think about it and get back to you" and then saying "no"
- pencilling in "self-care" in our appointment journals and treating this as just as important as all the other appointments

The research project conducted by Green and Thomas (2007) suggested that self-care includes taking care of the spiritual, emotional, physical, and mental aspects of self and:

> Workers strongly believed that helpers must have a self-care plan. This plan must include identifying who your support people are. Other questions that must be contemplated included, "what role does the agency that you work within play in self-care?" [In addition], each worker talked about how important laughter and fun is when the work that they do is so intense. (p. 21)

Workers had the following to say about how support from one another and from the agencies they are employed by is an important component of self-care:

> The support and the relationships that we have with one another are very strong and I don't think that I could do this work without it. Especially from a management level.... I never lack for support from them for direction, for advice, for compassion, for whatever. They really take care of our needs—personal, professional, whatever.
>
> We take the time that we need to sit with each other or listen to each other. (p. 21)

Each of us needs to come up with our own list of self-care activities and regularly implement them simply because we need and want to be well and healthy for ourselves and our loved ones. We also need to be well for those we are attempting to help. Indigenous teachings tell us that we need to be as healthy as possible in all four aspects of ourselves if we are to truly help others. I have heard this expressed in several ways, such as "You need to make sure your own house is in order before you try to help someone else put theirs in order" or "In a helping relationship, you can only help take a person as far as you are willing to go yourself." In other words, it is difficult and inappropriate to be in the work of helping if you are not helping yourself. In fact, research indicates that when social workers are not able to attend to their own symptoms of secondary traumatic stress, their abilities to help those who seek their services may be impaired (Bride, 2007; Figley, 1999; Rosenbloom, Pratt & Pearlman, 1999).

PROTECTION FROM ISOLATION

Protecting oneself from isolation is connected to help for the helpers or self-care in the work of helping/social work. Help for the helpers is certainly not only the responsibility of individual social workers. Rather, it is also a collective and political endeavour involving educators, researchers, practitioners, managers, supervisors, and members of boards of directors, who all need to care for those on the front lines.

Both social work education and the professional associations of the occupation need to be concerned with working environments and working conditions for practitioners. They, along with researchers and practitioners, need to work together to create and then evaluate ways in which social workers are cared for within their agencies and organizations. Social work managers need to carefully assess their agencies on an ongoing basis for situations that can contribute to the distress of their front-line practitioners. Supportive supervision—which addresses how social workers are feeling, addresses any concerns they may have about a service user's situation and makes room for self-care—is a must. Social workers need to be encouraged to ask for help before they are overwhelmed, and supervisors and managers need to encourage their calls for assistance. If all of these collective efforts do not occur, then it will not matter how much time researchers put into improving services for service users or how much time educators spend in teaching how to best deliver such services. None of these efforts will matter if social workers are not cared for and supported (Siebert, 2004).

Within Indigenous world views, being part of a collective is much more powerful, safer, and educational than being on one's own. There is only so much that an individual can do, but when groups come together for a common purpose, a great deal more can be accomplished. Social workers need allies, alliances, and to be with like-minded people for support, problem-solving, and activism. The following suggestions, based on Indigenous world views and values, can be useful for all social workers as they consider the importance of being a part of a group:

- humour
- learning lasts forever
- storytelling
- sharing food
- circle work

I have heard from relatives and old people from various Indigenous Nations all my life that laughter is good medicine. I could not agree more. Cree educator and writer, Ida Swan (1998), writes:

> Psychologically, the Northern Cree have used humour to its full advantage. The person who can laugh at himself or herself is held in high esteem by his or her peers. Humour and the ability to see humour in events and incidents has kept the Northern Cree from being swallowed by the hardships they have to endure. It has helped them keep their perspectives, able to respond to the demands of the land, and has allowed them to keep their reverence for the environment. (p. 54)

This is healthy advice for all social workers as it is an excellent way to relieve stress, distract us from the seriousness of our work, bring us together, and have fun.

Learning, or education, does not end once one completes a Bachelor of Social Work or a Master's or a Ph.D. There is only so much learning that can take place in a classroom, no matter how exemplary the professor is at teaching or how relevant the reading materials are. Rather, as emphasized within Indigenous world views, education "is a life long quest which require[s] patience, introspection, mistakes, sacrifices and spirituality" (Fiddler & Sanderson, 1991, n.p.). Furthermore, learning comes in many ways other than through the mind. It comes through all four aspects of self and "the spirit and the heart are essential ways of knowing" (Katz & St. Denis, 1991, p. 31). This means that we can learn through spiritual experiences, such as dreams and emotions. This could mean moving through feelings of loss and emerging feeling okay. Social workers learn through professional development training, attending conferences with diverse professionals, reading, talking with one another, paying attention to their bodies and emotions, raising children, looking up resources, and so on.

More than likely, though, social workers learn the most from those who come to their agencies for services. Who else can teach us so intimately what it is like to live below the poverty line, to try to get off and stay off of crack cocaine, to live with the scars of an abusive childhood, or to struggle with living on their own after being thrown out of their home at the age of 16? Service users also teach social workers how to be resourceful, resistant, and resilient, traits that we, too, need to do good social work. Storytelling is the oldest form of the arts. It is the basis of all other arts—drama, art, dance, and music. It has been and is an important part of every culture and

> is necessary for the revitalization of First Nations cultures and can be a starting point for moving away from assimilationist to liberationist education. Stories provide the intergenerational communication of essential ideas. Stories have many layers of meaning, giving the listener the responsibility to listen, reflect and then interpret the message. Stories incorporate several possible explanations for phenomena, allowing listeners to creatively expand their thinking processes so that each problem they encounter in life can be viewed from a variety of angles before a solution is reached. All people, young and old, love stories. (Lanigan, 1998, p. 113)

Getting together with other social workers—whether in supervision sessions or on the way home after work with a co-worker—to talk about one's experiences and concerns with practising social work is indeed revitalizing, liberating, and offers new angles to situations in which we may be stuck. Telling our stories affirms our thoughts and emotions. Listening to someone else's story shows respect and a desire to be helpful. We gain ideas and suggestions from others that we may not have considered before. We acquire a fresh outlook on a situation. Telling and listening is a reciprocal process. Today, one social worker needs the other's opinion on an issue; tomorrow it will be the other way around. In addition, as Lanigan, of the Métis Nation, states in the previous quote, all peoples of the world have been telling their stories in one form or another since the beginning of time.

Like telling stories, sharing food is another life experience that all peoples participate in. Many people, including Indigenous peoples around the world, view food as not only sustenance, but as a way to holistically nurture the self and others. Having lunch dates with co-workers or social workers in other agencies, gathering for potluck suppers at each other's houses, and going out to dinner occasionally breaks isolation while offering opportunities to tell our stories, relax, and enjoy cooking and one another's company.

Lastly, in this section, I will write a little about circle work as a way for social workers to connect and stay more connected. Of course, circles are important for sharing, telling stories, resolving conflicts, teaching, and so on, and are a much implemented method within most Indigenous Nations. The circle is significant and symbolic as it represents everything in the natural world around us—the seasons, the shape of the planets, stars, sun, and moon. The circle also represents the cycle of life, which has no beginning and end since human beings come from the spirit world and return to the spirit world. The circle is also important because within the circle, everyone is equal. There is no "head" of a circle. Everyone in a circle is able to look at every person there rather than look at someone's back.

Cree educator, Laara Fitznor (1998), articulates that:

> ... sharing circles embrace such concepts as learning from one another, and learning from what is said, gaining information and knowledge to incorporate into one's life, honoring and respecting what is heard, honoring the confidentiality of who said what, sharing the joy and pain of others, recognizing that what each person says is placed on an equal footing (no one person's voice is more important than another's), and the willingness to share information about one's experiences in light of personal growth and development. Sharing circles promote personal well-being and the well-being of Indigenous peoples. They reflect the traditional concept of interconnectedness. (p. 34)

Cree educator and author, Michael Hart (2002), supports Fitznor's understanding of Sharing Circles by writing that they:

> ... are both helping techniques and processes which set the stage for people's ongoing healing, growth and self-development. The general purpose of circles is to create a safe environment for people to share their views

and experiences with one another. They have several goals, including the initiation of the healing process, promotion of understanding, joining with others and growth. (p. 61)

There is a wide variety of activities and rituals that are a part of Sharing Circles, depending on which Nation the participants or the circle facilitator belong to. I do not support the implementation of any of these activities or rituals in a circle without Indigenous peoples' involvement in it. Even if there is an Indigenous person in the circle, this certainly does not mean that she or he will want to bring her or his specific cultural practices into the circle to share with non-Indigenous peoples. This is the individual's decision and will be based on her or his comfort with sharing these practices, her or his teachings about doing so, and the attitudes and behaviours of the others who are in the circle.

When social workers come together in a circle, I suggest that they decide as a collective how the circle will be run. Clearly, Indigenous peoples do not own the circle as it shows up as a significant symbol in many parts of the world, nor are we the only ones who are spiritual. Social workers can come up with their own particular activities and rituals to be used each time they have their gatherings. Alternatively, they can take turns in bringing activities and rituals from their own cultural and spiritual teachings to guide the circle process.

TURNING ANGER INTO ACTIVIST POWER

Social work is doing and taking action. Social workers do not wait passively to be told what to do. Rather, they interact with people, communities, policymakers, and politicians. The work ranges from one-to-one counselling to community development to organizing social movements. The profession is wide open as social workers are visible in many diverse areas and agencies, from hospitals to grassroots initiatives, and from government to youth shelters. There is continuous opportunity for social change within all of these positions and places, and social change is most definitely the business of social workers. However, involving oneself in social justice issues is not only about protesting at Queen's Park or Parliament Hill. Activism expresses itself in many ways. Examples of activism include: advocating for adequate housing for one person or a whole community; writing letters to politicians to support raising the minimum wage; conducting research that leads to policy changes in eligibility for subsidized daycare; and organizing the workers of an agency to become unionized so their working conditions can be improved. Activism is more than marching with placards on major urban streets.

What feelings motivate you to engage in social action? For me, fear and sadness about the conditions of the world tend to immobilize me. Anger, on the other hand, energizes and pushes me to take action. When a particular situation stirs up anger in me, I know that there is something wrong with that situation and I am motivated to speak up about it and join in some action to try to change it. When used constructively, anger is a powerful force that can greatly help social workers to achieve positive change. We were born with the emotion of anger and ought not to push it down or be afraid to feel it. We can also assist service users to see anger as a motivator, rather than have it come out in destructive ways that hurt themselves and others, or to hold onto it until it makes them sick.

Non-Indigenous peoples can learn a great deal from Indigenous peoples about activism. Indigenous peoples have always resisted colonization and its ongoing impacts in many ways, despite our meagre resources, low numbers, and our powerful opponent, the state. Throughout history, Indigenous activists have rallied their people, such as Métis leader Louis Riel, who led a movement of resistance in western Canada in 1885 and who is seen as the father of Manitoba, and Lakota warrior, Crazy Horse, who resisted the American army and protected the sacred Black Hills territory in South Dakota for 10 years until his death in 1877 (Matthiessen, 1980; Stanley, 1963). In more recent times, there has been Anishnawbe-Cree politician, Elijah Harper, who, as a member of the Manitoba Legislative Assembly, was frustrated with the exclusion of Indigenous issues in the 1990 Meech Lake Accord talks on the status of Quebec, and refused to waive a request for a two-day waiting period to start the debate, which led to other events that squashed the accord (CBC, 1990). Then there is Leonard Peltier, another Lakota from South Dakota, who was part of a resistance against massive energy developments on treaty lands, and who supported sovereignty for Indigenous peoples; he also has been imprisoned since 1977 (Matthiessen, 1980). Further, activism has also led to several mandated, Indigenous-controlled child welfare agencies, successful land reclamations, and inroads into education, health, and justice.

The Indigenous activists I am personally most proud of are women. In particular I am drawn to Jeanette Corbiere-Lavell and Sandra Lovelace-Nicholas. Corbiere-Lavell is an Anishnawbe woman from Ontario, who challenged the discriminatory provisions of the Indian Act, which dispossessed Indigenous women of their status when they married non-Indigenous men or Indigenous men without status. She became involved in this work in 1971 and took the issue all the way to the Supreme Court. Corbiere-Lavell continued her fight as one of the founding members of the Native Women's Association of Canada. In 2006, she and her daughter, D. Memee Lavell-Harvard, edited a book titled, *"Until Our Hearts Are on the Ground": Indigenous Mothering, Oppression, Resistance, and Rebirth*, which includes Jeanette's journey, as well as other stories of Indigenous women's resistance. Sandra Lovelace-Nicholas followed in the footsteps of Jeanette Corbiere-Lavell. Lovelace-Nicholas, a Maliseet woman from New Brunswick, was instrumental in bringing the case of discrimination in the Indian Act before the United Nations Human Rights Commission and lobbying for the 1985 legislation, which reinstated the rights of First Nations women and children. Sandra now sits in the Senate as a member of the Liberal Party of Canada.

These changes to Canadian legislation—the Indian Act—came about because of the efforts of Indigenous women during the 1970s and 1980s. Indigenous women are, according to every measurement scale, the most marginalized population in the country (CBC, 2006; Guccairda, Celasun & Stewart, 2004; Health Canada First Nations and Inuit Health Branch, 2003; Leschies, Chiodo, Whitehead & Hurley, 2006; Raphael, 2007; Shah, 2004). In fact, Sandra Lovelace-Nicholas was homeless during her activism when she challenged and brought about changes to the Indian Act. Imagine what a large group of organized social workers with various privileges and resources could accomplish if they were to try. What if such a group of social workers were to ask Indigenous women activists for guidance on how to achieve such incredible change with so little resources to work with? It seems obvious how much could be learned from such women.

Spirituality (which will be discussed at length in a later chapter) has a major place within activism, as each of us has a responsibility to use our spirituality in creating a better world. I explain my existence in terms of how I value my own life, the lives of others, and honour my connections within my community and the world. This connection and its emphasis on spirituality is succinctly explained by Kurt Alan Ver Beek (2000), who writes: "a sick child, dying livestock, or the question of whether to participate in risky social action are spiritual as well as physical problems, requiring both prayer and action" (p. 33). Ver Beek's description of Lenca "pilgrims" marching on a day of protest, "singing religious songs … and blowing on their conch shells—all traditional means of calling villagers to worship" (p. 33), reminds me of my own community's spiritual and holistic approach to social action. When Indigenous peoples engage in social justice activities, our Elders, prayers, medicines, songs, sacred fire, and the drum are always present as sanctions of the spiritual importance of the activities. They are also present as ways to support those who are participating in the activities of social movements. Once again, I encourage all social workers to consider how their own particular spirituality can be connected to social movements, social justice, and change, and to take guidance from Indigenous peoples in how to do this.

CONCLUSION

This chapter offers encouragement to *all* social workers who believe and engage in forms of activism as one of the paths to social justice and change. The chapter attempted to show how Indigenous approaches to social justice have made incredible inroads and positive changes in legislation despite great obstacles. Clearly, there is a need and an interest in creating bridges between Indigenous approaches to activism, which include methods that lead to structural change, and other ways of engaging in social movements. Indigenous approaches to helping and working toward social and political change have always been on the periphery of all that is seen as Canadian. An open mind will tell us clearly that a multiplicity within the centre can only bring about more options, creativity, and fresh outlooks that will help us understand particular situations and make positive changes for the collective good, which includes all the people who live in this country. When European peoples first landed on Turtle Island, they obviously had to rely on Indigenous peoples to ensure their survival. What better way to now give thanks than to engage in activism led by Indigenous peoples, which will lead to the equality of Indigenous world views and mainstream thought and action?

In addition, social workers may want to consider Indigenous ways of helping in developing more egalitarian relationships with service users, examining power imbalances on a micro level, and promoting self-care as an essential aspect for those who do the helping. It may be that these Indigenous teachings can assist social workers to further incorporate anti-oppressive social work theory on a more practice-oriented basis.

REFERENCES

Baines, D. (2007). Anti-oppressive social work practice: Fighting for space, fighting for chance. In D. Baines (Ed.), *Doing anti-oppressive practice: Building transformative politicized social work* (pp. 1–30). Halifax: Fernwood Publishing.

Beaton, R.D. & Murphy, S.A. (1995). Working with people in crisis: Research implications. In C.R. Figley (Ed.), *Compassion fatigue: Coping with secondary traumatic stress disorder in those who treat the traumatized* (pp. 51–81). New York: Brunner/Mazel.

Bride, B.E. (2007). Prevalence of secondary traumatic stress among social workers. *Social Work, 52*(1), 63–70. Retrieved from http://www.ingentaconnect.com

CBC. (1990, June 12). A vote of protest [digital archive]. *CBC digital archives.* Retrieved from http://archives.cbc.ca

CBC. (2006, May 22). UN committee again condemns Canada's treatment of people living in poverty. *CBC news.* Retrieved from www.cbc.ca

Chodron, P. (2000). *When things fall apart: Heart advice for difficult times.* Boston: Shambhala Publications Inc.

de Montigny, G. (2005). A reflexive materialist alternative. In S. Hick, J. Fook & R. Pozzuto (Eds.), *Social work: A critical turn* (pp. 121–136). Toronto: Thompson Education Publishing.

Fiddler, S. & Sanderson, J. (1991). *Medicine wheel concept from the world view of the Plains and Parkland Cree culture.* Unpublished manuscript, Saskatchewan Indian Federated College, Regina, Saskatchewan.

Figley, C.R. (1999). Compassion fatigue: Toward a new understanding of the costs of caring. In B.H. Stamm (Ed.), *Secondary traumatic stress: Self-care issues for clinicians, researchers, and educators* (2nd ed.) (pp. 3–28). Lutherville: Sidran Press.

Fitznor, L. (1998). The circle of life: Affirming Indigenous philosophies in everyday living. In D. McCane (Ed.). Life ethics in world religions (pp. 21–40). Winnipeg: University of Manitoba.

Green, J. & Thomas, R. (2007). Learning through our children, healing for our children: Best practices in First Nations communities. In L. Dominelli (Ed.), *Revitalizing communities in a globalizing world* (pp. 175–192). UK: Ashgate Publishing.

Guccairda, E., Celasun, N. & Stewart, D.E. (2004). Single-mother families in Canada. *Canadian Journal of Public Health, 95*(1), 70–74. Retrieved from http://journal.cpha.ca

Hart, M. A. (2002). Seeking mino-pimatisiwin: An Aboriginal approach to helping. Halifax: Fernwood Publishing

Health Canada First Nations and Inuit Health Branch. (2003*). A statistical profile on the health of First Nations in Canada.* Ottawa: Health Canada, First Nations and Inuit Health Branch. Retrieved from http://www.hc-sc.gc.ca

Katz, R. & St. Denis, V. (1991). Teacher as healer. *Journal of Indigenous Studies, 2*, 24–36.

Lanigan. M.A. (1998). Indigenous pedagogy: Storytelling. In L.A. Stiffarm (Ed.), *As we see ... Indigenous pedagogy* (pp. 103–120). Saskatoon: University Extension Press.

Lavell-Harvard, D.M. & Corbiere-Lavell, J. (2006). *Until our hearts are on the ground: Aboriginal mothering, oppression, resistance, and rebirth.* Toronto: Demeter Press.

Leschies, A.W., Chiodo, D., Whitehead, P. C. & Hurley, D. (2006). The association of poverty with child welfare service and child and family clinical outcomes. *Community, Work, and Family, 9*(1), 29–46. doi: 10.1080/13668800500420988

Matthiessen, P. (1980). *In the spirit of Crazy Horse.* New York: Penguin Books Inc.

Massaquoi, N. & Wane, N. (2007). (Eds.), *Canadian perspectives on Black feminist thought.* Toronto: Inanna Publications and Education.

Miehls, D. & Moffatt, K. (2000). Constructing social work identity based on the reflexive self. *British Journal of Social Work, 30*(3), 339–348. doi: 10.1093/bjsw/30.3.339

Raphael, D. (2007). *Poverty and policy in Canada: Implications for health and quality of life.* Toronto: Canadian Scholars' Press Inc.

Rosenbloom, D.J., Pratt, C. & Pearlman, L.A. (1999). Helpers' responses to trauma work: Understanding and intervening in an organization. In B.H. Stamm (Ed.), *Secondary traumatic stress: Self-care issues for clinicians, researchers, and educators* (2nd ed.) (pp. 65–79). Lutherville: Sidran Press.

Shah, C. (2004). Aboriginal health. In D. Raphael (Ed.), *Social determinants of health: Canadian perspectives* (pp. 267–280). Toronto: Canadian Scholars' Press Inc.

Siebert, D.C. (2004). Depression in North Carolina social workers: Implications for practice and research. *Social Work Research, 28*(1), 30–40. Retrieved from http://find.galegroup.com

Smith, L.T. (2000). Kaupapa Maori research. In M. Battiste (Ed.), *Indigenous voice and vision* (pp. 225–247). Vancouver: University of British Columbia Press.

Stanley, G.F.G. (1963). *Louis Riel.* Toronto: Ryerson.

Swan, I. (1998). Modelling: An Aboriginal approach. In L.A. Stiffarm (Ed.), *As we see ... Indigenous pedagogy* (pp. 49–58). Saskatoon: University Extension Press.

Ver Beek, K.A. (2000). Spirituality: A development taboo. *Development in Practice, 10*(1), 31–43. Retrieved from http://www.jstor.org

Womack, C. (1997). Howling at the moon: The queer but true story of my life as a Hank Williams song. In W.S. Penn (Ed.), *As we are now: Mixblood essays on race and identity* (pp. 28–49). Los Angeles: University of California Press.

Chapter 3

Current Theories and Models of Social Work as Seen through an Indigenous Lens

INTRODUCTION

Although Indigenous approaches to helping/social work stand on their own as theories and practice, there are some connections between these approaches and anti-oppressive, structural, postmodernist, and post-colonial theories of social work. Both anti-oppressive and structural theories include the history of Indigenous peoples in their critique of power, while postmodern theories acknowledge that there are many ways, including Indigenous ways, of seeing the world. Post-colonial theory goes further and focuses on Indigenous knowledges. Indigenous approaches to helping arise out of Indigenous world views, which emphasize introspection, connectedness, reciprocity, and spirituality. These four concepts are intertwined and will be explained in this chapter.

ANTI-OPPRESSIVE AND STRUCTURAL SOCIAL WORK THEORIES

Anti-oppression social work theory and practice contends that "the contemporary social order is characterized by a range of social divisions (class, race, gender, age, disability and so on) that both embody and engender inequality, discrimination and oppression" (Thompson, 1998, p. 3). Similarly, Jane Dalrymple and Beverley Burke (1995) point out that we live in a society characterized by difference, and that "differences are used to *exclude* rather than include. This is because relationships within society are the result of the exercise of power on individual, interpersonal and institutional levels" (p. 8).

Furthermore, according to social work scholar, Bob Mullaly (2002):

> ... oppression—not individual deficiency or social disorganization—is the major cause of and explanation for social problems. This, of course, necessitates an anti-oppressive form of social work practice to deal with these problems in any meaningful way. Such a practice requires an understanding of the nature of oppression, its dynamics, the social and political functions it carries out in the interests of the dominant groups, its effects on oppressed persons, and the ways that oppressed people cope with and/or resist their oppression. (p. 15)

Mullaly (2002) also links anti-oppression theory and practice with anti-racism and anti-colonialism. He writes:

> The "personal is political" analysis forces the social worker beyond carrying out mere psychological manipulations, which in effect pathologize people. This type of analysis has relevance and utility for understanding all forms and sources of oppression in our society. It can be used to understand better the nature and extent of racism in our society and how

it contributes to the oppression of visible minority groups. It can be used to understand better the nature of colonialism and how it contributes to the oppression of Indigenous persons in our society.... (p. 180)

Similar to anti-oppression theory, structural social work understands social problems as originating from a particular liberal or neo-conservative societal context (Mullaly, 1997). Structural social work theory focuses on the structures in society—such as education, employment, and justice—that create barriers for specific populations based on oppressions such as racism, capitalism, and sexism. Thus, instead of blaming individual people or groups for their social condition, structural social work examines the structures that create barriers to accessing resources, services, and social goods. Like anti-oppression theory, it emphasizes consciousness-raising, advocating with and on behalf of service users, incorporating a historical analysis, and recognizing internalized oppression.

Such an emphasis is necessary in order to uncover the roots of the oppression of Indigenous peoples and begin to dismantle the institutions that continue to perpetuate the ongoing effects of colonization. As Anishnawbe writers, Kathy Absolon and Elaine Herbert (1997), critically argue:

Structural analysis provides a way of examining how structures and institutions in Canadian society promote and perpetuate oppression. For example, rather than identifying individuals as unmotivated and lazy, a structural analysis of poverty in many First Nations communities reveals the lack of access to educational, social, and political opportunities for First Nations peoples and identifies the institutional omission in our culture. (p. 209)

However, although both anti-oppressive and structural social work theories include a historical analysis in their understanding of the detrimental impacts of colonization on Indigenous peoples, they lack any discussion of world views that might include values that could guide helping approaches. This is problematic from an Indigenous perspective as a majority of Indigenous social work scholars stress the significance of world views in community social work practice. Thus, from an Indigenous perspective, anti-oppressive and structural social work approaches are not very different in this regard from more conventional social work theories. However, conventional social work theories are grounded in Western world views, which tend to believe that spirituality should be contained within the realm of religious institutions (Hill, 1995).

Furthermore, despite the commonalities between structural social work and anti-oppression theories, these theories tend not to recognize that the marginalization of Indigenous peoples is different from other oppressed groups. As community development worker and educator, Anne Bishop (1994), asserts, "the tendency of many people to throw the struggle of Indigenous people in with all other human rights disregards the unique nature of Indigenous rights …" (p. 63). In Canada, the struggles of Indigenous peoples differ from those of other populations because the oppression of Indigenous peoples is the result of colonization. *All* Canadians, and in particular the privileged sector of society, benefit from the stolen land of Indigenous peoples, the exploitation of resources, and the violation of treaties. In fact, Indigenous peoples across the world face similar situations.

POSTMODERNISM

Postmodernism, which was first used in architectural criticism, and then became a theory that rejected Enlightenment-era Eurocentric thought that promoted one knowable reality, has been taken up by a growing number of academics in the social sciences (Lather, 1991). At the core of postmodern theory is the thinking that reality is socially constructed through language, maintained through narrative, and carries no essential truths. Reality is multiple and fluid, as well as historically specific. There is no way to be certain of social reality. All one can do is interpret reality based on one's own values, culture, biases, etc. Thus, in their analysis, postmodern theorists do not make normative statements about social reality or when visioning social justice claims (Moosa-Mitha, 2005).

As in both anti-oppressive and structural social work theory, power is also taken up by postmodern theorists as well. According to Michel Foucault (1965, 1975, 1980a, 1980b, 1985), language is an instrument of power and those who have the most power in society are the ones who have the most ability to participate in the discourses that shape society. Societal discourses determine what knowledge is viewed as true or right, so those who control the discourses also control the accepted knowledge. Again, like the first two theories, postmodernism asks the critical question of *whose* languages, knowledges, and voices are being privileged and heard. Yet, within postmodernism, power is also seen as something that moves about within a society rather than something that is always held by a particular group. This contradicts an understanding that it is the state and powerful corporations that support the state that hold the most power, which is imposed on others (Strega, 2005).

Postmodern theorists also reject what might be called "identity politics." Identity politics tend to support the idea that only women can speak about women's experiences, only Black people can talk about Black people, and only Indigenous peoples can tell the stories about Indigenous peoples. This means that individual and group identity may be reduced to one identity characteristic, aspect, or label. Identity politics also shape who is allowed to speak on behalf of a particular community, what moral position can be taken, and what is allowed to be spoken (Brown, 1998). Postmodernist theory recognizes that identity politics may be reductionist or limiting.

Even though I agree with many aspects of postmodernist theory, there are some areas that I find difficult to accept, as do some of the Indigenous and non-Indigenous students I teach. I agree that language has power and that there are multiple ways of interpreting social reality. I also believe that postmodern theories have much to offer and can challenge other social work theories. However, I disagree that there are no essential truths and there is no right or wrong. Tell that to the Indigenous survivors of the residential school system! For Indigenous peoples, organizing under a common identity is the backbone of political action that has helped to bring about much needed social and political change. It continues to be very important for Indigenous peoples to be able to assert our truths. Organizing under a common identity has been important for many other populations as well, such as women of colour, gay men, and people with disabilities.

This notion of no truth or many truths connects to the idea of identity politics as well. As will be seen throughout this book, identity is a crucial concept for Indigenous peoples and communities throughout the world. Connecting with others in terms of a common identity as Indigenous peoples emphasizes our unique place in this territory or country. This connection speaks to a specific and shared colonial oppression. This connection has also led to massive healing and reclamation initiatives across the country and has mobilized Indigenous peoples to fight for critical social change and Indigenous rights. It is not possible to be an Indigenous person without being political. Politics is interwoven into our day-to-day existence, and it revolves around shared world views, a shared history, and our inherent rights.

A postmodern view that says that there is no ultimate holder of power, such as the state and/or corporations, and says that there are no determining factors related to power, such as race, class, or gender, may be misleading. A more fluid view of power should not ignore the stories, experiences, and concerns of those who have faced and continue to face the terribly real effects of structural inequalities that shape our current society.

Of course, there are different forms of power and lenses from which to view power. A structural analysis of power is relevant because it focuses on the relationship between Indigenous peoples and the state. However, such an analysis cannot be allowed to limit the power of Indigenous knowledges and peoples themselves. The great strength of many Indigenous peoples, both past and present, is expressed through the ability of Indigenous peoples to survive and, at times, thrive, sometimes against all odds. Such strength can, at times, poke holes in this idea of fixed structural oppression. In Canada, this strength was evident when Indigenous peoples mobilized in the so-called "Oka crisis" of 1990 and was reinforced by the creation of the northern territory of Nunavut in 1999 and the responses to the 2008 state apology for the horrors of the residential school era (CUPE, 2009; First Nations Drum, 2000).

The fact that some of our languages, spirituality, and teachings in areas such as medicine and science continue to survive today speaks to the strength of global Indigenous knowledges. There is also power in Indigenous ways of helping, for they, too, continue to exist in adapted ways. Our ceremonies heal. Our customary laws restore. Our emphasis on the collective is inclusive. Furthermore, as this book asserts, the power of these knowledges is greater when we come to appreciate that these knowledges have value for *all* peoples of the world.

Finally, many of the tenets that postmodern theorists advocate are very familiar. Many ways of knowing? Alternative world views? I agree with Strega (2005), who writes:

> ... although Hekman believes that poststructural, Foucauldian "analysis also suggests the possibility of the creation of a discourse that does not constitute itself as inferior" (1990, 21), it seems that such a discourse cannot, however, be created by those who *are* "inferior": women and other marginalized people—or perhaps it is that we cannot be credited with the creation of such a discourse. Feminists and other holders of subjugated knowledge, such as Indigenous scholars and critical race theorists,

have for some time been delineating "ways of knowing," and of researching, that challenge Enlightenment epistemologies and methodologies.
Thus, it is difficult to believe Hekman's contention that "postmodernism
involves a crisis of cultural authority" (1990, 13) when the poststruc-
turalist challenge to authority resides primarily in the hands of white,
privileged men. (p. 212)

POST-COLONIAL OR ANTI-COLONIAL THEORY

Post-colonial, or anti-colonial, theory grew out of literary criticism and was
developed by writers from countries that had been colonized (Bhabha, 1994;
Deloria Jr., 1969; Fanon, 1963, 1967; Said, 1978, 1993; Spivak, 1999). The term
"post-colonial" was originally intended to replace the term "Third World," but
has been expanded to include non-Western critiques originating in the West
that are presented as credible knowledges.

According to Appiah (1992), the hyphen in post-colonial writing is a mark-
er that separates post-colonial theory from post-structural and postmodern
theories. However, this hyphen can be misleading, "particularly if it suggests
that post-colonialism refers to a situation in a society 'after colonialism', an
assumption which remains tediously persistent despite constant rebuttals by
post-colonialists" (Ashcroft, 2001, pp. 20–21). On the contrary, "post-colonial
discourse is the discourse of the colonized, which begins with colonization and
does not stop when the colonizers go home" (Ashcroft, 2001, p. 23). Thus, the
post-colonial dialogue examines Eurocentric Western thinking and colonization from the world view of people who have been colonized. This dialogue
can provide a language and concepts that may help explain the experiences of
people who have been, and/or continue to be, colonized.

Post-colonial theorists discuss how colonization has affected Indigenous
peoples, as well as the particular relationships that exist between colonized
peoples and between colonized peoples and colonizing peoples. Post-colonial
theory does not provide specific answers about how social work should func-
tion within Indigenous communities. However, post-colonial writers in diverse
countries such as India, Guyana, Australia, Kenya, and the United States have
examined issues of colonization, exploitation, resistance, and transformation
and have suggested some important questions. The answers to some of these
questions may come from Indigenous peoples and communities and also from
other groups. Together in partnership, Indigenous peoples and other groups

can work together to help inform the social work profession and work toward a process of decolonization.

Post-colonial theory also provides a message that Indigenous peoples in Canada are not alone in their struggles to decolonize. Post-colonial writers around the world look at patterns among colonized peoples and provide information about decolonization strategies that have been attempted in other places. Post-colonial theory can help to create space and credibility in the academy and bring the knowledges of Indigenous writers from the margins into the centre. By examining patterns of colonization and decolonization in other countries, Indigenous peoples in Canada can gain insights and strategies in their efforts to decolonize this country. Of course, the social context from country to country varies. However, the patterns of colonization and the themes of decolonization—such as remembering Indigenous histories and languages and the need for self-determination and control over economics and education—are similar. The universal need to make space in social work education, research, and practice for world views other than a Western world view is something Indigenous peoples have in common. This need makes post-colonial theory useful for social work.

When it comes to the discourses of power, post-colonial theory not only critiques the notion of power, but also focuses on resistance. This resistance takes the form of a post-colonial analysis. According to Loomba (1998), such an analysis "indicates a new way of thinking in which cultural, intellectual, economic or political processes are seen to work together in the formation, perpetuation and dismantling of colonialism ... by examining the intersection of ideas and institutions, knowledge and power. Colonial discourse studies... seek to offer in-depth analysis of colonial epistemologies, and connect them to the history of colonial institutions" (Loomba, 1998, p. 45).

CULTURAL COMPETENCY MODELS

In attempting to address "issues of diversity," the social work profession has attempted to create service providers who are culturally competent or cross-culturally sensitive. Basically, this model directs social workers to become more aware of, and sensitive to, the specific norms, practices, and behaviours of "cultural" and "ethnic" groups (Hines, Garcia-Preto, McGoldrick, Almeida & Weltman, 1999; McGoldrick, 1982). Developing heightened sensitivity to these norms, practices, and behaviours is seen as beneficial to the relationship between the social worker and the service user. Services may then be offered within the framework of a particular culture. The cultural competency model was the popular means of addressing "difference" in social work practice during the 1980s and 1990s and continues to be taught, written about, and practised in some areas of the profession (Jeffery, 2005). Not unlike anthropology, cultural competency creates a set of attributes, which are assigned to "the other" and then catalogued and managed as collective cultural profiles or identities. This emphasis on management and service provision is assumed to provide mostly White social services providers with an increased ability to communicate with non-dominant populations. As Nestel and Razack (n.d.) articulate, "the cultural competence approach proceeds on the assumption that what may be wrong in encounters between lawyers, educators, physicians and other health care providers, and their non-white, non-western clients, patients, or students, is that the professionals lack knowledge about how to manage these populations, and thus cannot adequately serve them" (p. 2).

Various scholars have critiqued the cultural competency model, taking the position that it reproduces simplistic assumptions about the various populations that are reminiscent of the imperialism, racism, and paternalism of an earlier social work era (Baskin, 2006; Dyche & Zayas, 1995; Gelfand & Fandetti, 1986; Gross, 2000; Jeffery, 2005, 2009; Miller & Maiter, 2008; Nestel & Razack, n.d.; Pon, 2009; Razack, 1998; Sakamoto, 2007; Yee & Dumbrill, 2003). For example, in African, Indigenous, and South Asian cultures, there are numerous languages spoken, several forms of spirituality, and multiple traditions, which are further complicated by class, gender, age, sexual orientation, and context. Without an understanding of this complexity, ideas about cultures can then become simplified and practitioners can fall into the trap of seeing culture as the only variable in the lives of individuals, families, or communities. Furthermore, an emphasis on attempting to learn about cultures may also create generalizations that limit rather than enhance cross-cultural encounters.

A cultural competency model can also reduce the understanding that social workers may have the difficulties that particular individuals face when accessing social services and attribute these difficulties to cultural differences, rather than attending to the social, economic, and political realities that support systemic inequalities. Thus, when structural power inequities are conceptually removed from our understanding, oppression may easily be attributed to individual prejudice and/or attributed to "cultural barriers." Needless to say, the cultural competency model is limited because it doesn't take into account power differences and the ways that power is maintained through a social hierarchy that marginalizes particular groups of people.

There is also an assumption within the cultural competency model that the social worker is "culture free." The assumption that social workers are White, and therefore have no culture, is prevalent. Only the "other" has culture. However, the reality is that everyone has a culture and is influenced by culture. Social workers need to examine their own cultural standpoint. The ways that social workers regard service users, understand particular challenges, and work on possible solutions to these challenges will be shaped by cultural understandings. Further, the culture of the social work profession itself is largely shaped by the particular understandings of the dominant group. Even if the social worker is a member of an Indigenous or other minority group, she or he will inevitably practise social work, at least in some measure, using the cultural understandings of the dominant group. It is likely this social worker has also been educated in these more dominant world views and perspectives. Despite the critiques, cultural competency discourse remains popular with some students as evidenced in classroom dialogues and papers and with many social services providers.

Gordon Pon (2009), a faculty member of the School of Social Work at Ryerson University, describes "cultural competency as new racism" (p. 59). By this, Pon (2009) means that racial discrimination has moved away from exclusion based on biology and toward racial discrimination based on culture. Through this notion of cultural competency, the social work profession unwittingly essentializes culture, which leads to a reinforcement of cultural stereotypes and a freezing of culture that renders it fixed or static. Of course, it is whiteness that constructs cultural "others," who are supposedly different from White Canadians, and who do not belong and come from somewhere else (Pon, 2009). However, it is important to understand that the Indigenous peoples of Turtle Island did not come from anywhere else. Nevertheless, they are still most definitely seen as "other" within White Canadian culture. I agree with Pon's (2009) assertion that "when cultural competency constructs knowledge of cultural 'others', it forgets the history of non-whites in Canada and how this troubles, even renders absurd, any notion of a pure or absolute Canadian culture" (p. 63).

As some social work scholars (Baskin, 2006; Gross, 2000; Pon, 2009) have written, culture is extremely complicated and there is too much information associated with what constitutes "culture" for anyone to become competent in every aspect of it. I don't think I am fully competent in understanding my own culture, never mind anyone else's. Fortunately, both Indigenous world views and postmodern theory challenge the idea of fixed cultures and identities (Gosine, 2000; Hall, 1989; Yon, 2000). A much more realistic understanding of culture comes from Yon (2000) as cited in Pon, (2009), who states that "postmodern understandings of culture shifted from being 'a stable and knowable set of attributes' to a view of culture as a 'matter of debate about representations and the complex relationships that individuals take up in relation to them'" (p. 64).

Pon (2009) then asks why some people within the social work profession continue to engage with ideas and practices of cultural competency even though cultural competency is an outdated theory about culture embedded in modernist and colonialist discourses. I agree with Pon's (2009) answer to his own question, when he suggests that this clinging to cultural competency is based in Canada's desire to forget about its genocide of Indigenous peoples, and to see itself as a fair and tolerant country. Thus, social work can hold on to an identity of innocence and goodness by focusing its attention on the "other" who is being helped, rather than on itself. Pon (2009) identifies this phenomenon as "a manifestation of a rush to practice," which is, according to Britzman (2000) as cited in Pon (2009), "often related to a refusal to engage with learning about social violence, such as colonialism, racism and slavery" (p. 69). Such learning can be difficult for both educators and learners since it requires them to examine how they are implicated in benefiting from colonization. Hence, those who benefit from colonization may run to cultural competency, rather than engage in the necessary processes of self-reflexivity that help develop self-knowledge. As this book emphasizes, running away from oneself is the last thing we want to do if creating a better world is our intention.

INDIGENOUS WORLD VIEWS GUIDE APPROACHES TO HELPING

Chickasaw academic Eber Hampton published an article in 1995 in the *Canadian Journal of Native Education* titled "Memory Comes before Knowledge." For me, this magical, mysterious, and completely sensible title captures the connections inherent in Indigenous world views. It is inclusive of spirit, blood memory, respect, interconnectedness, storytelling, feelings, experiences, and guidance. It also reminds me that I do not need to know about or understand everything with a sense of absolute certainty. It reinforces the concept that it is perfectly acceptable and appropriate to believe that there is much that I am aware of and rationally cannot explain. I am also aware that this is the way it is supposed to be. I accept and am comfortable with what cannot be known, and I recognize that this is part of my world view.

Cree scholar Willie Ermine's (1995) statement that: "Indigenous epistemology speaks of pondering great mysteries that lie no further than the self" (p. 108) is aligned with this understanding. Thus, in order to find meanings in the world around us, we must continually explore our inner selves. Indigenous world views incorporate ways of turning inward for the purpose of finding meanings through, for example, prayer, fasting, dream interpretation, ceremonies, and silence. Our ancestors left us these methods through the generational teachings that are passed on by our Elders and through our blood memories.

Within Indigenous epistemologies, there is an explicit acceptance that each individual has the inherent ability for introspection. Although there is great community guidance, this inward journey is conducted alone and is unique to each of us. It provides us with our purpose and, therefore, what we have to offer the whole of creation. Knowledge, then, is based on experience. One's experiences through inward journeys and living life provide both individual learning and teachings for the collective. Within Indigenous world views, the personal experiences of helpers contribute to the helping process. There is an understanding that experience, rather than "book learning," leads to knowledge that will benefit others. For example, in the area of contemporary social work, it is often those healing from substance misuse who are the best addictions counsellors, or those who have survived domestic violence who are the most informed about making positive policy changes for the safety of women and children. Furthermore, within Indigenous societies worldwide, it is the older people, often called Elders, rather than people with Ph.D.s, who are held in the highest regard. Why? It is because Elders have knowledge based on experience rather than merely on theory. It would be wonderful if Western societies and the profession of social work valued elderly people in this way.

Collective Indigenous cultural and spiritual experiences across the planet strongly emphasize this notion of connection. Many Indigenous writers (Baskin, 2002, 2005, 2006; Battiste & Youngblood-Henderson, 2000; Cajete, 1994; Couture, 1991; Fitznor, 1998; Hart, 2009; Shilling, 2002) speak to the idea of interconnectedness as an important concept within our world views. As Laguna-Sioux writer Paula Gunn Allen (1986) states, "all things are related and are of one family" (p. 60). Thus, I am connected to my family, community, Mi'kmaq Nation, and to everything on Mother Earth and in the spirit world. To divide any of these realities into separate categories is a dishonour to Indigenous ways of thinking.

This understanding of interrelatedness applies to each individual as well. Cherokee author Carol Locust (1988) writes: "as Native people, we cannot separate our spiritual teachings from our learning, nor can we separate our beliefs about who, and what we are from our values and our behaviours" (p. 328). Hence, all of the aspects of a person—spiritual, physical, emotional, and psychological—are connected and cannot be viewed in isolation. Cree academic Laara Fitznor (1998) emphasizes the importance of the concept of holism to the well-being of each of us and reminds us "that we are all related and all have a responsibility to each other's healing and growth" (p. 33). In turn, this concept of interconnectedness leads to a holistic approach to healing and learning whereby "all of the senses, coupled with openness to intuitive or spiritual insights, are required" (Brant-Castellano, 2000, p. 29).

When people can live as whole persons, then they can connect with everything around them and attend to their responsibilities. In Indigenous world views, a focus on individual and collective responsibility for all members of one's community is highlighted. Blood scholar Leroy Little Bear (2000) articulates this focus beautifully:

Wholeness is like a flower with four petals. When it opens, one discovers strength, sharing, honesty, and kindness. Together these four petals create balance, harmony, and beauty. Wholeness works in the same interconnected way. The whole strength speaks to the idea of sustaining balance. If a person is whole and balanced, then he or she is in a position to fulfill his or her individual responsibilities to the whole. If a person is not balanced, then he or she is sick and weak—physically, mentally or both—and cannot fulfill his or her individual responsibilities. (p. 79)

Is it not possible that teachings of connectedness can lead to a sense of responsibility and greater compassion for all? Is compassion not a deeply rooted value of the profession of social work? I would guess that the vast majority of social service users who seek the assistance of social workers may come away from the experience not feeling connected to much of anything. This disconnect or lack of wholeness leads to the exclusion of some populations, which causes so much pain for many people. A focus on connecting marginalized peoples, both to their own inner worlds and to the worlds of other people, needs to be a major focus of the profession of social work. After all, we as educators and practitioners need to keep in mind that the work we are involved in is "social," which clearly includes facilitating connections among people.

Writing about their work in a Dine community in southwestern Turtle Island (North America), Dine social work practitioners, Margaret Waller and Shirley Patterson (2002), focus on what it means to offer and receive help within Indigenous world views. According to these writers, helping one another is a way of life; there is no distinction between the helper and the person in need and no stigma attached to the need for help. Unlike the stigma that is often attached to need in a Western context, in this Dine community, it is "assumed that everyone has problems at one time or another and therefore that everyone will be a recipient of help as well as a helper" (Waller & Patterson, 2002, p. 11). Hence, there is no sense of social distance between people in need and those who are helping. In addition, the writers highlight the importance of natural helpers, such as family, clan members, and friends, as people who may greatly support those in need.

This concept of a reciprocal relationship among people speaks to the notions of connectedness and compassion outlined previously. It also suggests an egalitarian way of living in which helping is understood through values of sharing. Today, I will help you simply because I can. Next week, next year, when I am in need, you will help me because you can. This way, the well-being of everyone is considered. When each individual is okay, then it follows that the whole community benefits. In addition, many peoples throughout the world share the belief that help comes from natural networks such as family, friends, and other community members. In fact, social work is a Western concept that is foreign to many societies. It must be rather puzzling to some people to hear that they would have to go to a stranger who is paid a salary through government funding to help them sort out particular personal concerns.

Spirituality, of course, is another significant component of Indigenous world views. My understanding of Indigenous spirituality, according to the teachings that have been passed on to me, is that it is about our interconnectedness and interrelationship with all life. Everything in the world (both "animate" and "inanimate") is seen as equal. Everything has a spirit and is also an interdependent part of the great whole. This inclusive view permeates the entire Indigenous vision of life and the universe. Georges Sioui, of the Huron Nation (1992), further explains:

Where their human kin are concerned, the Amerindians' attitude is the same: all human beings are sacred because they are an expression of the will of the Great Mystery. Thus, we all possess within ourselves a sacred vision, that is, a unique power that we must discover in the course of our lives in order to actualize the Great Spirit's vision, of which we are an expression. Each man and woman, therefore, finds his or her personal meaning through that unique relationship with the Great Power of the universe. (p. 9)

Many Indigenous helpers and writers speak about a revitalization of spirituality in the lives of Indigenous peoples. The findings from a research project, published in the *Canadian Journal of Native Education*, looked at the facilitation of healing for Indigenous peoples in British Columbia (McCormick, 1995). In this research, "establishing a spiritual connection" and "participation in spiritual ceremonies" were ranked among the most important components of healing by research participants. Métis scholar Jean Fyre Graveline (1998) refers to this revival as "spiritual resistance [which] flourishes through treasuring our children and honouring the visions and words of our ancestors" (p. 45). In her research regarding Indigenous women, Métis writer Kim Anderson (2000) shares that "many Native women told me it felt like they had finally found something that was 'ours' when they began to practice Native spirituality" (p. 133).

Often this reclaiming of spirituality begins in healing processes with Indigenous social workers and other helpers. It is important that these helpers adopt this work because "spiritual healing requires special attention, the spiritual aspect of Indigenous identity having suffered most from the effects of cultural colonialism" (Morrissette, McKenzie & Morrissette, 1993, p. 99). Thus, some healing programs ensure that emphasis is placed on activism, resistance, and social change, as well as community recovery (Avalos, Arger, Levesque & Pike, 1997; Baskin, 1997).

Within Indigenous world views, spirituality has a central place in healing. In fact, I do not believe that healing can occur apart from spirituality. As Hart (2002) states, "Indigenous philosophy and ways of knowing encompass spirituality to such a degree that it necessitates including spirituality in this approach" (p. 46). Within specific Indigenous cultures, traditional teachings, ceremonies, rituals, stones, water, the pipe, herbs, sitting on the earth, fasting, prayer, dreams, visions, channelling, out-of-body experiences, touch, and food may be part of the journey to spiritual balance and well-being.

In addition, those who are the helpers are said to be containers or channels for healing. Their abilities come from the spirits and live inside them through blood memory. The assistance that helpers or healers pass on to others is more spiritual than anything else. According to Anishnawbe helper, Calvin Morrisseau (1998), "without the recognition of spirituality, our relationships are superficial at best" (p. 103). Thus, helping or social work practice from Indigenous world views deeply involves spirituality and cannot be truly effective without it.

A significant area that I believe to be of great concern within helping processes is the connection and confusion between mental health and spirituality. I think that the line between a spiritual and a psychotic experience may be blurred. However, practitioners tend to diagnose some spiritual experiences and practices as "pathological symptoms of delusions, immaturity, regression, escapism, or neurosis" (Gilbert, 2000, p. 79). In fact, what some people see as spiritual strength is often pathologized by practitioners. Service users learn that they cannot discuss their spiritual beliefs and experiences with social workers for fear of being judged or pathologized as "crazy." This is problematic for many Indigenous peoples. For example, within Indigenous world views, a major focus of spirituality is the ability to communicate with the spirit world. There are many practices, such as fasting and ceremonies, that are designed to help us enhance this ability. To hear the voices of spirits is considered to be a strength. However, in the dominant society, the spiritual experiences of Indigenous peoples may be constructed as schizophrenia by medical professionals who are supported by social workers (Baskin, 2007a, 2007b).

Another issue that concerns the connection between spirituality and mental health is depression. According to many Indigenous Elders and healers, the roots of depression are due to an "abandonment of respect for a spiritual way of life in exchange for materialistic things which overwhelm people, preventing them from looking at themselves as they really are" (Timpson et al., 1988, p. 6). Abandoning spirituality involves losing conscious contact with the Creator and the spiritual parts of all life. The more this conscious contact is lost, the more our consciousness becomes numb. We lose our sense of where we come from and the direction in which we are going. In addition, I would argue that, due to material depravity and spiritual abuse, and because of social oppression, many Indigenous peoples are suffering from spirit injuries that manifest as depression. Hence, depression is considered to be a spiritual illness and, therefore, spiritual practices must be a part of the healing process.

Once again, I am reminded that many societies of the world, such as those in Africa and the Far East, incorporate spirituality within their helping and healing practices. In fact, like Indigenous peoples, these societies do not separate spirituality from day-to-day living. A chapter in this book is dedicated to the topic of spirituality and this commonality will be explored.

CONCLUSION

This chapter briefly explored critical, structural, postmodern, and post-colonial social work theories as they relate to Indigenous approaches to helping. Viewed through an Indigenous lens, this exploration concludes that the first three theories have both strengths and challenges as they relate to Indigenous approaches. Post-colonial, or anti-colonial, theory fits best with Indigenous approaches as it originates with and is written by Indigenous peoples. I believe, however, that all of these theories, when applied to the area of social work, can operate alongside Indigenous approaches toward common goals. All of these theories can strengthen the work that social work students, educators, researchers, and practitioners do. Having allies helps everyone to create a more credible public position.

However, critical social work perspectives continue to be critiqued for their day-to-day usefulness and applicability to social work practice because they are thought to be too sociological in nature. Indigenous world views attempt to extend beyond critical theory to include processes of agency, resistance, and transformation, which are just as important to social work theory and practice as are critical perspectives. Social work educators, students, and practitioners are encouraged to explore these processes within their own practices.

The chapter also critiqued the cultural competency model, concluding that it fails both service users as a helpful approach to practice and social workers as it sets social work practitioners up to do the impossible. The cultural competency model also allows social workers to ignore the role that their own identities and positionalities, in terms of how they see themselves, how the state views them and how they are seen by service users, particularly in terms of power, play in social work practice and obscures social justice concerns. This critique from an Indigenous lens can be considered by all social work educators, students, and practitioners in how they work with those who do not come from a social location similar to theirs.

Finally, some aspects of Indigenous world views were described as the foundation for helping approaches. This book takes the position that Indigenous approaches to helping are theories that do not belong to any other theory. As theory is transferred into practice, the value of Indigenous approaches to helping practices will be demonstrated in later chapters.

REFERENCES

Absolon, K. & Herbert, E. (1997). Community action as a practice of freedom: A First Nations perspective. In B. Wharf & M. Clague (Eds.), *Community organizing: Canadian experiences* (pp. 205–227). Toronto: Oxford University Press.

Allen, P.G. (1986). *The sacred hoop: Recovering the feminine in American Indian traditions*. Boston: Beacon Press.

Anderson, K. (2000). *A recognition of being: Reconstructing Native womanhood*. Toronto: Second Story Press.

Appiah, A.K. (1992). *In my father's house: Africa in the philosophy of culture*. London: Methuen.

Ashcroft, B. (2001). *Post-colonial transformation*. New York: Routledge.

Avalos, C., Arger, L., Levesque, E. & Pike, R. (1997). Mooka'am (a new dawn). *Native Social Work Journal, 1*(1), 11–24.

Baskin, C. (1997). Mino-yaa-daa: An urban community based approach. *Native Social Work Journal, 1*(1), 55–67.

Baskin, C. (2002). Circles of resistance: Spirituality in social work practice, education, and transformative change. *Currents: New scholarship in the Human Services, 1*(1). Retrieved from http://wcmprod2.ucalgary.ca/currents/

Baskin, C. (2003). Structural social work as seen from an Indigenous perspective. In W. Shera (Ed.), *Emerging perspectives on anti-oppressive practice* (pp. 65–80). Toronto: Canadian Scholars' Press Inc.

Baskin, C. (2005). Centring Indigenous world views in social work education. *Australian Journal of Indigenous Education, 34*, 96–106.

Baskin, C. (2006). Indigenous world views as challenges and possibilities in social work education. *Critical Social Work, 7*(2). Retrieved from http://www.uwindsor.ca/criticalsocialwork/

Baskin, C. (2007a). Conceptualizing, framing, and politicizing Indigenous ethics in mental health. *Journal of Ethics in Mental Health, 2*(2), 1–5. Retrieved from http://www.jemh.ca/issues/v2n2/documents/JEMH_v2n2_Article_Part1_AboriginalEthicsMentalHealth.pdf

Baskin, C. (2007b). Working together in the circle: Challenges and possibilities within mental health ethics. *Journal of Ethics in Mental Health, 2*(2), 1–4. Retrieved from http://www.jemh.ca/issues/v2n2/documents/JEMH_v2n2_Article_Part1_AboriginalEthicsMentalHealth.pdf

Battiste, M. & Youngblood-Henderson, J. (2000). *Protecting Indigenous knowledge and heritage: A global challenge.* Saskatoon: Purich Publishing Ltd.

Bhabha, H. (1994). *The location of culture.* London: Routledge.

Bishop, A. (1994). *Becoming an ally: Breaking the cycle of oppression.* Halifax: Fernwood Publishing.

Brant-Castellano, M. (2000). Updating Indigenous traditions of knowledge. In. G.J. Dei, B.L. Hall & D.G. Rosenberg (Eds.), *Indigenous knowledges in global contexts: Multiple readings of our world* (pp. 21–36). Toronto: University of Toronto Press.

Brown, C. (1998). Essays on postmodernism and social work. In A. Chambon & A. Irving (Eds.), *Feminist postmodernism and the challenge of diversity* (pp. 35–48). Toronto: Canadian Scholars' Press Inc.

Cajete, G. (1994). *Look to the mountain: An ecology of Indigenous education.* Durando: Kivaki Press.

Couture, J. (1991). Explorations in Native knowing. In J.W. Friesen (Ed.), *The cultural maze: Complex questions on Native destiny in western Canada* (pp. 201–215). Calgary: Detselig Enterprises Ltd.

CUPE (2009). First anniversary of residential schools apology. Retrieved from http://cupe.ca

Dalrymple, J. & Burke, B. (1995). Some essential elements of anti-oppression theory. In J. Dalrymple & B. Burke (Eds.), *Anti-oppressive practice: Social care and the law* (pp. 7–21). Buckingham: Open University Press.

Deloria Jr., V. (1969). *Custer died for your sins: An Indian manifesto.* New York: Avon Books.

Dyche, L. & Zayas, L.H. (1995). The value of curiosity and naiveté for the cross-cultural psychotherapist. *Family Process, 34,* 389–399. doi: 10.1111/j.1545-5300.1995.00389.x

Ermine, W. (1995). Indigenous epistemology. In M. Battiste & J. Barman (Eds.), *First Nations education in Canada: The circle unfolds* (pp. 101–112). Vancouver: University of British Columbia Press.

Fanon, F. (1963). *The wretched of the earth.* New York: Grove Weidenfeld.

Fanon, F. (1967). *Black skin, white masks.* New York: Grove Press.

First Nations Drum. (2000). Crisis inspired many Native people. Retrieved from http://firstnationsdrum.com

Fitznor, L. (1998). The circle of life: Affirming Indigenous philosophies in everyday living. In D. McCane (Ed.), *Life ethics in world religions* (pp. 21–40). Winnipeg: University of Manitoba.

Foucault, M. (1965). *Madness and civilization: A history of insanity in the age of reason.* New York: Vintage Press.

Foucault, M. (1977). Discipline and punish: The birth of the prison. Paris, France: Gallimard.

Foucault, M. (1980a). Two lectures. In C. Gordon (Ed.), *Power/knowledge: Selected interviews and other writings, 1972–1977* (pp. 78–108). New York: Pantheon.

Foucault, M. (1980b). *Language, counter memory, practice.* Ithaca: Cornell University Press.

Foucault, M. (1985). *The history of sexuality, vol 2: The uses of pleasure.* New York: Pantheon.

Foucault, M. (1989). On literature. In S. Lotringer (Ed.), *Foucault live: Collective interviews, 1966–1984* (pp. 113–119). New York: Semiotext(e).

Gelfand, D. & Fandetti, D. (1986). The emergent nature of ethnicity: Dilemmas in assessment. *Social Casework, 67,* 542–550. doi: 10.1606/0037-7678.2518

Gilbert, M. (2000). Spirituality in social work groups: Practitioners speak out. *Social Work with Groups, 22,* 67–83. doi: 10.1300/J009v22n04_06

Gosine, K. (2000). Essentialism versus complexity: Conceptions of racial identity construction in education scholarship. *Canadian Journal of Education, 27*(1), 81–99.

Graveline, F.J. (1998). *Circle works: Transforming Eurocentric consciousness.* Halifax: Fernwood Publishing.

Gross, G.D. (2000). Gatekeeping for cultural competence: Ready or not? Some post and modernist doubts. *Journal of Baccalaureate Social Work, 5*(2), 47–66.

Hall, S. (1989). Cultural identity and cinematic representation. *Framework, 36,* 69–81.

Hampton, E. (1995). Towards a redefinition of Indian education. In M. Battiste & J. Barman (Eds.), *First Nations education in Canada* (pp. 5–46). Vancouver: University of British Columbia Press.

Hart, M.A. (2002). *Seeking mino-pimatisiwin: An Indigenous approach to helping.* Halifax: Fernwood Publishing.

Hart, M.A. (2009). Anti-colonial Indigenous social work. In R. Sinclair, M.A. Hart & G. Bruyere (Eds.), *Wicihitowin: Aboriginal social work in Canada* (pp. 25–41). Winnipeg: Fernwood Publishing.

Hill, D. (1995). *Indigenous access to post secondary education: Prior learning assessment and its use within Indigenous programs of learning.* Toronto: First Nations Technical Institute.

Hines, P.M., Garcia-Preto, N., McGoldrick M., Almeida, R. & Weltman, S. (1999). Culture and the family life cycle. In B. Carter & M. McGolrick (Eds.), *The expanded family life cycle* (3rd ed.) (pp. 69–87). Boston: Allyn & Bacon.

Jeffery, D. (2005). What good is anti-racist social work if you can't master it?: Exploring a paradox in social work education. *Race, Ethnicity, and Education, 8,* 409–425. doi: 10.1080/13613320500324011

Jeffery, D. (2009). Meeting here and now: Reflections on racial and cultural difference in social work encounters. In S. Strega & J. Carrière (Eds.), *Walking this path together: Anti-racist and anti-oppressive child welfare practice* (pp. 45–61). Black Point, NS: Fernwood Publications.

Lather, P. (1991). *Getting smart: Feminist research and pedagogy with/in the postmodern.* New York: Routledge.

Little Bear, L. (2000). *Jagged worldviews colliding.* In M. Battiste (Ed.), *Reclaiming Indigenous voice and vision* (pp. 77–85). Vancouver: University of British Columbia Press.

Locust, C. (1988). Wounding the spirit: Discrimination and traditional American Indian belief system. *Harvard Educational Review, 58*(3), 315–330.

Loomba, A. (1998). *Colonialism/postcolonialism: The new critical idiom.* New York: Routledge.

McCormick, R.M. (1995). The facilitation of healing for the First Nations people of British Columbia. *Canadian Journal of Native Education, 21*(2), 251–322.

McGoldrick, M. (1982). Through the looking glass: Supervision of a trainee's trigger family. In J. Byng-Hall & R. Whiffen (Eds.), *Family therapy supervision* (p. 17–37). London: Academic Press.

Miller, W. & Maiter, S. (2008). Fatherhood and culture: Moving beyond stereotypical understanding. *Journal of Ethnic and Cultural Diversity in Social Work, 17,* 279–300. doi: 10.1080/15313200802258216

Moosa-Mitha, M. (2005). Situating anti-oppressive theories within critical and difference-centered perspectives. In L. Brown & S. Strega (Eds.), *Research as resistance: Critical, Indigenous & anti-oppressive approaches* (pp. 37–72). Toronto: Canadian Scholars' Press Inc.

Morrisseau, C. (1998). *Into the daylight: A wholistic approach to healing.* Toronto: University of Toronto Press.

Morrissette, V., McKenzie, B. & Morrissette, L. (1993). Towards an Indigenous model of social work practice: Cultural knowledge and traditional practices. *Canadian Social Work Review, 10*(1), 91–108.

Mullaly, R. (1997). *Structural social work.* Toronto: Oxford University Press.

Mullaly, R. (2002). *Challenging oppression: A critical social work approach.* Toronto: Oxford University Press.

Nestel, S. & Razack, S. (n.d.). *Wrestling with the "ghost of anthropology past": Cultural competency approaches in medical education* (pp. 1–58). Unpublished manuscript, Toronto.

Pon, G. (2009). Cultural competency as new racism: An ontology of forgetting. *Journal of Progressive Human Services, 20*(1), 59–71. doi: 10.1080/10428230902871173.

Razack, S. (1998). *Looking White people in the eye: Gender, race, and culture in courtrooms and classrooms.* Toronto: University of Toronto Press.

Said, E. (1978). *Orientalism.* New York: Vintage Books.

Said, E. (1993). *Culture and imperialism.* London: Chatto & Windus.

Sakamoto, I. (2007). An anti-oppressive approach to cultural competence. *Canadian Social Work Review, 24*(1), 105–118.

Shilling, R. (2002). Journey of our spirits: Challenges for adult Indigenous learners. In E.V. O'Sullivan, A. Morrell & M.A. O'Connor (Eds.), *Expanding the boundaries of transformative learning: Essays on theory and practice* (pp. 151–158). Toronto: Palgrave Publishers.

Sioui, G. (1992). *For an Amerindian autohistory: An essay on the foundations of a social ethic.* Montreal: McGill University Press.

Spivak, G. (1999). *A critique of postcolonial reason: Toward a history of the vanishing present.* Cambridge: Harvard University Press.

Strega, S. (2005). The view from the poststructural margins: Epistemology and methodology reconsidered. In L. Brown & S. Strega (Eds.), *Research as resistance: Critical, Indigenous, and anti-oppressive approaches* (pp. 199–235). Toronto: Canadian Scholars' Press Inc.

Thompson, N. (1998). *Promoting equality: Challenging discrimination and oppression in the human services.* London: Macmillan.

Timpson, J., McKay, S., Kakegamic, S., Roundhead, D., Cohen, C. & Matewapit, G. (1988). Depression in a Native Canadian in northwestern Ontario: Sadness, grief, or spiritual illness? *Canada's Mental Health,* (June/September), 5–8.

Waller, M. & Patterson, S. (2002). Natural helping and resilience in a Dine (Navajo) community. *Families in Society, 83,* 73–88. doi: 10.1606/1044-3894.46

Yee, J.Y. & Dumbrill, G. (2003). Whiteout: Looking for race in Canadian social work practice. In A. Al-Krenawi & J.R. Graham (Eds.), *Multicultural social work in Canada* (pp. 98–121). Don Mills: Oxford University Press.

Yon, D. (2000). *Elusive culture: Schooling, race, and identity in global times.* New York: State University of New York Press.

Chapter 4

Centring All Helping Approaches

INTRODUCTION

During ongoing self-reflexivity, helping professionals create space for themselves to explore who they are and what they bring to their work. Through these opportunities, helpers can consider ideas of universalism, difference, essentialism, and knowledge, which will be discussed in this chapter. Through self-reflexivity, social workers and other helping professionals can also consider what might be the challenges in incorporating Indigenous knowledges into their work and explore possible solutions to such challenges.

BEING SECURE IN WHO YOU ARE

To be an effective social worker, particularly with service users who are not members of one's specific objectivity, each of us needs to understand *our own* values, beliefs, and cultures. Social work is never neutral or objective. Rather, feelings, thoughts, and experiences all contribute to what we see as good social work practice.

Then there is the larger, dominant culture of the country in which one lives. It is this dominant culture that sets community standards of what is acceptable within the areas that social workers practise, such as child welfare, criminal justice, or addiction. However, the views of the dominant culture are rarely discussed and analyzed, as they are widely seen as what is "normal" and "right".

In a course I developed and teach—"Aboriginal Approaches to Social Work"—one of the assignments for students is to write about how they are influenced by their values, beliefs, cultures, and experiences and how this may affect their practice with Indigenous peoples. An initial response to this assignment from many White students is "But I'm Canadian. I don't have a culture." I would guess that White students across countries such as Canada, the United States, Australia, and New Zealand would have similar responses to such an assignment. This response, however, is really a denial that the dominant culture is actually a culture because it is so taken for granted and rarely "seen" even though it is all around us. Dominant White culture informs all of our institutions—education, media, law, government, officially recognized holidays, shopping, entertainment, advertising; how our families, streets, and communities are designed; what is valued (youthful appearances, materialism); and who are considered to be the carriers of knowledge.

Becoming aware of one's own culture, comes about through critical self-reflexivity and questioning. This involves an ongoing process of looking inward and being open to learning more about the self and how we might practise social work. Kondrat (1999) suggests that this ongoing process focuses on three broad questions about "the world," "my world," and "correspondences and contradictions between those worlds" (p. 465). Based on these broad areas, I would suggest asking more specific questions, such as the following:

- Why am I working with this specific population (e.g., street-involved youth of colour, Indigenous single mothers) in this particular place (e.g., agency, organization)?

- What do I have to offer (e.g., knowledge of appropriate resources, non-judgmental attitude) to this population?
- Will I stand by these service users when the work becomes difficult?
- What are the areas of my work that challenge my values and beliefs and why?
- Am I committed to ongoing learning from service users and through self-reflexivity?
- What social policies and social work practices do I see as oppressive in the context of my work with this population, including within my place of employment, and how can I work toward changing these practices?

Knowing who you are in terms of your culture requires ongoing self-reflexivity that can help you as a social worker become more secure in your own identity. Security in knowing who you are and what your purpose is helps you to resist appropriating cultures that are not your own. There is no need to search other cultural practices in order to fill up emptiness inside you. This sense of security also leads to a greater openness to many ways of knowing, rather than staying with only one way or your way of knowing. Often it is insecurity about who one is that leads one to view the "other" as inferior.

Charlene Avalos, who was first introduced in Chapter 2, is a good example of a non-Indigenous social worker who successfully works with Indigenous peoples. The following is some of Charlene's story about her early days working in the Bela Bela First Nation in B.C.:

My social work education did not prepare me for doing social work out in a community. However, my learning was balanced out when I moved to the First Nations community, where I gained an understanding of the teachings there, which led to my deep respect for the people. This was my first social work job—being the first band social worker in the community. The people saw me as "the welfare lady" who could take children away.

The people were not much interested in my degree. They were more interested in who I was, what I could do for them, and would I stay there. For a while, most people didn't like me. They asked what I was doing in their community; told me I didn't know anything about them or their lives; they were unfriendly, cold, and they excluded me. I was pushed to the extreme where I was asking myself why I was there and what I was doing. (C. Avalos, personal communication, February 14, 2009)

Needless to say, these were exactly the kind of questions Charlene needed to ask herself. Once she began, she was able to uncover the issues:

I realized that when I first got to the community, I wanted to jump in and do the kind of social work I was taught to do through my education. This did not work! I suggest to all social workers that instead of doing this, you watch, observe, take your time, learn, and receive when people want to teach you. When I started to do this, I arrived at a place of collaboration with the people of the community. I joined committees to help get people what they needed, such as a daycare. I gradually became a part of helping to build back the community after the destruction caused by the residential schools. (C. Avalos, personal communication, February 14, 2009)

Charlene's process of self-reflexivity assisted her in coming to some important insights into her work with Indigenous peoples:

I was insecure when I came to Bela Bela. As a non-Aboriginal social worker in an Aboriginal community, I carried guilt about what had been done to Aboriginal people in the past. I also had to learn about not taking things personally. One time I was at a party where some of the people were cutting down White people. I began to pull away, but when someone asked what was wrong, I told them. Everyone was surprised and saying, "We don't mean you." This taught me that when Aboriginal people talk about what White people have done, it's not directed at any individual one of us. (C. Avalos, personal communication, February 14, 2009)

Charlene's example refers to the concept of "whiteness," which is defined as "a complex social process that perpetuates and maintains the dominant and/or majority group's power" (Yee, 2005, p. 89). What is being critiqued here is not Charlene or any other individual White person, but discourses of power that maintain whiteness in a privileged position. The Aboriginal peoples in Charlene's story were referring to the colonizing power, which is a part of whiteness, but is not inherent within any individual who is of this identity.

Another equally important component to critical self-reflexivity is one's analysis of how power and oppression affect our interactions with service users. Social work educator, Barbara Heron (2005), writes about how she teaches this type of analysis to students. She wants students to see:

> ... how power and oppression shape their sense of self and their approach to practice. I want students to think about how this plays itself out in the "helping" relationship: how the complexities of their and their clients' identities may interact, how domination may be reinscribed at the moment of helping, and how their participation as social workers in such relationships inevitably works to shape their identities. (pp. 341–342)

Most of us, both social workers and service users, carry multiple identities that carry a combination of power and oppression. For example, I am oppressed as an Indigenous woman who has little power in society. However, as a university professor with a Ph.D., I hold significant power in my classroom, and my knowledge is sought after and valued (as evidenced by my writing this book!). A low-income, White female social service user may hold very little power. In some aspects of her identity, she may be oppressed. However, she also may exert power if she refuses the services of a Black Muslim social worker. A White female social worker may carry power in her work with service users, but perhaps the power that she exerts may be reduced when the service users with whom she interacts are male. Further, the power that she exerts may be significantly reduced when she interacts with a male executive director of her agency.

I agree with Heron (2005), who suggests that such issues of power and their effects between social workers and service users, front-line practitioners and management, and professors and students are rarely examined. Heron also brings privilege into this discussion:

> The acknowledgement of privilege seems to strike a chord for racially-aware members of the dominant group, but I would propose that admitting one's privilege does not necessarily unsettle its operation. For this is a concept that has the potential to leave those who name it in a place

of double comfort: the comfort of demonstrating that one is critically aware, and the comfort of *not* needing to act to undo privilege. (p. 344)

It is clear that awareness of one's privileges does not always lead to action. However, action is what is needed. The next section of this chapter takes up the action of privileging Indigenous world views and ways of helping as social work theory that can occupy a position of equality with respect to other social work theories.

Here is a final word from Heron (2005) before I go on: "Since as a subject one is not taken to be a unitary, all-of-one piece identity, it becomes more possible to 'forgive' oneself for an imperfect resistance to dominance" (p. 356). Please read on, but be kind to yourself for doing so. A process of self-reflexivity requires one to be kind to oneself.

SAMENESS OR ACCEPTANCE OF DIFFERENCE?

Centring all helping approaches involves creating space for all of us in the circle. It asks Western knowledge to move over, so that Indigenous knowledges can occupy a place in the circle that is neither in front nor behind. Everyone's knowledge is not the same and everyone also has something of value to offer to the whole. People are not the same. We are all different. This stand, then, rejects universalism within the social work profession. This universalism is currently being challenged not only by Indigenous voices, but also by many marginalized peoples.

When we come to understand one another's world views, then we will be more likely to accept differences and begin to value them. Valuing differences means letting go of one's comfort zone and arrogance about what is the "right" way to help or to do social work. Valuing differences asks us to listen to what others have to say, keep our minds open to new learning, and consider how we can be enriched by these teachings.

Challenging universalism involves questioning whether or not Western social work theories and practices are relevant within all contexts. It is unlikely that these practices can simply be transplanted within non-Western communities. Like plants, if they are not indigenous to their environment, they may not survive. This challenge involves "authentication," which means in this case "to become genuine" or "to go back to one's roots to seek direction" (Gray, Coates & Hetherington, 2007, p. 61). This is precisely what I am advocating for *all* peoples. It is important that we all look toward the values and beliefs of *all* our world views in order to guide us in shaping social work practice. In doing so, we will come to realize that many peoples around the world do not support Western social work concepts such as individualism, professionalism, and objectivity. In fact, I have met many non-Indigenous peoples from India to Australia to Canada working in the social work profession who do not base their practice on these concepts.

Gray et al. (2007) write about Indigenous perspectives on helping, which they believe can enrich social work practice regardless of who the service users are. Some of these aspects are:

- Everyone has a common humanity.
- There are many ways of knowing and all are significant.
- Social work inherently carries humanistic goals.
- Context needs to always be kept in mind.
- Connecting with service users and ensuring that our practices are meaningful to them is key.
- Self-fulfillment can only be truly realized when there is group/community fulfillment.

Our differences may be large or small, but do not have to be based on binaries. I encourage readers to have deep discussions about these seven points and keep them in mind when reading the rest of this book.

Undoubtedly, there is an interest in Indigenous world views as sites of assistance in several areas of concern to the West. A literature review in this area revealed a number of examples of the importance of Indigenous world views within diverse professions, places, and publications. Here are some examples:

- Documentation of the positive impacts of culturally based programming rooted in Indigenous world views for survivors of Indian residential schools in *Australian Psychiatry* (DeGagne, 2007)
- The work of the Aboriginal Healing Foundation in the *Canadian Public Administration Journal* not only in the area of culturally based practices, but also in the field of administration where its high standards were emphasized (DeGagne, 2008)
- Increased concern for the environment has resulted in more openness to world views other than those of the dominant society,

including an openness to Indigenous ways of healing (Coates, Gray & Hetherington, 2006)

- A holistic approach is becoming more valued in health care education (Hunter, Logan, Goulet & Barton, 2006)
- Indigenous and non-Indigenous helping approaches have been combined and used in healing work. For example, the Wellbriety Movement blends the teachings of the Medicine Wheel with the 12-step Alcoholics Anonymous program (Coyhis & Simonelli, 2008)
- The Canadian International Development Agency's (CIDA) Policy Document on Indigenous Knowledge and Sustainable Development (2002) states that "some see Indigenous knowledge as a last hope in implementation of a sustainable future" (p. 3)
- According to Berry (1997), some writers have argued that Indigenous world views can guide humanity

More than 25 years ago, research was conducted with Russell Willier, a Cree Medicine Man from Sucker Creek First Nation in northern Alberta. Swartz (1987) documented Willier's treatment of non-Indigenous participants suffering from psoriasis.

Willier permitted researchers to conduct an intrusive investigation, including a chemical analysis of the plants used in his treatments, and photographing and videotaping participants' skin conditions before and after treatments (Swartz, 1987). This example is evidence of an Indigenous value of knowledge sharing. According to Willier, the Earth offers many medicines for human beings, including plants, animals, water, and soil. At the same time, the Earth is also suffering. Some argue that pollutants, the destruction of ecosystems, and the genocide of some animal species has resulted in a state of chronic sickness for human beings (Swartz, 1987).

Within social work specifically, Gray et al. (2007) take a similar position to the writers above, stating that "... Indigenous beliefs and values have gained recognition and credibility among the world views that provide a re-conceptualization of the universe and humanity's relationship to it. In social work, this has opened avenues of acceptance toward Indigenous approaches to helping" (p. 60). I believe that the social work profession is not only ready to listen to Indigenous world views, but is actually taking the lead within the helping professions to create a space for these world views within social work discourse. Indigenous world views are acknowledged by a rising number of Indigenous and non-Indigenous peoples, both students and educators, within social work education. There is also a growing amount of literature by Indigenous writers that has been published within peer-reviewed journals, and Indigenous content is included within the curriculum of a number of college and university-level social work programs. The number of Indigenous social work practitioners, both within Indigenous and other social services agencies, has also increased. It may be said that we are beginning to Indigenize the profession of social work in numerous pockets throughout the West!

CHALLENGES TO INCORPORATING INDIGENOUS APPROACHES

First, let me tell you about one of the challenges I am having right now while writing this book. No, it's not the one I have already mentioned about walking the fine line between world views and cultures. This one is about writing about Indigenous approaches on topics of helping as though they are separate from one another. Indigenous approaches in helping areas cannot be separate, which is the whole point!

Within Indigenous world views, everything is connected. Therefore, it is difficult to write chapters about chosen topics such as values and ethics, caring for families and children, and research without saying something from other chapters about areas that include holistic approaches and spirituality. Should I include a disclaimer here?

Spirituality, holistic approaches, and values and ethics are all a part of the knowledge that is taught, learned, and practised within Indigenous helping approaches. They are woven into our helping practices and so will show up in every chapter of this book. Therefore, I may repeat myself many times, causing readers to exclaim, perhaps in frustration, "She already said that!"

I fear I have no choice but to refer to these foundational aspects of Indigenous world views repeatedly and hope that I do not bore you. I will do my best to not repeat exactly the same words, but to instead explain in a variety of ways how these aspects apply to each particular chapter.

Wendy Martin is a non-Indigenous ally with an M.S.W. who has taken social work courses with Aboriginal professors on the history of colonization and Aboriginal world views in both her undergraduate and graduate education. She works in the area of youth in conflict with the law. She is also one of my dearest friends. When I asked Wendy what her greatest challenge was in terms of her work regarding Indigenous peoples, she responded with the following:

Educating colleagues! I do a lot of this, especially when I talk about the impacts of colonization, for example. I'm often tuned out, negated, ignored; others don't want to hear at times, they get angry, shut me down. Then I get hurt. It gets so that I feel I'm doing more of a disservice to Aboriginal people if I'm not listened to.

I don't want to ever invalidate Aboriginal people's pain, but being an ally can give one a bit of an idea of what it's like to be shut out and pushed away, which is what Aboriginal peoples experience daily.

I can get apathetic: there are times when I just can't muster up the strength to address colleagues' ignorant statements, so I'm now learning how to choose my battles and be strategic. It seems that successful strategies are often about timing. Sometimes I use my intuition or ask myself "Will I be helping with Aboriginal causes by saying something right now or will I actually be alienating non-Aboriginal people from them?" (W. Martin, personal communication, February 8, 2009)

Doing the "right thing" is not always doing the easiest thing, which is clearly what Wendy is experiencing. No doubt, non-Indigenous practitioners everywhere face similar practice challenges. However, White people and Indigenous peoples working together to educate other White people is exactly the work that is required of a true ally, especially when the work gets tough. As Indigenous peoples, it is not our responsibility to do all the educating. However, our allies need to be kind to themselves, take care of themselves, and receive support, so that they, too, can continue their important work of helping to educate others. Wendy spoke to me about how she does this:

I have a support group, which I believe is essential to doing the work of an ally. I have a circle of Aboriginal friends who are also in the helping professions who support me and who[m] I support. I also have non-Aboriginal people in my life who think similarly to me. These supports are vital to the work of an ally. When I need some guidance about a particular situation, my Aboriginal friends and colleagues are there to help me in the moment. We support each other, which helps prevent burnout and compassionate fatigue. Being an ally in an agency or working in an institution often means you are alone in the work you are trying to do. Sometimes when you are on your own, you just feel like giving up, but when I connect with Aboriginal helpers, I get energized again! (W. Martin, personal communication, February 8, 2009)

I invited the students from the course, "Indigenous Knowledges in Social Work," who participated in a Sharing Circle for this book, to talk about what they saw as challenges to incorporating Indigenous approaches within social work, which I believe students in many other parts of the world will relate to. The following is their discussion on some of the challenges they identified and suggestions on how to address them:

Eddy: I see it as a struggle to figure out where to fit within Indigenous social work. This is my second Indigenous knowledges in social work course in the School of Social Work at Ryerson, and I believe that continuous learning is crucial. I never want to feel like I know enough, that I can stop learning.

Flo: I agree with Eddy that as non-Indigenous social workers, we need to continue to learn in the future. We need to be diligent about deconstructing and really take a good look at things like I had to do regarding the song "Onward Christian Soldiers." Let me remind you about that learning for me.

I was raised in a Christian family and grew up in church singing the song "Onward Christian Soldiers" on occasion. I never considered its meaning. The song is a popular one and is sung in church, so I never thought of questioning it. Why should I? After all, all hymns have a good meaning, or so I thought. But then I read an article about this hymn for the presentation I was doing for our course and found out about the origins of the song. This had quite an emotional impact on me, but the experience taught me to see how important it is for all of us to continuously aim to gain new knowledge, which brings awareness. I think if we are not aware, then we can easily be manipulated or influenced about what is taught to us. It became important then for me to take some sort of action by talking to others who attend my church to see what we could do about not having it sung there.

But it turned out that there was another layer to my experience that Cyndy taught me, which led me to understand that it is not this hymn or any other hymn that I have a relationship with since, after all, they have been man-made, but my relationship is with God.

Meliza: My greatest challenge is when do we as non-Indigenous social workers pass on information that we have learned about Indigenous world views? When do we as non-Indigenous social workers call people on their inaccurate information or racist comments about Indigenous peoples? Those we challenge may respond with "Who made you the expert?" or "What makes you think you can speak on this?"

Carolina: We need to listen to our inner voices when they tell us to speak up and resist. We need to listen to our own ancestral voices inside us. Indigenous ways speak to those of us who are searching for better ways, so we need to do this.

Karen: I agree. Intuition is our cue as to when to speak up or not. And we can speak up without having to know it all.

Lorraine: Our work can be to engage people who don't care by showing them they need to care because we are all connected. The work of non-Indigenous peoples is to dedicate ourselves to creating equitable partnerships with Indigenous peoples and deal with whatever arises in a productive way. An example is appropriation—to challenge ourselves about it and to initiate conversations, rather than simply rejecting what people do or walking away all the time.

It's easy to be critical, but not so easy to form partnerships. This is what I started to understand in this course in the middle of a critically focused, anti-oppressive curriculum. It is a quick decision to reject or dismiss something that is not working or will not work or should not work. I think this is about expecting perfect plans and rejecting messy processes, but we don't know if something will work at first glance. There isn't enough time to make this judgment, so it often seems easier to just reject something at the first sign that it does not fit with what one knows. I think the message for us non-Indigenous people is you made this mess, so you stay and be a part of cleaning it up; you stay and work at relationships and partnerships. (Eddy, Flo, Meliza, Carolina, Karen, Lorraine, personal communication, April 6, 2009)

A strong and gifted Two-Spirited Anishnawbe Kwe (woman) from Couchching First Nation also contributed her thoughts on what are the most challenging

out exactly what is expected. If children do not learn what is expected, then they "fail."

Jennifer Ajandi, who was previously introduced, shared with me how some of the teachings on Indigenous ways of raising children influenced her in her parenting:

I appreciate the information I have received on raising children within Aboriginal world views: an understanding that there are many ways of parenting, that it does not have to be so directive and authoritarian as in mainstream practices. It allows for a child to think through challenges, learn from experiences, and understand that there are natural consequences to one's behaviour.

I have an example of this with my own daughter, who is three-and-a-half years old, which was truly a learning moment for me. When she asked to bring something to school that could break, instead of answering "No, go find something else," which is what I usually do when we're rushing in the morning, I discussed with her what I thought might happen if she chose to bring this snow globe with her to school—that it was not a toy in the same way her other stuff was—it could break, that maybe she could bring it, but put it in her locker. She stood for a moment and thought about it and then said, "I will go put it back and get something else instead." That moment made me realize how we had just had a discussion about her options, and that I provided the space for her to make her own decision and feel confident with it. This was an approach I had learned in class with you, Cyndy, about Aboriginal ways of parenting, which are more non-directive and come about through discussion or storytelling. (J. Ajandi, personal communication, January 10, 2009)

Further, Indigenous world views emphasize that children are gifts from the Creator. Indigenous world views emphasize that children do not belong to us. We may borrow them for a while and we have responsibility for them. In addition, biological parents are not the only ones who are expected to raise children. Rather, extended families and entire communities share a responsibility for raising children. Children are seen as precious because it is believed that they come directly from the spirit world. Today, within Western world views, children are no longer regarded as their parents' property, but there is still this notion of "my" children. This notion of "my" children implies that the parent is the sole one responsible for raising a child. The parent is responsible for whatever that child does or does not do. It is possible to hear stressed-out single mothers saying, "Don't tell me how to raise my child!"

There are many societies that view the raising of children in ways similar to Indigenous peoples. According to Flo, one of the students in the class who participated in the Sharing Circle:

> There are many similarities between Aboriginal world views and those of the peoples of the Caribbean. In both of these world views, the community raises children. Why can't everyone practise this so that everyone is looking out for each other and taking care of children? (Flo, personal communication, April 6, 2009)

Non-interference is an Indigenous value that Liz Arger referred to in one of my earlier chapters. This value is about not getting in the way of another person's journey or process or preventing someone from doing something simply because we do not agree with it. It means not giving advice, not being directive, and not participating in another person's process unless invited to do so. In the West, however, most helping professions do not adopt these kinds of values. There is a great deal of interference. People who require assistance are told what services to access with very little consultation. People are told how to take care of themselves, how to raise their children, and how to manage their relationships. There is also a considerable amount of entertainment on national television that focuses on people's misery and how people ought to deal with it.

FROM AN ETHICAL PLACE

A review of the literature reveals that very little has been published on the subject of Aboriginal ethics in the area of social work. This may be, in part, because Indigenous ethics are rooted in the context of oral history and storytelling. Indigenous ethics are framed within a process rather than as a specific code (Ellerby, McKenzie, McKay, Gariepy & Kaufert, 2000). Ethical decisions are always related to context and involve collaboration with community members and families.

In defining ethics generally from an Indigenous world view, Brant-Castellano (2004) states that:

Ethics, the rules of right behaviour, are intimately related to who you are, the deep values you subscribe to, and your understanding of your place in the spiritual order of reality. Ethics is integral to the way of life of a people. The fullest expression of a people's ethics is presented in the lives of the most knowledgeable and honourable members of the community. Imposition of rules derived from other ways of life in other communities will inevitably cause problems, although common understandings and shared interests can be negotiated. (p. 103)

Indigenous world views inherently include an epistemology that has ethical and moral dimensions. For example, when someone comes into a relationship with specific knowledge, that person is not only honoured and transformed by it, but must also take responsibility for it (Newhouse, 2004). A relational perspective teaches individuals to take social responsibility for living an ethical and moral life in the present, to honour the past through the spiritual care of those who have passed on, and to always keep the future in mind by taking care of the Earth for the next seven generations to come as stated in the Great Law of the Haudenosaunee (A. Jock, personal communication, May 1986). Living an ethical life is particularly important for Elders, healers, and other service providers as they are known and respected within both rural and urban communities. Their efficacy and moral behaviour must be open to scrutiny. Being a healer or helper involves issues of power and there needs to be open and ongoing critical examination of these issues by everyone involved, including those accessing services, community members, and the helpers themselves.

Another issue that needs to be considered in our work is the idea of objectivity. I do not think objectivity, as defined in conventional usage, exists. We bring who we are and what we believe—our values and ethics—into everything we do. Everything from a social work assessment of a family living in poverty or the approach that we might take when working with a child who has been sexually abused is affected by our values and ethics. The decisions we make are neither neutral nor objective. Rather, they are based on our values and ethics and on the ways that we express our values and ethics through our actions. It is important to ask questions about what kind of lens we are using, where our particular values come from, and what these values really mean. The helping professions are not neutral or objective, and neither are the people who do this kind of work.

I would argue that what is needed is respect, rather than holding on to a notion that objectivity exists. At its roots, the meaning of respect involves "looking twice" at something, which allows for an open mind (M. Thrasher, personal communication, October 1991). It means moving beyond one's own initial reactions or assessment and looking at a situation again in a closer, deeper way, taking every possible dimension into account.

MOVING AWAY FROM INDIVIDUALISM

One of the most fascinating activities I am currently engaged in is learning about different ways of knowing. I am interested in the diverse and connected world views of the peoples of the world. And I am particularly struck by the common values that many of us coming from non-Western societies share. For example, I meditate, which is a common spiritual practice for many people around the globe. I meditate when I fast, but I also meditate almost every day for anywhere between one hour to five minutes in a sitting. I meditate because it's good for me. It helps me as an individual to focus, relax, and stay in the moment. Like exercise and prayer, if I don't meditate, I don't feel grounded and balanced. I believe meditation is one way of knowing myself and my relationship with the world I live in.

However, like prayer and my participation in the spiritual ceremonies of my Mi'kmaq Nation or those of the Anishnawbe whose territory I live in, I also meditate because it helps the planet. I do it because I believe that it helps all people who are ill or who are in difficult situations. For me, meditation is a move away from individualism and toward caring for the collective—all people and for the planet that we all share.

Pema Chodron is a Buddhist nun whose teachings I relate to because they connect closely with those of my Indigenous world views. In one of her books, *When Things Fall Apart: Heart Advice for Difficult Times*, Chodron (1997) writes about a breathing practice called "tonglen," which involves breathing in the pain of others and breathing out relief to all those who are feeling pain. She provides a touching example of this practice:

> For instance, if we know of a child who is being hurt, we breathe in with the wish to take away all of that child's pain and fear. Then as we breathe out, we send happiness, joy, or whatever would relieve the child. This is the core of the practice: breathing in others' pain so they can be well and have more space to relax and open—breathing out, sending them relaxation or whatever we feel would bring them relief and happiness. (p. 94)

Such teachings, which emphasize the well-being of all who make up the collective, rather than the well-being of the self or those who are part of one's inner circle such as family and friends, have existed since the beginning of time in many non-Western societies.

Within the profession of social work, individualism is often manifested in the ways that we choose to work with people. Perhaps we might individualize a person's difficulties. We might choose to work with that individual on a one-to-one basis, but avoid actively engaging in community outreach and practice. We might have rigid guidelines about confidentiality. It also might be that by focusing on one person or one family, we are reinforcing a condition of isolation that is also often a large part of the problems people are dealing with. By focusing on individual concerns, are we putting the larger community at risk? By seeing the world in a more narrow way, are we hurting ourselves and others? By not bringing the collective together, are we missing out on many helpful possibilities, suggestions, and opportunities that might help us to assist one another?

Social workers are also impacted. Are we not imposing an impossible amount of work on the role of individual social workers? Because social workers often work in isolation, how many of these workers see themselves as part of a larger collective or part of a movement toward social justice? By working with one individual or one family at a time, how many of these social workers see themselves as contributing to significant social justice initiatives? How many see themselves as caring for all peoples and the Earth we share?

Such questions can be explored in large part from a values and ethics perspective. Indigenous knowledges and spiritual beliefs, which exist throughout the world on many continents and have no boundaries in terms of "race," teach us that to focus only on the self has long-lasting negative consequences. For centuries, many countries of the world have focused solely on their own national well-being without any thought to other peoples on the Earth. Today, because the globalization of the mass media has engendered an increased awareness of global issues, many of us are faced with the consequences of the selfishness of individualism. The values of individualism and competition are not working and many of us know this. Rather than continuing on this path, perhaps it may help us all if we begin to look at how we relate to others, to the world, and to our profession in ways that honour and care for the collective well-being.

In her contribution to the student Sharing Circle, Sondra took up the idea of how the mentality of those in the West is not working and she sees that:

... a lot of un-learning is now happening. People in the West have been taught about survival of the fittest; that one needs to be a conqueror or will be conquered. There has been a mentality of faster, better, stronger, but this is making people sick. Aboriginal ways have healing in them, such as medicines, which could be helpful for all people. (Sondra, personal communication, April 6, 2009)

Rupert Ross is an assistant Crown attorney in Kenora, Ontario. He has been working with, and writing about, Indigenous peoples and the justice system for many years. Not Indigenous, Ross has written a number of progressively insightful writings over the years. These days he writes about what he calls "the relational lens" in his attempts to understand Indigenous world views. Ross (2007) states that within these world views:

... the world can be understood as primarily composed of ever-changing relationships of dependency, as all things are seen as essential to a healthy whole. That basic conviction drives a further conclusion: our relationships are fundamentally centred on dependencies, and human beings are not, as the western view seems to hold, fundamentally a collection of rights against others, but a bundle of responsibilities towards others, towards all aspects of Creation. (p. 24)

Ross goes on to discuss how these connections and responsibilities are expressed to community members:

To be told, especially within powerful ceremonies, of your intrinsic worth within Creation, and of the importance of your contribution to maintain its healthy equilibrium, is to be given a precious gift indeed.... They [teenage girls] were ... almost desperately grateful for being told that they were important somewhere, that they had roles to play, that they were part of something larger than themselves—especially something as huge and magical as the universe itself! (pp. 24–25)

Jacquie Green, of the Haisla Nation, and Robina Thomas, of the Lyackson of the Coast Salish Nation (2007), conducted research with Indigenous social work practitioners on what they saw as "best practices" in the area of child welfare. Throughout their interviews, Green and Thomas reported that almost all of the social workers described their work as "family-centred" walking with families to "collectively make decisions" (p. 182). As one worker explained:

> Our workers include, as much as we can, family, community and anyone the child feels connected to ... because once we have community, once we have family, they have control, and that's where it belongs, with the family, not with us. (p. 182)

RELATIONSHIPS

Charlene Avalos strongly advocates that Indigenous values and ethics have much strength and can be applied to all peoples. In talking about relationships as a significant value within Indigenous ways of helping, she first begins with understandings of a relationship with the self:

> Aboriginal helping approaches are holistic, always viewing a person in relationship with their family and community. I believe every social worker can learn from this. The holistic approach is also about the four aspects of a person, which, of course, applies to all peoples. Let me explain this according to the teachings of the four directions as I have been taught about them.
>
> The eastern doorway represents vision, which means having a purpose in life. Each of us needs a sense of the future and our role in it. We can't get healthy without this.
>
> The doorway of the south is all about relationships and connections, which are the foundation of helping approaches or social work for all people.
>
> Then in the west are emotions. Aboriginal ways of helping have always looked at trauma and how to release it. It's understood and accepted that people need to do this. Social work has begun to do the same.
>
> And finally in the northern direction is the area of the physical, such as nutrition and exercise. If a person doesn't eat properly and exercise, then this affects everything else so there will be a greater chance that the person will be unbalanced.
>
> For all human beings, these aspects are interconnected and healing needs to take place in all areas so balance can be achieved. (C. Avalos, personal communication, February 14, 2009)

I then asked Charlene about her understanding and experiences about the relationship between a social worker and a service user from an Indigenous viewpoint. Her response focused on trust:

> Service users are supposed to trust social workers, but we don't trust them since we don't reveal anything about ourselves to them. This creates a hierarchy and inequality with an expert-client relationship. Within an Aboriginal perspective, we are all equal, but each of us can be at a different place in our healing journey. Sharing one's journey with a client helps to balance out the playing field while deepening the relationship and connection between the two. It wasn't until I lived and practiced social work in an Aboriginal community that I realized how the disclosure of a helper's story can greatly increase trust. In Aboriginal helping processes, there is often some form of disclosure between client and worker because this helps to balance out the relationship while normalizing and de-stigmatizing the need for help. (C. Avalos, personal communication, February 14, 2009)

Cree Elder Joanne Dallaire, from Attawapiskat First Nation, is a Traditional Counsellor/Healer with over 25 years of experience. She is an adviser to many Aboriginal agencies and programs throughout Ontario. Joanne supports what Charlene emphasizes about self-disclosure and trust:

> Actually, I told a woman today who was in an abusive relationship for eight years that I had been in one for 14 years and know how difficult it is to get out of such a situation. Service providers need to give service users a reason to trust them. This is why I share some of myself with them. If one is recovering from drug abuse, for example, it helps to see someone who had this issue in the past and overcame it. (J. Dallaire, personal communication, July 23, 2009)

I agree with Joanne that a helper's disclosure about how she overcame adversity, what helped her, and what she may still struggle with at times can be encouraging for those who come to us for assistance. If, for example, a social worker discloses that she was once a victim of domestic violence, then the woman sitting across from her who is attempting to get out of the same situation may believe that the worker understands her ambivalent feelings and, therefore, sees the social worker as more credible. When a worker says to a service user, "I know what you mean," there must be authenticity in this. I also believe that when such a woman hears how the worker got help and created a different story for herself, she may begin to have hope that she will be able to do the same.

However, both service users and social workers need to *choose* what they wish to share with one another. The time social workers spend with service users is not about them. It is not an opportunity for them to go into detail about their life experiences or to disclose information that is not directly intended to assist the service users about specific concerns. The service user is not the worker's sounding board or therapist, and disclosure is not to be used as a way to be liked by the service user.

In their research, Green and Thomas (2007) also heard from their research participants about "building trusting relationships with the community" (p. 183). They share how one worker stated "that she approaches all relationships as if they will be lifelong relationships ... [which] requires commitment and time" (p. 183). Green and Thomas stress how connection, such as knowing "the community, the kinships, the history, [and] the culture ... help us in establishing powerful helping relationships" (p. 187). Such relationships are crucial when helping work becomes difficult:

> ... [W]e might have to go into a family member's home to "protect" a child and are met with rage. This anger is not easy to overlook. And then, we have to know that we have done everything right when we walk in our communities and face the rest of the family and community. This is when the importance of building "relationships" is critical—the stronger the relationship, the more able we are as workers to work through the anger. (p. 187)

Ross (2008) writes about the relationship between service provider and service user, using his observations from his work in Indigenous communities. He states that there are no concepts that express the grey areas between service provider and service user. Within Western concepts, the relationship between service provider and service user is defined by the idea of "I [the service provider] am well, but you [the service user] are ill" (p. 22). Rather, from an Indigenous perspective:

> The distinction between healer and patient seems to lose its force, as do the boundaries between them. Instead, the sense that "we are all on this

journey together" seems to characterize most interactions, and gives people the critical message that they are not some lower order of humanity destined never to rise above their pain or their sins. (p. 22)

Like Avalos, Ross (2008) also raises issues of power, hierarchy, and inequality within Western approaches to helping. He states that "western therapies … engage patient and therapist in one-on-one relationships conducted within strict professional boundaries" (p. 23). He goes on to quote Judith Herman (1992):

> The Patient enters therapy in need of help and care. By virtue of this fact, she voluntarily submits herself to an unequal relationship in which the therapist has superior status and power (p. 134).... The dynamics of dominance and submission are re-enacted in all subsequent relationships, including the therapy. (p. 138)

Ross then raises the use of Healing Circles as part of Indigenous approaches to helping and how they may achieve something different from one-to-one counselling:

> I find myself wondering whether the circle, as opposed to the therapist's couch, is a *qualitatively* different place, and whether the circle participants, all speaking of their own healing journeys, are not *qualitatively* different from the single therapist forced by her profession to maintain strict boundaries.... [I]s it possible that aboriginal healing circles can be seen as potentially powerful processes with perhaps a *lesser* risk of obstructions like transference? (pp. 24–25)

Ross concludes from his observations and understandings of Healing Circles that

> … it seems that the stories in the circle send another critical message, that healing is indeed *possible*, for every person speaking [has] been exactly where the victim now [sits].... I also suggest that no one, even the best-trained therapist, can simply *tell* them that it could be different; instead, they have to feel it to believe it. And if they feel the celebration of others, maybe that's a source of optimism and celebration for them as well. (p. 25)

In Chapter 6, I take up Ross's ideas about the efficacy of the Healing Circle as a powerful place of learning, sharing, and hope.

WHOLENESS

Liz Arger sees Indigenous ways of helping as focusing primarily on the value of holism, which can be applied to all people. Liz has been taught by the Cree and Anishnawbe Elders and colleagues where she works on how to use the Medicine Wheel as a holistic assessment tool. She explained some of her understanding about how the Medicine Wheel works:

> The Medicine Wheel helps practitioners to keep all aspects of a person in mind, especially if they have a tendency to focus on only one or two of them. As an example, if a person is challenged with depression, it will affect all four of their aspects. A person is not compartmentalized nor is their life, so all areas need to be respected. A holistic approach to helping asks how a person is doing physically—for example, asking how sugar affects the person's moods. (L. Arger, personal communication, June 18, 2009)

Another example is if one takes up a cognitive behavioural approach, then the psychological aspect is being looked at, but what about the person's spirit? This can't be addressed by only talking about it. There's actual research now that shows how all aspects of a person are interconnected and impact upon one another, but this has been a part of Aboriginal world views forever. This is only one example of how Aboriginal people have so much of value to contribute to the world. (L. Arger, personal communication, June 18, 2009)

Values and ethics are of prime concern in all areas of social work. Let's consider how they can be applied within the frameworks of both Western and Indigenous world views in the area of mental health. For someone struggling with mental health challenges, part of the role of medications, crisis intervention, and hospitalization in a Western framework is to re-establish needed connections to reality, the here and now, etc., and to alleviate symptoms. The goal of, for example, sweat lodge ceremonies, the meals that follow them, and the use of herbal medicines is to activate a new relationship between body, mind, emotion, and spirit. Both of these approaches may calm people and ground them in human relationships so they can make an informed choice about treatment and/or healing (Baskin, 2007).

A mental health issue is not seen as located only within a person, but is also reflected in the problems in that person's family, peer group, and community. The individual and community are not seen as separate. Relatives, community members, and support people need to work together in order for health and well-being to be re-established for this person. Thus, it is necessary for all the relatives of a person with mental health challenges to be present, involved, and working toward common goals for that person (Baskin, 2007). Restoration of a person's health must include restoring relatedness within that person's family and with others whom she or he identifies as significant to her or him. Ceremonies often help to achieve this connection. Family members of a person with mental health challenges often speak about how ceremonies help them understand how they can help their loved one (Baskin, 2007).

Western practitioners can also work with families using modelling in their responses to those who are struggling with mental health issues. For example, modelling calmness for people who are experiencing anxiety attacks can help them to cope with ongoing symptoms of anxiety. Such modelling can also help to increase the skill and competence of the family while assisting them in building the confidence to know that they *can* help (Baskin, 2007).

It appears to me that there are similarities between Indigenous and Western values with respect to direct service work with those who face mental health challenges as demonstrated in the above examples. Western and Indigenous world views may not agree about the origins or meanings of mental health challenges or about the specific practices used to address these challenges. However, the intentions of the helping practices are similar and include:

- calming the person and grounding her or him in human relationships
- ensuring informed choice about treatment/healing
- acknowledging that mental health challenges are not only within a person, but are connected to problems with other people
- restoring relatedness to others
- acting as a role model for others

These observations may be a starting point for Western and Indigenous helpers to begin talking about helping practices within the mental health field.

LEARNING

I invited Liz Arger to speak about her experiences of how helpers are taught to help within Indigenous world views. She shared the following:

> An Elder that I work with often says, "We are involved in the university of the universe," which means learning how to live with everything around us. It means learning about values, principles, relationships, roles, the importance of family, and how to be with each other in a healthy way.
>
> Helpers are taught that service to others is thoughtful; that they are students of life who learn through paying attention and truly listening. They are taught to respond, rather than react. They develop leadership, which is about giving of themselves and what they learn to the community through their actions. They learn how *not* to interfere in someone else's journey, growth and development through the values of respect and non-interference. (L. Arger, personal communication, June 18, 2009)

I then invited Liz to reflect on why she believes such learning for Indigenous helpers can be of value to non-Indigenous ones. She responded with:

> This learning process I'm talking about means immersing oneself subjectively or from the inside out. It entails letting go of comfort zones of what is familiar and feels safe. This enriches a person and teaches them to respect their own process so that they are better able to do the same for others. It is a process of coming to *know* rather than believing something that is outside of the self. Believing is a mental concept that can be about looking to the future for an idea, hope, or vision. Yet this is often prescriptive where we are asked to suspend an aspect of our intuitive intelligence or pass our process over to some "authority." Knowing is lived experiences and comes from deep inside of ourselves. It needs to be nurtured to mature into an insightful and knowledgeable tool. All helpers would benefit from this way of learning. (L. Arger, personal communication, June 18, 2009)

While listening to Liz, I thought about how the learning process she spoke of could be applied to service users as well as social workers, as each individual is his or her own expert. I recall hearing from somewhere the phrase that "the client is the expert on their own life." I think this is what Liz is referring to when she speaks of "intuitive intelligence"; each of us has the capacity for insight and healing within ourselves. We do not need to believe in or take advice from anyone with authority, including a social worker. Rather, a helper will learn through his or her own experiences and she or he will, in turn, assist others to do the same. This fits nicely with what Charlene Avalos spoke of earlier about avoiding hierarchy and inequality within the service user-social worker relationship.

I also think that this way of learning teaches the Indigenous value that everyone has a role and purpose for his or her life, and that each individual can contribute to the betterment of the community. There is also an understanding that everyone has something to give back in return for what they receive or, as Liz creatively puts it, "everyone is a part of the giveaway." As well, this notion of giving and receiving represents the Indigenous value of reciprocity.

Ross (2007) would appear to agree. This is his description of the role of a helper within Healing Circles:

> In aboriginal processes, the professional seems to act not so much as an author, but as a process-provider, not as a creator of remedies but as prompter of creation, and not as a prescriber of choices but as the provider of a context in which healthy choices can be discovered and adopted by those directly involved.... [T]he aboriginal professional retreats very substantially from the spotlight to become only a single member of a multi-party process, and that ... as well as the exploration processes undertaken by everyone together, [is what] lend the circles their power to heal. (pp. 34–35)

Jennifer Ajandi also spoke about learning how to become a helper who pays attention to an Indigenous perspective:

> Aboriginal world views teach social work students and practitioners how to practice anti-oppressive social work in terms of being non-judgmental, linking individual issues with structural causes or contributions, that behaviour is learned and can be changed, and that there are many different paths a person can take. There is no *one* right answer; options depend on the person, family, and their community at the particular time. Self-determination has always been a part of Aboriginal world views and it is an important part of social work's code of ethics as well.
>
> Aboriginal approaches tend to be non-judgmental. There is much more

of an equalizing dynamic between people. There is a strong emphasis on building relationships with those seeking help rather than mechanically running through a list of questions. Trust building happens before talking about personal issues. "Intakes" and "assessments" are discussions rather than standardized forms to complete. (J. Ajandi, personal communication, January 10, 2009)

Wendy Martin and I had a conversation about Indigenous values and ethics in an interview we did together. Wendy believes, practises, and lives many Indigenous values. She is adamant that the profession of social work would be greatly enriched if social workers could pay more attention to these values. She listed those that she implements in her work:

- developing relationships with the families and communities of a client
- being more non-directive
- focusing on a client's strengths
- emphasizing wellness and what that means to clients
- being creative in the helping process, such as using visual presentations to discuss concerns or wellness (W. Martin, personal communication, February 8, 2009)

Most of Wendy's social work experience is in the area of youth justice. She challenges mainstream notions of justice, and believes that Indigenous approaches to justice are more effective because they focus on the value of community responsibility for young people:

It's helpful for everyone to take some responsibility when a youth becomes in conflict with the law. Society is letting these youth down. We all need to look at how we have contributed to the problems of a young person. Why have we allowed youth to struggle so much for their whole lives by, for example, putting them in foster homes, then group homes, pushing them out of school? Is it any big surprise that they then end up in youth justice? (W. Martin, personal communication, February 8, 2009)

Flo supports Wendy's position here about the importance of considering both strengths and responsibilities in our work with people:

Each of us has some kind of strength and I believe that we can learn from each other according to our strengths. At the same time, however, we cannot forget about the systemic barriers we face. How do we learn from each other or even begin to teach others with all the different forms of oppression that are weighing us down? Most marginalized people already know what they would like to achieve, but they cannot obtain it because of systemic issues, such as institutionalized racism. When we work with people, we need to take into consideration that it is not that they do not have strengths or that they are not trying to achieve their goals, but that they have to face obstacles way beyond their control. We need to acknowledge social injustice and not down play structural forms of oppression when we talk about resiliency or strengths. I believe this is what Indigenous peoples do when they work with one another and the rest of us can learn from that. (Flo, personal communication, April 6, 2009)

In pulling together and concluding this section on learning, I will finish with the words of Lindsay, another student who participated in the student Sharing Circle. She spoke about the value of Indigenous teachings, and also asks that social workers be cautious in their approach:

Indigenous ways teach that helping is *who* a person is, rather than that it's a job. As social workers we need to keep this in mind and pay attention to where we are going as a helping profession. We do not want to be disconnected from those we seek to assist, which is the danger of becoming professionalized. (Lindsay, personal communication, April 6, 2009)

SEVEN GRANDFATHERS

One of the major purposes of helping work is to help people restore their relationships with other people and with everything around them. (This holistic approach is the topic of the next chapter.) Healthy relationships need to be based on universal Indigenous values. Within Anishnawbe teachings, these values are called "the Seven Grandfathers/Grandmothers." They are:

1. To cherish knowledge is to know WISDOM.
2. To know LOVE is to know peace.

3. To honour all of creation is to have RESPECT.

4. BRAVERY is to face the foe with integrity.

5. HONESTY in facing a situation is to be brave.

6. HUMILITY is to know yourself as a sacred part of creation.

7. TRUTH is to know all of these things.

My understanding is that the Seven Grandfathers/Grandmothers teachings are about ethics. Love is one of these ethics, but it has a different connotation than it has for mainstream society. In Indigenous world views, love is about connectedness. In my experience, students can relate to this concept of love within social work and discuss it. They acknowledge that a relationship is being built between the social worker and service user, and they acknowledge that it is okay to care about people we are working with. It is significant to note that the Feminist Ethics of Care Model emphasizes the interconnectedness of people, including connections among people and between people and the Earth, and also emphasizes that building relationships can be "therapeutic" (Herman, 1992). All of these ideas have been a part of Aboriginal world views since the beginning of time.

CONCLUSION

Values and ethics frame how we conceptualize helping. This chapter has looked at differences between Western and Indigenous values. It is clear that there are some similarities among Indigenous values and those of non-Western societies, as well as spiritual practices such as meditation. The chapter also provided ideas for opportunities in which social work educators, students, and practitioners (as well as those in other helping professions) can come together to begin a dialogue about values and ethics.

Both Indigenous and non-Indigenous voices in this chapter emphasized the significance of Indigenous values, such as connectedness to everything around us, the importance of relationships, wholeness, learning through introspection and experience, and basing all our interactions on foundational principles such as love. Since values underpin all that we do as helping professionals, including theories and practice, this may be one of the areas of Indigenous world views that has the most applicability for the helping professions. It would appear that many helpers agree, as evidenced from their contributions to this chapter. Chapter 6 explores the values of connectedness and wholeness in deeper ways through what is often referred to as a "holistic approach."

REFERENCES

Baskin, C. (2007). Working together in the circle: Challenges and possibilities within mental health ethics. *Journal of Ethics in Mental Health*, 2(2). Retrieved from http://www.jemh.ca/issues/v2n2/documents/JEMH_v2n2_Article_Part1_AboriginalEthicsMentalHealth.pdf

Brant-Castellano, M. (2004). Ethics of Aboriginal research. *Journal of Aboriginal Health*, 1(1), 98–114. Retrieved from www.naho.ca/jah/english/journal_V01_01.php

Chodron, P. (1997). *When things fall apart: Heart advice for difficult times*. Boston: Shambhala Publications Inc.

Ellerby, J., McKenzie, J., McKay, S., Gariepy, G. & Kaufert, J. (2000) Bioethics for clinicians: Aboriginal cultures. *Canadian Medical Association Journal, 163*(7), 845–850. Retrieved from www.cma.ca/cmaj/series/bioethic.htm

Green, J. & Thomas, R. (2007). Learning through our children, healing for our children: Best practices in First Nations communities. In L. Dominelli (Ed.), *Revitalizing communities in a globalizing world* (pp. 175–192). UK: Ashgate Publishing.

Herman, J. (1992). *Trauma and recovery: The aftermath of violence—from domestic abuse to political terror*. New York: Basic Books.

Kovach, M., Thomas, R., Montgomery, M., Green, J. & Brown, L. (2007). Witnessing wild woman: Resistance and resilience in Aboriginal child welfare. In L.T. Foster & B. Wharf (Eds.), *People, politics, and child welfare in British Columbia* (pp. 97–116). Vancouver: UBC Press.

Limb, G. & Hodge, D. (2008). Developing spiritual competency with Native Americans: Promoting wellness through balance and harmony. *Families in Society, 89*(4), 615–622. doi: 10.1606/1044-3894.3816

Locust, C. (1988). Wounding the spirit: Discrimination and traditional American Indian belief systems. *Harvard Educational Review, 58*(3), 315–330. Retrieved from Research Library (Document ID: 1660176).

Newhouse, D. (2004). Indigenous knowledge in a multicultural world. *Native Studies Review, 15*(2), 139–154. Retrieved from the Academic Search Premier database.

Ross, R. (2007). *Discussion paper: Exploring criminal justice and the Aboriginal healing paradigm*. Unpublished manuscript. Retrieved from http://www.lsuc.on.ca

Ross, R. (2008). Colonization, complex PTSD & Aboriginal healing: Exploring diagnoses & strategies for recovery. Adult Custody Division Health Care Conference. Vancouver: British Columbia Ministry of Public Safety and Solicitor General.

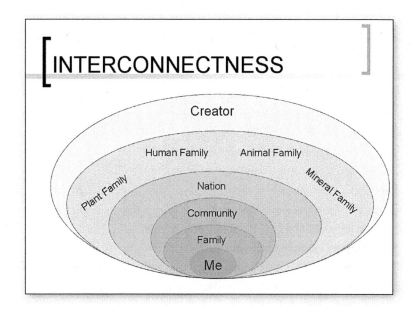

INTERCONNECTNESS

Creator

Human Family   Animal Family

Plant Family

Nation

Mineral Family

Community

Family

Me

Chapter 6

Holistic or Wholistic Approach

INTRODUCTION

I have seen both spellings of this word in the literature and in conversations with Indigenous authors, so I want to acknowledge both spellings by putting them in the title. I also want to note that common usage of both of these spellings tend to give them the same meaning, but there is some recent literature that explains how they have different connotations. According to Anishnawbe scholar Renee Linklater (2010), wholism refers to wholeness and is, therefore, an "all encompassing term" (p. 230). The author goes on to explain that Elders have told her that holism refers to what is holy and, therefore, is seemingly linked to patriarchal power and force. One woman also shared with Linklater that she believes holism to be "an empty space word" (p. 230).

The Elders I know have never told me about these differences between the two spellings, nor have I read a discussion about it by anyone other than Linklater. Research via a dictionary and a thesaurus states that the two are alternative spellings for the same meaning, but cites "holistic" as the more common usage and defines its meaning as the view that a whole system of beliefs, rather than individual components, needs to be taken into consideration. That is what I mean when I use the term "holism." I am used to spelling the word like this—holistic—so this is the spelling I will use throughout this chapter. The concepts connected to holism have come up repeatedly in previous chapters. (Remember, I cautioned that this might happen!) However, because the concept of holism is so foundational to helping approaches within Indigenous world views, and so many authors include this idea in their writing, I believe it needs its space in this book. This chapter will explore a holistic approach based on the following areas:

- the four aspects of a person
- interdependency of individuals, families, and communities
- interconnectedness of all creation
- healing

THE PERSON

According to a holistic approach, each person is made up of four aspects— spiritual, physical, emotional, and psychological (Bopp, Bopp, Brown & Lane, 1984; Hart, 2002; Sterling-Collins, 2009; Verniest, 2006). The ideal state of well-being is to be balanced in all of these areas. However, many people rarely achieve this ideal state of balance, which means that we need to be involved in activities that assist us in our attempts to stay balanced. Because the four aspects—spiritual, physical, emotional, and psychological—are connected, they constantly impact on one another. Should a person become ill or be harmed in one area, then the other three areas will also be affected. For example, should someone fall into a depression (emotional aspect), the body (physical) may be impacted because she or he is not eating or sleeping properly; the person's mind (psychological) can be affected and she or he may have self-deprecating thoughts, or might be forgetful and have trouble focusing. On a spiritual level the person may begin to lose hope, stop praying, and avoid practices that ordinarily sustain her or him, such as ceremonies and meditation.

It could be said that such a person is out of balance. In order to return to a place of balance, since all four aspects of this individual are affected, all four aspects must be engaged in a process of returning to balance. In other words, the whole person must be included in the healing process. Using the example of a person experiencing depression, it is not enough to focus only on the emotional aspect of healing. Hence, Indigenous methods of restoring balance include ceremonies that address all four aspects. An example of this integrated approach to addressing all aspects of healing is the sweat lodge ceremony, practised by such Nations as the Cree, Lakota, and Anishnawbe. Within this ceremony, one sweats (physical), releases feelings (emotional), hears teachings (psychological), and prays and sings for spirits to come into the lodge to help (spiritual).

A recent research study shows the possibilities of how a holistic approach can assist people with physical illnesses. Mehl-Madrona (2008) conducted research with 47 Indigenous peoples living with cancer whose Western doctors, at the outset of the study, had given them a prognosis of five years to live. Although it is only a preliminary study, the results are promising for those who wish to learn Indigenous holistic healing approaches. The life expectancy of the participants who had adopted traditional Indigenous healing methods taught by traditional Indigenous healers ranged from five to 21 years. Mehl-Madrona (2008) points out that these results show a plausible relationship between the mind and body, and that they also influenced the life expectancy of the study participants.

Consider how what I have written thus far compares to the following writing about behavioural medicine:

Behavioural medicine represents a new current within medicine itself, one that is rapidly expanding our ideas and knowledge about health and illness. New research findings and new ways of thinking about health and illness in behavioural medicine are rapidly producing a more comprehensive perspective within medicine, one that recognizes the fundamental unit of mind and body....

Perhaps the most fundamental development in behavioural medicine is the recognition that we can no longer think about health as being solely a characteristic of the body or the mind because body and mind are inter-connected. The new perspective acknowledges the central importance of thinking in terms of *wholeness* and *interconnectedness* and the need to pay attention to the interactions of mind, body, and behaviour in efforts to understand and treat illness. (Kabat-Zinn, 2005, pp. 150–151)

Dr. Kabat-Zinn is a renowned scientist, writer, and meditation teacher who focuses on mindfulness, which is one of the types of meditation I practise. He is the founder and former director of the world-renowned Stress Reduction Clinic at the Centre for Mindfulness in Medicine, Health Care, and Society. He is also a board member of the Mind and Life Institute, which establishes collaborative partnerships between modern scientists and Buddhists, includ-ing the Dalai Lama. Dr. Kabat-Zinn is someone whom I admire very much and who is making incredible contributions to our planet. It is clear that there are important connections between the work of Dr. Kabat-Zinn and an Indigenous approach to well-being that makes connections between the mind and body. At the same time, I noticed that Dr. Kabat-Zinn (2005) uses the word "new" three times in his description of behavioural medicine in the above quote, and he also talks about "new ways of thinking" (p. 150). I am disappointed because Dr. Kabat-Zinn does not acknowledge that the mind-body connection has existed in Indigenous world views since the beginning of time. Even those who position themselves as enlightened allies of Indigenous peoples can fail to acknowledge where their "new" ideas originate.

THE FAMILY AND COMMUNITY

Every person starts life as a connected being. Each one of us exists because of a connectedness between two people. This connection could exist because of a sexual relationship, a loving relationship, or a giving or donor relationship. Each of us was once entirely connected—spiritually, physically, emotionally, and psychologically—to another human being. An Indigenous perspective would say that we come from the spirit world into the physical world through our mothers' bodies. This connectedness is physical, symbolized by the belly button. This is why there are many spiritual practices around the world that are associated with the severing of the umbilical cord (Dempsey & Gesse, 1995; Gonzales, 2007; Greenberg, 1982).

Within a holistic framework, individuals are connected to all other people around them. First, there are connections to one's family and then connections to the members of one's community. The interconnectedness of all creation means that everyone is both dependent upon and connected with other people and the environment (Bopp et al., 1984; Lowe, 1982). Each person has unique contributions to make that also affect the whole. Every contribution—positive or negative—has an impact on all other people and on one's physical environment in some way.

But who constitutes one's family? For Indigenous peoples, as it is in many other world views, family can include a wide group of people, some of whom may be biologically related and others who are not. Family is made up of parents, grandparents, siblings, aunts, uncles, and cousins. In some Indigenous traditions, such as those of the Anishnawbe, Haudenosaunee, and Mi'kmaq, family includes members of one's clan and our sponsors, who are there when we receive our spirit names or get married. In my own life, my Elder refers to me as her younger sister, and in my community, many people call female Elders they are particularly connected to as "grandmother." A good friend's daughter refers to me as "auntie" and my son as "cousin." These are all important and unique relationships.

Further, Indigenous peoples have always had family adoptions within their societies. This not only occurred with children, but also took place in order to replace relationships that were severed through death. Many years ago, when my only brother passed on, the Elders who assisted my family and me with the ceremony and grieving process told me something that I initially could not comprehend. They said that at some point in the future, a young man would enter my life, and that I would immediately recognize him as my brother. In that moment, I wondered how it could be possible that another person would come along and replace my brother. But that wasn't what the Elders were trying to say. The Elders were not saying that *my brother* could be replaced. They meant that the *relationship* needed to be replaced. Sure enough, in time a young man did come along. I knew he was the one and I adopted him through ceremony as my brother. He is my brother forever, just as my blood relatives are. He is my brother, and I cannot divorce him even if our relationship isn't going well as I might if he were a marriage partner.

In Indigenous traditions, this concept of replacing relationships is an expression of the value of interconnectedness. It seems to me that this understanding is valuable for all peoples to understand because many people face the loss of familial relationships through death, conflict, estrangement, lack of safety, abuse, and prejudice. Having the freedom to *choose* some family members for ourselves can be both a source of support and healing.

Another connection between Indigenous world views and Buddhism, meditation, and other spiritual traditions can be made with respect to the connections between family and community. According to Kabat-Zinn (2005):

> The web of interconnectedness goes beyond our individual psychological self. While we are whole ourselves as individual beings, we are also part of a larger whole, interconnected through our family and our friends and acquaintances to the larger society and ultimately to the whole of humanity and life on the planet. (p. 157)

Many major research studies conducted in several countries demonstrate the importance of social connections and health. This is also explained by Kabat-Zinn (2005):

> ... [S]ocial factors, which of course are related to psychological factors, also play an important role in health and illness. It has long been known, for instance, that, statistically speaking, people who are socially isolated tend to be less healthy, psychologically and physically, and more likely to die prematurely than people who have extensive social relationships....

There seems to be something about having ties to others that is basic to health. Of course this is intuitively understandable. We all have a strong need to belong, to feel a part of something and associate with other people.

However, Indigenous world views about holism take the connection between one's individual health and relationships to other people to a deeper level. These teachings on holism emphasize that family and community members play a direct role in helping to heal individuals. Ross (2007) explains that his collective experiences in Healing Circles and ceremonies gave him:

> ... a powerful, emotional certainty of intimate and healthy connection with other humans struggling through common human challenges that I can only describe them as experiences of spiritual connection. It was not just that we joined each other, but that we all felt joined to something much larger than our collective sum.

The challenge seems to involve nourishing a conviction of healthy and meaningful connection in the hearts, minds and spirits of all of us, regardless of whether, in a particular instant of our lives, the world wants to describe us as a victim, an offender, a healer—or a supposedly disinterested stranger. (p. 26)

Ross's experiences speak to the belief that the healing of any one person is dependent on the health of other community members. Thus, the community heals the individual, and the individual contributes to the healing of the community. Reliance on the "expertise" of one person—for example, a social worker or counsellor—might not be enough (McCabe, 2008). In addition, community members have a duty to help others take responsibility (Hill, 2008). This may involve taking responsibility for harmful behaviour or for actively participating in one's healing journey.

ALL OF CREATION

From the individual to the family, to the community, and then to all of creation—*all* of the peoples of the world, the plants and animals that feed and sustain us, the water, rocks, air, the planet, and the cosmos—*everything* is connected. From an Indigenous perspective, everything has a spirit and impacts upon everything else. Part of the human condition is that we have a kinship with *all* living things, and also to those things that are considered to be inanimate objects.

From a holistic and Indigenous perspective, rocks have a spirit. I have been taught that rocks are the oldest and strongest part of creation. When we are in need of strength, we go to the mountains. Around my neck I carry a pouch with a stone from a sacred place, where I have attended many ceremonies. This stone helps me to be strong when I need to be. Should you ever see me clutching my medicine pouch, you will know it is because I am asking for strength in that particular moment!

Knowing that everything on the planet is related and connected has been written about by numerous Indigenous authors. Battiste and Youngblood Henderson (2000), Cajete (1994), Couture (1991), Fitznor (1998), and Shilling (now Linklater) (2002) all emphasize interconnectedness as an important concept within Indigenous world views. As Paula Gunn Allen (1986) says, "all things are related and are of one family" (p. 60). Thus, I am connected to my family, my community, the Mi'kmaq Nation, and to everything on Mother Earth and in the spirit world. To divide any of these realities into separate categories is a dishonour to Aboriginal ways of thinking.

When people can live as whole persons, then they can connect to everyone and everything around them and attend to their responsibilities. In Aboriginal world views, a focus on individual and collective responsibility for all members of one's community is highlighted. Blood scholar Leroy Little Bear (2000) articulates this perspective beautifully:

> Wholeness is like a flower with four petals. When it opens, one discovers strength, sharing, honesty, and kindness. Together these four petals create balance, harmony, and beauty. Wholeness works in the same interconnected way. The whole strength speaks to the idea of sustaining balance. If a person is whole and balanced, then he or she is in a position to fulfill his or her individual responsibilities to the whole. If a person is not balanced, then he or she is sick and weak—physically, mentally or both—and cannot fulfill his or her individual responsibilities. (p. 79)

Again, I turn to the writing of Dr. Kabat-Zinn (2005) to show how there are other peoples of the world alongside Indigenous peoples who share similar understandings of wholeness and connectedness. Dr. Kabat-Zinn (2005) states that there are:

> ... larger patterns and cycles of nature that we only know about through science and thinking (although even here traditional peoples always knew and respected these aspects of interconnectedness in their own ways as natural ways).... [O]ne scientific view, known as the Gaia hypothesis, is that the earth as a whole behaves as one self-regulating living organism, given the name Gaia after the Greek goddess of the earth. This hypothesis affirms a view based on scientific reasoning, that was, in essence, also held by all traditional cultures and peoples, a world in which humans were interconnected and interdependent with all beings and with the earth itself. (p. 157)

I am certain that if these knowings were a part of the world views of *all* peoples of the world, then collectively we would never have participated in the literal slow death of our Mother, the Earth. People everywhere need to awake to the reality that if we do not stop this death of our Mother, we will *all* die as well. The colour of one's skin or how much money one has in the bank will not matter if the Earth dies. If She dies, we *all* die. Ross (2007) echoes that, even though many people might still think so, people are not the boss of creation.

> The Bible puts us right at the top, set on earth to rule all the fishes in the sea, everything. Aboriginal teachings seem to present an opposite hierarchy. Mother Earth (with her life-blood, the waters) plays the most important role in Creation, for without the soil and water there would be no plant realm. Without the plants there would be no animal realm, and without soil, water, plants and animals, there would be no us.... [Human creatures are understood to be the least essential and the most dependent aspects of Creation; no longer its Masters, we are its humble servants instead. (p. 14)

EVER CHANGING

In viewing all of creation through a holistic lens, one also comes to appreciate that everything is continually changing. One season moves into another, day becomes night, babies become children, then youth, then adults, and eventually, when they are old, they leave this world. Thoughts, feelings, understandings, our bodies, and relationships all change, sometimes over the long term and at other times from moment to moment. Mountains, beaches, oceans, the stars, and galaxies change over time (Bopp et al., 1984). Everything on the planet and in the universe is in a state of perpetual change. Everything comes full circle as well—babies come from the spirit world, and when they become old people, they eventually return to the spirit world. Change is inevitable and everything is constantly evolving. Nothing is permanent. Nothing is forever.

If we choose not to fight against impermanence, then we will begin to understand that impermanence is another aspect of a holistic understanding in which balance and harmony are continually in flux. Change is part of connectedness. Many world views appreciate and celebrate the impermanent aspect of connectedness. Within Indigenous world views, changes are often marked with ceremonies. There are a lot of ceremonies! There are ceremonies for the birth of a baby; the naming of a baby; for the changes that occur when a child begins to grow into a youth; and ceremonies for marriage, adoption, initiations, and passing on into the spirit world. There are ceremonies for the full moon, planting and harvesting, and the changing of each season. Every significant change is acknowledged and celebrated. Impermanence is the essence of all of creation, but, unfortunately, many people have no respect for this. Pema Chodron (2000) notes this when she writes: "in the process of trying to deny that things are always changing, we lose our sense of the sacredness of life. We tend to forget that we are part of the natural scheme of things" (p. 61).

CONCLUSION

Perhaps what stands out the most from the insights in this chapter is that Indigenous peoples have always had a holistic approach to life. Now, when the entire world is in crisis, the West is searching for possible solutions that may have been here all along. Rather than continue the same behaviours that have led to the current crisis, those who make up dominant societies could perhaps pause and consider for a moment other ways of viewing creation and living within it.

Many changes happening in the world today aggravate the current global crisis. However, there are also many changes that are helping us move in a direction of balance, understanding, and healing. As we are all able to bring our collective knowledge together—spiritually, physically, emotionally, and psychologically—a healing movement can begin to grow. I believe that Indigenous peoples are moving toward healing for themselves and the planet and they have a desire to share their knowledges with other peoples of the world in accomplishing this. Apparently, many non-Indigenous peoples are also starting to see the world in a similar way that views all life on the planet as connected. Viewing everything in creation from a holistic lens is one of the gifts that Indigenous knowledges have given to the world.

REFERENCES

Allen, P.G. (1986). *The sacred hoop: Recovering the feminine in American Indian traditions*. Boston: Beacon.

Battiste, M. & Youngblood-Henderson, J. (2000). *Protecting Indigenous knowledge and heritage: A global challenge*. Saskatoon: Purich Publishing Ltd.

Bopp, J., Bopp, M., Brown, L. & Lane, P. (1984). *The sacred tree*. Lethbridge: Four Winds.

Cajete, G. (1994). *Look to the mountain: An ecology of Indigenous education*. Durando: Kivaki Press.

Chodron, P. (2000). *When things fall apart: Heart advice for difficult times.* Boston: Shambhala Publications Inc.

Couture, J. (1991). Explorations in Native knowing. In J.W. Friesen (Ed.), *The cultural maze: Complex questions on Native destiny in western Canada* (pp. 201–215). Calgary: Detselig Enterprises Ltd.

Dempsey, P. & Gesse, T. (1995). Beliefs, values, and practices of Navajo childbearing women. *Western Journal of Research, 17*(6), 591–604. doi: 10.1177/019394599501700602

Fitznor, L. (1998). The circle of life: Affirming Indigenous philosophies in everyday living. In D. McCane (Ed.), *Life ethics in world religions* (pp. 21–40). Winnipeg: University of Manitoba Press.

Gonzales, P. (2007) *Birth is a ceremony: Story and formulas of thought in indigenous medicine and indigenous communications.* Doctoral dissertation. Retrieved from ProQuest Dissertations and Theses Database (AAT 3278871).

Greenberg, L. (1982). Midwife training programs in highland Guatemala. *Social Sciences & Medicine, 16*(18), 1599–1609. doi: 10.1016/0277-9536(82)90290-8

Hart, M.A. (2002). *Seeking mino-pimatisiwin: An Aboriginal approach to helping.* Halifax: Fernwood Publishing.

Hill, L.P. (2008). *Understanding Indigenous Canadian traditional health and healing.* Unpublished manuscript, Department of Social Work, Wilfred Laurier University, Kitchener, ON, Canada.

Kabat-Zinn, J. (2005). *Full catastrophe living: Using the wisdom of your body and mind to face stress, pain, and illness.* New York: Bantam Dell.

Linklater, R. (2010). Decolonizing our spirits: Cultural knowledge and Indigenous healing. In.S. Marcos (Ed.), *Women and Indigenous religions* (pp. 217–232). Santa Barbara: Praeger.

Little Bear, L. (2000). *Jagged worldviews colliding.* In M. Battiste (Ed.), *Reclaiming Indigenous voice and vision* (pp. 77–85). Vancouver: University of British Columbia Press.

Lowe, D.M. (1982). *History of bourgeois perception.* Chicago: University of Chicago Press.

McCabe, G. (2008). Mind, body, emotions, and spirit: Reaching to the ancestors for healing. *Counselling Psychology Quarterly, 21,* 143–152. doi: 10.1080/09515070802066847

Mehl-Madrona, L. (2008). Narratives of exceptional survivors who work with Aboriginal healers. *Journal of Complementary and Alternative Medicine, 14*(5), 497–504. doi: 10.1089/acm.2007.0578

Ross, R. (2007). *Discussion paper: Exploring criminal justice and the Aboriginal healing paradigm.* Retrieved from http://www.lsuc.on.ca/media/third_colloquium_rupert_ross.pdf

Shilling, R. (2002). Journey of our spirits: Challenges for adult Indigenous learners. In E.V. O'Sullivan, A. Morrell & M.A. O'Connor (Eds.), *Expanding the boundaries of transformative learning: Essays on theory and practice* (pp. 151–158). Toronto: Palgrave Publishers.

Sterling-Collins, R. (2009). A holistic approach to supporting children with special needs. In R. Sinclair, M.A. Hart & G. Bruyere (Eds.), *Wicihitowin: Aboriginal social work in Canada* (pp. 65–88). Winnipeg: Fernwood Publishing.

Verniest, L. (2006). Allying with the medicine wheel: Social work practice with Aboriginal peoples. *Critical Social Work, 7*(1). Retrieved from http://www.uwindsor.ca/criticalsocialwork/

Chapter 7
The Answers Are in the Community

INTRODUCTION

In all of my reading and what was shared with me through the interviews I conducted for this book, I found that community was significant for people regardless of what particular topic was focused on. Because individuals, families, and communities are so connected, it is not possible to write about any one of them without the other.

WHY COMMUNITY FIRST?

I have chosen to place this chapter on community before the one on families and children because I see community first and families and children second, rather than the other way around. This is due to an emphasis on the collective rather than the individual. The well-being of the community takes precedence over any individual. Collectivism is central to Indigenous world views, and Indigenous peoples across the globe have been taught to conduct themselves in ways that create positive relationships with everyone in their community.

In many Indigenous languages, there is a phrase that translates into "all my relations." It is intended to express that one's community is an extension of one's family, that interdependence is valued, that we must care for one another, and that it is important to focus all our efforts on the betterment of our community. Everyone has the ability to participate in the well-being of the community. Each of us is expected to put the community before our individual gain, and that we will take into account everyone's well-being in all that we do.

This emphasis on collective well-being is based on Indigenous values, such as caring for all, sharing what one has, and interdependence. But it is also based on necessity and logic. Centuries ago, the original peoples of this land endured often harsh environmental conditions, such as extreme cold and shortages of food. Families gathered to live together so they could support one another by working together for the betterment of all. They needed each other.

Communal living meant sharing the raising of children and providing for old people. It meant that when food was plentiful, everyone had enough and when it was not, no one had more than any other member of the community. No one moved ahead of anyone else. There were ceremonies in place to ensure this. If any one family accumulated a lot of things, then this family was required to give away things to others; this is what we call the "giveaway" today. In this way, what everyone had was more or less the same.

For the work and betterment of the community, there were hereditary clan systems. Each clan had a specific purpose. Some clans were protectors, others were carriers of medicines, some were mediators. Every person belonged to a clan.

PEOPLE KNOW WHAT IS NEEDED

If we pay attention, listen, and watch what people are doing in their communities today, we will learn that communities' sustainable development is needed and is being addressed. Indigenous communities are leading the way in terms of healing and transformation. According to activist and academic Jim Silver (2006), who is non-Indigenous:

> The process of people's healing, of their rebuilding or recreating themselves, is rooted in a revived sense of community and a revitalization of Aboriginal cultures; this in turn requires the building of Aboriginal organizations. The process of reclaiming an Aboriginal identity takes place, therefore, at an individual, community, organizational and ultimately political level. This is a process of decolonization that, if it can continue to be rooted in traditional Aboriginal values of sharing and community, will be the foundation upon which healing and rebuilding are based. (p. 133)

When it comes to community rebuilding, many Indigenous authors focus on children and women. When it comes to the power to protect children, communities take up the role of parents because in an Indigenous community, everyone is understood to have a connection to *all* children, can participate in raising children, and needs to be involved in decisions that affect children. When it comes to child protection, the community can take responsibility for the safety of its children, including meeting such legal obligations as conducting risk assessments and developing safety plans.

Kim Anderson (2000), a Cree/Métis scholar, writes extensively about women and motherhood in relation to community revitalization. She describes inclusiveness in terms of who is recognized as a mother, as well as the community responsibility that goes along with this:

> In the Aboriginal ideology of motherhood, all women have the right to make decisions on behalf of the children, the community and the nation. The Aboriginal ideology of motherhood is not dependent on whether, as individuals, we produce children biologically. Women can be mothers in different ways. I have heard many stories of magnificent "mothers" who have adopted children as well as adults and provided them with the guidance and love that they needed. (p. 171)

WHAT'S MISSING?

There are a number of theories about identity formation in children and youth. Indigenous world views have a "theory" about this as well. According to Gregory Cajete (2000), of the Tewa Nation, the importance of a community identity needs to be recognized. Cajete explains that "Relationship is the cornerstone of tribal community, and the nature and expression of community is the foundation of tribal identity. Through community, Indian people come to understand their 'personhood' and their connection to the communal soul of their people" (p. 86).

Many other Indigenous writers speak about identity as being inexplicably connected to one's community. Jeannine Carrière (2008), a Métis woman originally from the Red River area of Manitoba, states that "this collective view of identity is linked to the traditional view of children. When children are viewed as gifts from the Creator, their identity is recognized as having a critical place in the family and community they are from" (pp. 70–71). Authors Larry K. Brendtro, Martin Brokenleg of the Lakota Nation, and Steve Van Bockern (1990) refer to "the spirit of belonging," in which children are seen to develop an identity where they can begin to understand themselves as related to everyone in their community as well as to the land (p. 37).

In a research study with 90 Inuit people, Kral (2003) identified that family and kinship are viewed as determinants of well-being. Kral (2003) states that this research taught him that Inuit people are "collective selves [who] see group membership as central to their identity whereas individualistic selves are more autonomous from any particular group and may value individualism quite highly" (p. 8). Kral's observation also applies to other Indigenous peoples as well.

This sense of a collective self or community identity is supported by theorists such as Branch, Tayal, and Triplett (2000), who write that most theories about identity ignore the significance of ethnic or place-based identity. They state that "ethnic identity refers to the application and connectedness to a place of origin and history associated with it" (p. 778). This, too, is a critical part of Indigenous world views as identity is strongly linked to a person's original territory, the history of that territory, and how this connection stays intact regardless of where the person lives. As Carrière (2008) reminds us, when it comes to raising children, "it takes a community.... How often have we heard this in different circles? It is, however, the core of Aboriginal child development and identity" (p. 77). I believe that community is the core of identity development for *all* children of the world.

WEALTH OF RESOURCES

Several Elders participated in interviews for this book, and some focused on their views of community. Each of their contributions fit well together.

Dan (Oneida Nation) and his partner, Mary Lou Smoke (Anishnawbe Nation), travel mostly around southern Ontario, sharing their teachings with others. They also teach a course in the School of Journalism at the University of Western Ontario. Dan explained to me that he has been a part of many communities throughout his life, several of which were created by groups of Indigenous peoples who came together for a united purpose. As a young man in the 1970s, Dan began to volunteer for a community newspaper in Akwesasne, a Mohawk community whose territory straddles the Ontario, Quebec, and New York borders. The building in New York where the newspaper was published was called Nation House, and many Indigenous peoples from all across the United States lived there. Each person contributed to the Nation House community by chopping wood, cleaning, and cooking. Everyone did his or her part to ensure that the community functioned well. Dan described this experience as an immersion into a sense of community.

Dan also shared another example of this sense of community. He explained how he and Mary Lou travelled to Alberta to attend a Sundance ceremony, but before the ceremony could begin, everyone present spent a week clearing the land to prepare for it. This experience taught Dan and Mary Lou about the importance of a strong sense of community, as everyone worked hard together to make the Sundance ceremony happen. After the work was completed, everyone who helped participated in a sweat lodge ceremony together, which further reinforced a sense of community.

I can easily relate to what Dan is talking about. There is much preparation in holding a ceremony, which is all a part of the experience. Preparations that I have participated in have included cooking traditional foods, gathering medicines such as cedar, and building a fasting lodge. Sometimes these activities are done alone and sometimes they are done with others. Sometimes these activities are done in silent prayer, using mindfulness meditation or in conversation with others. For me, these activities were usually done with other women. I have participated in activities with people I know well, people I do not know so well, and people I have just met.

I would say that, in many ways, once the preparation begins, the ceremony has already begun. The preparation is like part one of a series of parts. During the preparation, people come together on all four levels: spiritual, physical, emotional, and psychological. They share teachings, songs, stories, and information about themselves with each other and a connection is formed, which deepens as the ceremony progresses.

When I am unable to participate in the preparation for a ceremony, I feel like I've missed out on something. I can't help feeling that the workers/helpers have bonded and I'm on the outside. I'm just not quite as connected to the others. There is something about being a part of building something, whether it is for a single ceremony or for the creation of community, that brings people together in a connected way that goes beyond being just physically present. This kind of connected participation seems to help us *know* in a deeper way that we are an integral part of whatever is happening, that we belong, and that we have a right to have the experiences that we do. This experience of community-building has a direct bearing on social work if we choose to practise from a place of inclusiveness and social justice. Helping work is *social*, meaning that this work isn't just about talking; it's about doing, and there is also a focus on societies or communities. Indigenous world views about working with communities can be valuable to all social workers. These world views focus on working *with* groups of people to assist them to move toward what they want and need. Helpers are not expected to do all of the work. Everyone who makes up a community is invited to participate in rebuilding that community because everyone has a contribution to make. We are reminded to consider one of the Seven Grandfathers/Grandmothers teachings—humility—which teaches that each of us is merely one tiny part of creation. No individual is an expert on other people's lives. We listen and learn from the people who make up the community we are attempting to assist. Perhaps, most importantly, we take the time to connect with the community, we develop relationships, get to know people, and people get to know us. We also work hard at reminding everyone that they belong, that they are important, and that no work can be accomplished without them.

As a social worker working within a particular community, are you really a part of that community? Community can be many things—a geographical area, a group of people with similar concerns, a group of people with similar subjectivities. Do you live in the community you work in or do you leave that community at the end of each working day? Are the concerns of the community in which you work also among your concerns? Although different approaches will be necessary depending on how you answer the above questions, being part of the community we serve is not what is most important. I do not have to be a part of the Muslim, Two-Spirited, or youth population to care about how Muslims, Two-Spirited people, or youth are doing. I do not have to live in Iraq or Guatemala or northern Ontario to care about what is happening in these communities. It all matters to me because, like everyone else, I am a human being. We are all connected and what happens to everyone on the planet affects my humanity. This is why I care.

Eileen Antone is an Oneida woman, originally from Oneida of the Thames First Nation, who currently lives in Toronto. She is an associate professor at the University of Toronto's Transitional Year Program and in the Department of Adult Education and Counselling Psychology. She is also the director of Aboriginal Studies and the director of the Centre for Aboriginal Initiatives at the University of Toronto. Eileen shared a great story about her experiences growing up in a community that embraced two distinct spiritual traditions found in the Longhouse and in a Christian church. She told me:

> My grandfather was such a peaceful person and I wanted to have what he had. He went to church so I thought that was where he got it. When I was six years old, I started to go to the Baptist church in my community. For a while I walked until someone started taking me. I saw that church was about teaching love. An Aboriginal person was the pastor at this church; we sang hymns in Oneida, but everything else was in English.
>
> At the Longhouse, everything was spoken in Oneida, so I couldn't understand most of it as my parents chose not to teach me the language so I wouldn't have as much trouble in school.
>
> I started going to the Longhouse as a teenager to learn the social songs and dances. Other teenagers who attended churches such as Baptist and Pentecostal like me also went.
>
> When I went to church I was told not to sing and dance. I decided to not sing and dance *in church*, but I would in the Longhouse. The teaching for me in all this was that God loves everyone. If a particular church accepted me, then it was good, but if it didn't, then it wasn't good.
>
> Both the Longhouse and the church taught me that community and family is vitally important—no one gets left behind. Community is about teamwork, responsibility, and co-operation. People must work together. And through the support one gets, what needs to happen, happens. (E. Antone, personal communication, July 10, 2009)

Three other women who were interviewed also spoke about the importance of community in Indigenous world views. These women include Charlene Catchpole, whom we heard from earlier in this book; Traditional Teacher, Mary Lou Smoke, mentioned above; and Joanne Dallaire, who also appeared earlier. All three women focused on community within urban centres. Mary Lou related:

> Community is about people taking care of one another. It is about a sense of belonging. A sense of community can be lost in urban centres. In Toronto, for example, there are many Nations and we need to listen to all of them. We need to welcome and share all the gifts that come with diversity. "Cultural gatekeepers" who want things to always be done their way are not helpful. Community is also about people coming together to deconstruct stereotypes, myths, and misrepresentations. (M.L. Smoke, personal communication, February 20, 2009)

Joanne shares a similar message:

> Everyone wants to belong somewhere. Toronto is made up of pockets of communities of various populations. Many people go to cities because they are looking for something better for themselves and their families, or they are running away from something harmful. This is true of many people who immigrate here, as well as with Indigenous peoples, which is one of the many commonalities amongst human beings. It may be difficult in North America to hold onto one's community when you are coming from another part of the world. When people come here, they want to hold onto their identities, so they create communities.
>
> It's healthy for people of many communities to come together to learn from each other; to educate ourselves about other people's experiences. Coming together is not a compromise of self, but rather about a common humanity and finding common ground. (J. Dallaire, personal communication, July 23, 2009)

Charlene Catchpole offers an example from the shelter where she works of what Mary Lou and Joanne are speaking about:

> Ideas and values which focus on the importance of community, the collective, and ways of raising children bring women together as many of

them who are in the shelter are newcomers to Canada and/or Indigenous, so these values often apply to them as well—for example, that women are the centre of the community and children are seen as gifts. (C. Catchpole, personal communication, February 16, 2009)

As a social work practitioner, I have worked for many years in the violence against women (VAW) movement. Although my direct practice has been working with Indigenous communities, I have been a part of creating alliances with other populations of women as well, such as women of colour and newcomers to Canada. Through these alliances, I have learned that perspectives about community may differ between groups of women who are newcomers to Canada and women who have lived here for generations and, therefore, have had their identities shaped by Western norms. A newcomer woman's identity tends to be strongly linked to the identity of her community. Value conflicts can arise because many violence against women services often focus on individual women. VAW services often provide women with one-to-one counselling, and often family issues are not adequately addressed because of limited organizational mandates. This is often the case when a woman seeks support for both herself and her partner. There are very few social service agencies that are able to meet the needs of women's partners even though many front-line workers report that women have repeatedly requested this kind of assistance (Fong, 2010). It is true that concerns have arisen about maintaining safety while doing couple interventions and family-based support work. These concerns must be taken into consideration. Providing services to the abusing partner challenges the ways that mainstream services are typically delivered to women who have experienced or continue to experience, violence. However, this does not mean we should ignore what women are asking from us. Fortunately, some communities are currently exploring this issue. For example, social services agencies in Toronto—such as the Family Services Association of Toronto, Abrigo Centre, Native Child and Family Services of Toronto, and the Family Group Conferencing Model at the George Hull Centre—are beginning to explore more integrated services (Alcalde & Caragata, 2007; George Hull Centre, 2010).

It is also important to acknowledge that interventions, such as family group conferencing and community-based support in the area of violence prevention, have been a part of the work of Indigenous communities and urban agencies for quite some time. In fact, other communities and services often learn how to do their work by implementing models based on Indigenous practices. I have an example from a community program that I worked in for several years that focused on violence prevention. This program, called Mino-Yaa-Daa (meaning "Healing Together" in the Anishnawbe language), followed Indigenous world views, which emphasize the value of the well-being of the community and the family above that of the individual. The individual is seen in the context of the family, which is seen in the context of the community. Thus, from this holistic perspective, when an individual is harmed, it is believed that this affects all other individuals in that person's family and community.

A major purpose of the Mino-Yaa-Daa program's services for women was to bring the community's women together. Only when women join together can the disempowering silence around issues related to family violence be broken. By coming together in a circle, women learned that they were not alone, and that their situations and feelings were similar to those of other women. The women learned how to trust, take risks, and both give and receive support, while building relationships and a community of empowered women. This can only be achieved by individuals coming together in a circle. This kind of community-building cannot happen through individual counselling or therapy.

Two important elements were emphasized in the women's circles. The first was a focus on tools that women learned in the circle, which they then took with them to help them in their daily lives. It was important that what was learned in the circle had practical value for women. The second element encouraged women to support each other and develop friendships outside of the program. This kind of community-building was significant because it reinforced an Indigenous value of interdependency that emphasizes that everyone has gifts and resources and a natural ability to help others. Incorporated into all program services for women was a belief in the healing powers of laughter. We had fun!

When it comes to the importance of a community focus in anti-violence work, no one says it better than Andrea Gunraj (2005), who at the time was the outreach manager at the Metropolitan Action Committee on Violence against Women and Children (METRAC) in Toronto:

> True safety doesn't come from individuals. I can buy security gadgets and learn how to defend myself, but it won't do anything to make the world a safer place. And it definitely won't benefit those who are most vulnerable to experiencing violence. True safety comes from community, from diverse people creating an inclusive vision for safety and working together to make a difference. (p. 8)

To close this section, I turn to the writing of Australian social work educator Robyn Lynn (2001), who advises all social workers to question "the modernist assumptions of the universal standardized forms of social work" (p. 906), and to build multiple approaches to helping. She discusses how Indigenous values on the well-being of the community and family take precedence over individual well-being, and how these values are significant in all social work practice. Lynn cites mainstream social work's use of family participation in areas such as child protection and youth justice as evidence of how non-Aboriginal practitioners can learn from Indigenous ways.

I definitely agree with Lynn's proposal to build on the many approaches to helping within the practice of social work. Indigenous knowledges are significant sites of learning and are much more progressive than Western theories and practices in many areas. I am open and committed to sharing these knowledges for the good of all humanity.

SOCIAL WORKERS AS WARRIORS

Sharon Big Plume (2008) is an Anishnawbe/Métis woman who has written about the role of the warrior within Indigenous societies prior to colonization. She explores how the roles of warriors are akin to the ideals of social justice, which she defines simply and succinctly as "the ability to determine when something is not right, along with willingness to do something positive about it" (p. 235). Big Plume (2008) proposes that the role of the warrior can be understood in the context of setting standards for social work practice in Indigenous communities. She states that warriors have a mission that originates from their agreement with the Creator. Warriors prepare themselves to complete their mission through ceremonies and their own ongoing healing as it is understood that they will face challenges and adversities. Big Plume (2008) believes that both warriors and social workers have a vested interest in "strengthening people so the community can survive, flourish, and thrive" (p. 248).

Let's have a look at what Big Plume is advocating. Like warriors, social workers identify what is not right within societies, particularly regarding how certain populations are marginalized. As mentioned earlier, similar to a group of warriors, we are a helping profession whose role is tied to the notion of "doing." More on this will be taken up in the chapter on spirituality, but for now, within social work, choosing to have a relationship with one's Creator is an individual choice. Within Western social work codes of ethics, for example, there is no reference to spirituality as a guiding principle for practice. Social workers certainly prepare themselves for their work by attending university and participating in professional development, which, in part, offers people direction about how to address specific challenges. Social workers are also encouraged to engage in ongoing self-reflexivity and self-care, which relates to the warriors' teaching about the importance of personal healing. And, like warriors, one of the roles of a social worker is to help strengthen people in many areas, using many different methods. As this chapter emphasizes, social work with individuals and families cannot be separated from our work within communities.

I believe there are, and always have been, many types of warriors: academic, spiritual, and helping ones. In my opinion, social workers are a type of warrior, and I am happy to report that I am not the only who thinks so. We, as in some members of Toronto's Indigenous community and I who make up the Aboriginal Advisory Committee in the School of Social Work where I teach, named one of my courses "Ogitchita Lu Wa Ti Li Hu Nyu Nih." "Ogitchita" means "warriors" or "strong helpers" in Anishnawbe and "Lu Wa Ti Li Hu Nyu Nih" means "teachings" in Oneida.

CONCLUSION

This chapter emphasizes the overarching significance of community as the beginning point for helping within an Indigenous world view. This means that the overall well-being of everyone must be considered rather than the well-being of only a few. Communal societies around the world carry this perspective and within these multiple communal spaces, it may be possible to share our commonalities and form alliances and partnerships within helping.

The teachings are clear: A person cannot be viewed as separate from a community, however that community may be defined. Every community has a wealth of resources—teachers, natural helpers, warriors—and the answers to what we seek are there. This is a valuable Indigenous perspective that is influencing the area of social work more and more as seen by the profession's willingness to adopt practices, such as family group conferencing and kinship placements within child welfare, which are based on the importance of community in people's lives. For the good of the world, we must always keep in mind that each of us is a part of the human community. We *are* all related.

REFERENCES

Alcalde, J. & Caragata, L. (2007). Environmental scan of services and service coordination for woman abuse in Toronto: Final report. *Toronto Public Health*. Retrieved from http://www.womanabuse.ca

Anderson, K. (2000). *A recognition of being: Reconstructing Native womanhood.* Toronto: Second Story Press.

Big Plume, S. (2008). *Warriors, empowerment, and social work.* Doctoral dissertation, University of Calgary. Retrieved from Proquest Dissertations & Theses (AAT NR38039).

Branch, C.W., Tayal, P. & Triplett, C. (2000). The relationship of ethnic identity and ego identity status among adolescents and young adults. *International Journal of Intercultural Relations, 24*(6), 777–790. doi: 10.1016/S0147-1767(00)00031-6

Brendtro, L.K., Brokenleg, M. & Van Bockern, S. (1990). *Reclaiming youth at risk.* Bloomington: National Education Service.

Cajete, G. (2000). *Native science: Natural laws of interdependence.* Santa Fe: Clear Light.

Carrière, J. (2008). Maintaining identities: The soul work of adoption and Aboriginal children. *Pimatisiwin: A Journal of Aboriginal and Indigenous Community Health, 6*(1), 61–80. Retrieved from http://www.pimatisiwin.com

Fong, F. (2010). *Out of the shadows: Woman abuse in ethnic, immigrant, and Aboriginal communities.* Toronto: Women's Press.

George Hull Centre. (2007). *About the George Hull centre.* Retrieved from http://www.georgehullcentre.on.ca/FamilyGroupConferencing

Gunraj, A. (2005, Spring). Reaching out for safer communities. *Metropolitan Action Committee on Violence against Women and Children.* Retrieved from http://www.metrac.org/about/downloads/newsletter.spring.05.pdf

Kral, M.J. (2003). *Unikaartuit: Meanings of well-being, sadness, suicide, and change in two Inuit communities.* Final report to the National Health Research and Development Programs. Ottawa: Health Canada.

Lynn, R. (2001). Learning from a "Murri way." *British Journal of Social Work, 31*(6), 903–916. doi: 10.1093/bjsw/31.6.903

Silver, J. (2006). *In their own voices: Building urban Aboriginal communities.* Black Point: Fernwood Publications.

Chapter 8
Spirituality

INTRODUCTION

In the early 2000s, when I began to write and publish about spirituality in social work practice, education, and transformative change, there were few social work scholars, let alone Indigenous ones, who were publishing in this area (Baskin, 2002). Less than a decade later, as I conduct a literature review of this topic, I am encouraged by the amount of information I find. Clearly, spirituality is emerging as an area of interest within the helping professions, including social work, psychology, psychiatry, and the health sciences. I would like to think that such interest in spirituality also means that more helpers and educators are listening to the needs of service users and students who practise some form of spirituality. I also believe that this interest in spirituality means that practitioners and educators are beginning to see people and the world around them in more holistic ways, a view that has been influenced by Indigenous world views.

The literature on spirituality in social work states that, historically, spirituality has been excluded due to the:

> Separation of church and state, which has a huge impact since most social workers are employed in agencies funded by the government; drive toward professionalism and evidence based scientific practice where spiritual issues are viewed as unscientific; and tendency to link spirituality to pathology rather than seeing it as a strength and resource. (Zapf, 2005)

Why the rising interest in spirituality within the helping professions of today, then? Authors, such as Zapf (2005) and Drouin (2002), argue that this is because the Western mindset of individualism and materialism no longer works for many people, who are realizing that spirituality encompassing connections to others, to community, and to the land may bring some meaning and fulfillment into their lives.

HOW IS SPIRITUALITY DEFINED?

Over the years, the social work literature remains consistent in its definition of spirituality as encompassing an individual's values, relationships with others, and a perception of the sacred (Baskin, 2002; Canda, 1988; Gilbert, 2000; Ingersoll, 1994; O'Rouke, 1997; Pellebon & Anderson, 1999; Titone, 1991; Zapf, 2005). Carolyn Jacobs (1997) defines spirituality as "heart knowledge where wholeness, meaning and inner peace occur. Spirituality is a sense of being at one with the inner and outer worlds" (p.172).

The literature also emphasizes that although religion can be a part of spirituality, religion and spirituality are not interchangeable. Religion is a formalized practice that includes "an integrated belief system that provides principles of behaviour, purpose of existence, meaning of death, and an expression of reverence for a supernatural being (or beings)" (Canda, 1989, p. 37). Spirituality, on the other hand, is distinguished as "a set of personal beliefs derived from individual's perception of self and his or her relationship to both the natural world and some metaphysical realm" (Canda, 1989, p. 37). The significant difference between religion and spirituality is that religion is a structured form of spirituality that usually has a group following, whereas spirituality can include individual experiences with or without a structured belief system (Baskin, 2002).

My understanding of Indigenous spirituality, according to the teachings that have been passed on to me, is that spirituality embodies an interconnectedness and interrelationship with all life. Everyone and everything (both "animate" and "inanimate") are seen as equal and interdependent, part of the great whole and as having a spirit. This view permeates the entire Indigenous vision of life, land, and the universe.

According to Ruth Koleszar-Green, who was introduced in Chapter One:

> Our teachings are not only spiritual, they're about everything—about the Great Law of Peace and the Two-Row Wampum, which talk about peace, love, and respect in all of our interactions. We can't separate the spiritual from any of the other aspects. Mentally taking the time to speak in a good way is an example of how the spiritual influences the mind. The Great Law of Peace is about the traditional ways of interacting and acting within the Haudenosaunee Confederacy based on peace, unity, and the power of the good mind.
>
> Everything in one's body knows spirit. Spirituality is difficult to put into words. It's difficult to articulate on its own, to try and talk about it as separate from everything else when it isn't. This is an artificial way to discuss it. Spirituality isn't just about attending ceremonies; it's about how we walk in the world, what we believe, how we connect, how we practise our beliefs.
>
> Spirituality isn't stagnant. The ways in which we celebrate and acknowledge our existence and experiences change as we advance as a species. The underlying core or values of spirituality are always the same, but how this comes to fruition always changes. For example, our ways of practising spirituality had to change as our people went into hiding when spirituality was legislated illegal by the colonization process. Sometimes we just understand why some things are done, such as ceremonies, but not exactly how to do all of the things that are involved.
>
> Humility is paramount: We can't learn everything there is to know about spirituality, nor are we meant to. If we knew everything there is to

know, then we would not have anything left to learn. Learning is important even when one is already a teacher. (R. Koleszar-Green, personal communication, November 26, 2008)

Joanne Dallaire sees spirituality as a relationship with what one believes in. She shared that:

There is a sense or connection to community through spirituality. Spirituality brings people together, which is wanted and needed by all people. It is a way of expressing the self. Spirituality can create a bigger trust of the self. It is a process of going inward to look for answers.

Spirituality is a way of living that shows us that all is connected; everyone and everything has a reason, purpose, and value for being here, even though we may not know what this is in the moment.

Experiencing a health or emotional crisis is seriously difficult. Everyone needs something that will help with this. It is comforting [for] people to believe in something. The power of faith is much known to heal the body. This helps us to understand the spiritual piece of healing. Spirituality is about turning it over to faith or one's beliefs when one cannot solve things alone. Spiritual practices are designed to heal in many cultures of the world. It is humanity's quest to seek things spiritual, to have something outside of the self to believe in, to help explain things that happen. (J. Dallaire, personal communication, July 23, 2009)

After more than 30 years at the School of Social Work at Ryerson University in Toronto, Dennis J. Haubrich is now professor emeritus. He has conducted research in the psychosocial dimensions of HIV disease, and has done work with AIDS caregivers in the area of spirituality. He now lives in Thornbury, Ontario, on southern Georgian Bay. Dennis started out as a colleague of mine, but over time, he became a friend. He is one of only a few White men with whom I have been able to discuss spirituality. So, needless to say, I asked him to share his thoughts with me for this chapter. Dennis explains spirituality like this:

Getting to the core of who you are and validating this. It's so difficult to always try to be who everyone else wants us to be, like doing what you are told and blindly obeying, so spirituality is about letting go of all the roles and expectations that others have of us. Spirituality is engagement with all around us, but it is too often constructed as a private matter. We complicate our lives with social expectations: being part of the status quo, making money, getting married, having children. Although these things are neither positive nor negative, we construct ourselves according to what we are told to do, which includes these things usually.

Sometimes we cannot do anything to change the physical or outside of us, but we can change the inside of us. Spirituality is a search for the sacredness inside. It's about trying to find one's relationship with the world. It's a search for meaning and purpose. Making meaning of one's life is central to the spiritual endeavour.

Spirituality is relational: person to person, person to Earth. It tells us that the answers we search for are inside us and in nature around us. Spirituality is recognition of our connectedness to all things, including things past. It means that I am part of this very earth—"remember that thou art dust and to dust thou shall return." (D. Haubrich, personal communication, November 26, 2008)

Dennis also shared his notions about the impacts of not having spirituality and how it can be of help:

Most people are missing the spiritual dimension. They're searching for it, but they are not listened to by others when they try to speak of this because public social discourse is largely devoid of spirituality apart from the formal spiritual discourses generated by religions. Depression, despair, and suicide: these come from not having spirituality. We need to listen to people who want to speak about their spirituality, about the things that others in their ordinary lives don't want to hear.

Spirituality is so significant for people who need to be released from addictions, trauma, and resentments. It is healing. It unburdens us from what harms us. There are journeys that are unchosen in life, and spirituality can help us get through these challenging ones, such as a serious illness. (D. Haubrich, personal communication, November 26, 2008)

LAND-BASED SPIRITUALITY

Although Indigenous scholars who write about spirituality—such as Fyre Jean Graveline (Métis) (1998), Kim Anderson (Métis) (2000), Michael Hart (Cree) (2002, 2009), Calvin Morrisseau (Anishnawbe) (1998), Leilani Holmes (Native Hawaiian) (1999), and Rod McCormick (Haudenosaunee) (1995)—include the land in their discussions, Western scholars rarely do.

Within Indigenous world views and spirituality, there is no separation between people and the land. Place or the physical environment shapes Indigenous peoples' entire lives and everyone else's lives too, even though in Western culture people are largely removed from and unaware of the connections between themselves and the physical environment in which they live. Place or physical environment directly influences cultures, education, relationships, food security, transportation, and spiritual beliefs. Around the globe there are sacred physical places that Indigenous peoples fight to protect and where they conduct their ceremonies. The Earth is often referred to as our Mother, for she gives birth to us and provides all that we need.

Rarely do Indigenous peoples anywhere in the world need buildings to conduct their ceremonies or offer prayers. Ceremonies are held on the land; all sacred objects used for prayer and ceremony come from the land; the people sit directly on the land. When answers to questions are sought or healing is needed, many Indigenous peoples go off by themselves and sit with their Mother in a fast or enter her womb through a sweat lodge.

It is often the land that awakens blood memories within us, such as being in a certain place and knowing down to our core that we have been here before. The land has the ability to calm and restore us and to inspire creativity. The land is home. The land is in us. The land *is* us.

I am originally from a tiny community on the Atlantic coast, but currently live in Toronto. It is the land that I miss the most: the contrast of woods and fields, the smell of the salt from the ocean, my feet sinking in the sand, and the ocean itself, which goes on forever. As soon as I step onto the beach back home, my breathing begins to slow down, my muscles relax, and I feel calm. This is not what I feel as I go about my daily life in the city of Toronto, a place that always pushes me to go faster and do more.

My best writing happens when I am on the land and water. I am able to tap into my creativity more easily. I have fewer distractions. I do everything at a slower pace. I feel as though I am as much a part of the place as the chipmunks who befriend me. It is not merely that the beauty of my surroundings inspires me to write, but that my connection to place takes over and allows access to what I am *supposed* to be writing. A good part of my Ph.D. dissertation was written while I was back home on the ocean, and some of this book was written while I was on Manitoulin Island on Lake Huron. My writing is part of my spirituality.

Of course, there is land everywhere, even under the cement of cities. Indigenous spirituality goes with us wherever we go. It teaches that a person is a spiritual being and can practise spirituality anywhere. Spirituality is inside us, in a tree in a park, in a flower in a garden, and in the sunset at the end of each day. Land-based ceremony and prayer can happen every day in cities such as Toronto if we want it to.

In her work as a helper, Koleszar-Green often goes for a walk with the people she works with as she listens to their stories and offers teachings. In one of her previous workplaces, the agency had a backyard, where she would bring service users to talk. Notes Koleszar-Green, "I don't think about this. I just do it" (R. Koleszar-Green, personal communication, November 26, 2008). Spirituality is also a major aspect of Ruth's role as a member of the Aboriginal Legal Services of Toronto's Community Council. As she sees it:

> Council members see people through eyes with love and respect. The Council creates a space where people can begin to connect with the Aboriginal community in Toronto and with their spirituality. Many of the people who come through the Council have not had Aboriginal spirituality in their lives and state that they feel disconnected from it and the community. In many of the hearings that I have participated in, youth have expressed an interest in exploring Aboriginal spirituality and some specifically ask to speak to an Elder or Traditional Teacher. It's amazing to bear witness to them beginning to connect to medicines, beliefs, and ceremonies that are a part of Aboriginal spirituality. For many people, being through the Council has been the best thing that's happened to them as it has helped them to connect, to belong, and to be a part of something that is so much bigger than them as individuals. Spirituality heals. (R. Koleszar-Green, personal communication, November 26, 2008)

Oritz and Smith (1999) and Gause and Coholic (2007) conducted literature reviews on spirituality in the social work literature. Neither of the reviews, in their definitions of spirituality, includes mention of a connection to place or the physical environment. According to Hunkpapa Lakota scholar Vine Deloria Jr. (1999), Western society can "attribute to the landscape only the aesthetic and not the sacred perspective" because it relates to the environment through technology such as photography or television (p. 257). Tewa Native scholar Gregory Cajete (1994) writes about society's "cosmological disconnection from the natural world" (p. 25). Peat (1994), a non-Indigenous scholar, also writes:

> Unlike western science, the importance of the landscape, and specific places in it, is a characteristic of all Indigenous science.... Within Indigenous science there is an association of spirit or energy with particular places, and it is important to visit these places and carry out ceremonies there.... This idea of the significance of place and the energies associated with it is common to Indigenous sciences all over the world.... [W]estern science does not appear to have a corresponding concept. (pp. 265–267)

When people have been in a particular place for generation after generation, their identities include that place and their connection to it. Spretnak (1991) explains this understanding beautifully: "a people rooted in the land over time have exchanged their tears, their breath, their bones, all of their elements—oxygen, carbon, nitrogen, hydrogen, phosphorus, sulphur, all the rest—with their habitat many times over. *Here nature knows us*" (p. 19).

Generally speaking, Western social work and other helping professions focus on person-environment relationships. From this perspective, the person and the environment are viewed as two separate entities that relate to each other. This relationship needs to be changed in order to assist the person, family, or group to gain greater stability, health, or well-being. However, within the helping professions, environment refers to systems such as the school, workplace, or services. It does not tend to include the physical environment or nature. As non-Aboriginal social work educator Michael Zapf (2005) explains:

> We view the physical environment as separate from ourselves, as an objective thing, as a commodity to be developed or traded or wasted or exploited, as an economic unit, as property. The dominant western culture has been described as "hostile to nature" (Spretnak, 1991: 102) and antagonistic to any concept of personhood beyond individualism. It is little wonder that the treatment of spirituality in the social work literature has been limited

to a narrow person-centered perspective. Yet there are alternatives. If we are open to exploring the connection of person and environment from a different world view, we might have much to learn from the developing written knowledge base for Aboriginal social work. (p. 636)

My friend Dennis is certainly someone who understands the connection between himself and the environment. In 2005, Dennis went on a spiritual walk through France and Spain. He began walking on his 58th birthday, April 12. He arrived in Camino de Santiago de Compostela (The Way of St. James as it is the alleged burial place of St. James the Apostle) on June 18, and on June 22 in Finisterre, which is the medieval end of the world. He walked 994 miles in three months.

Dennis explained to me that people from many parts of the world go on this pilgrimage for all sorts of reasons: to be healed, forgiven, or to simplify their lives. He went on this walk just as he was coming out of a dark place of despair and addictions due to the many losses he had in his life. He lost both his partner and best friend, and was wondering why he was still here. The walk was about coming into the light, choosing life rather than a slow death.

He walked for all of his friends who had died of AIDS. Dennis said that they were all with him as he walked. He was never alone and there was much healing in this for him. Dennis became much more aware of the physical Earth he inhabits as he walked through Europe. He learned that the Earth and everything on it is sacred. He explained that he came to realize he is only a speck on the Earth, but a speck that is part of a much bigger existence:

I believe that I am a part of something much greater than myself, albeit a small part, but a part nevertheless. When I was walking, I became aware that I was not alone in what I was doing, but that I was walking in the footsteps of thousands upon thousands of others. However, I was also not alone in another way for I was walking this journey for the people in my life that I had so loved and lost to AIDS. I was walking for them because they were no longer here to walk for themselves. My walk was also representative of putting the capstone on the journey out of sorrow, grief, and addiction. (D. Haubrich, personal communication, November 26, 2008)

Dennis also built a different relationship with himself on the walk—with his body and with his spirit—and he came to understand that body and spirit are integrated. He said he believes that as he became more and more aware of all the relationships he had with everything around him, who he truly is became clearer to him. Considering his relationships to others who walked the pilgrimage at the same time as he did, Dennis explained:

> On the pilgrimage, everyone is on the same playing field. The freedom is that they don't have to be who they are in the rest of the world of work and all that. Equality doesn't have to be taught on the walk; people don't even ask what you do back home—this tends to only come out at the end—everyone is the same, a child of creation, connected by humanity. People let go of defences and methods of protection while on the walk. The pilgrimage allows for the authentic person to come out.
>
> People from all over the world go on this pilgrimage. There was an 18-year-old youth from L.A., a social worker from Holland, a judge from Germany, a middle-aged woman from Australia. Youth are sent by their parents as they are beginning to get in trouble. There is a program where youth walk the pilgrimage instead of going to jail.
>
> People are walking through the problems they have in order to find solutions inside themselves. I think that as a metaphor for life the Camino de Santiago de Compostela is representative of helping people find their way, thus it's called "The Way." As such, it may be seen as providing direction, assisting in life decisions. The Way is also constructed in ways that are representative of rehabilitation and penance, for example, using the Camino experience and its challenges as a means [of] rehabilitating young offenders. (D. Haubrich, personal communication, November 26, 2008)

Dennis concluded our conversation about his life-changing spiritual journey with:

> The walk is a metaphor of life. One only truly learns why one went on the walk, why and what one learned, when the walk is finished. It ended at Finisterre—the end of the world—which is a fishing village on the Costa de Morte—coast of the dead. It was believed that this was the literal end of the world in the days when people there believed that the world was flat and that the stars that shone above the sea were the souls of the dead. When I came to the end of the walk, I felt that I had been given the greatest gift in the world: the gift was having been able to walk the Camino, to finally reach the end,

which is yet another beginning. I felt that I had been blessed to be able to do this walk. (D. Haubrich, personal communication, November 26, 2008)

On the walk, Dennis made the decision to leave academia and take early retirement. He knew it was the right decision as he felt out of place when he returned to his ordinary life there. He knew he was different from how he was before he went on the walk. He could no longer relate to the values of academia, such as the "rugged individualism rather than collectivism" (D. Haubrich, personal communication, November 26, 2008).

WHERE ARE WE HEADING?

I think Zapf (2005) would agree that there is a slightly different thought emerging in the typical person/environment social work literature of late. This comes from writing about eco-spiritualism. One of the more prominent writers on this subject is social work scholar John Coates (2003, 2004) who has also published with Mel Gray and Tiana Hetherington (2006, 2007).

At this point in our history, it is beyond doubt that we are living amidst an environmental catastrophe whereby humans are slowly killing the Earth. The warning signs are climate change and the increasingly frequent and horrendous "natural disasters" taking place around the globe. The industrial and agricultural practices that exploit both the physical environment and human beings are supported by the values and beliefs of a Western society that believes economic well-being, which often translates into having more things and gaining material wealth, will lead to overall well-being. In other words, materialism and consumerism equals happiness. These beliefs also stress that technology will solve all of our problems. However, the kinds of material benefits that these claims support are not within reach of 80 percent of the Earth's population, nor is our current rate of consumption sustainable (Chossudovsky, 1998; Wackernagel & Rees, 1995).

The destruction of our planet ought to be of concern to the profession of social work because "progress" has contributed to vast social injustices, such as racism, sexism, and the abuse of women and children. Overproduction in the name of progress has generated pollution and increasing human exploitation as people engaged in low-paid and often dangerous subsistence-wage jobs struggle to keep up with an increasing demand for products. Coates (2003) writes that humanitarian values, which are also social work values, can play a leading role in the struggle to assert new perspectives about how the West currently operates.

Coates (2003) then goes on to discuss what he refers to as "new foundational assumptions" (New Foundational Assumptions, para. 3): all things are connected, everyone and everything has inherent value, there is wisdom in nature, diversity is natural, and identity and fulfillment happen within community. Sound familiar? At least Coates (2003) mentions that these beliefs are consistent with those of First Nations. He then offers a number of tasks for social workers to consider, based on the above assumptions:

> Nurture an understanding and appreciation of the connectedness of all things, and the hope and direction that can flow from this. This step is perhaps the most essential as it will involve, for many, the emergence of a transformed consciousness—the acceptance of an alternative world view. This is particularly significant in today's modern culture where politicians, transnational corporations and mainstream economics preach from the same modernist book—neo-liberalism and market forces. An unfolding world view moves away from an exclusively human-centered, materialistic, individualistic, and consumerist value system to one that is based on interdependence, community, the sacredness of all life, and sustainability. (New Tasks for Social Work, para. 3)

This time, however, Coates does not make reference to Indigenous world views, although the connection is obvious.

In another article by Coates, Gray, and Hetherington (2006), entitled "An 'Ecospiritual' Perspective: Finally, a Place for Indigenous Approaches," the authors advocate for the foundation of a new system of beliefs and values to guide human behaviour so that people will be more in harmony with the Earth. Coates et al. (2006) further point out that several scholars now "recognize the important contribution made by traditional indigenous beliefs and values" (pp. 389–391). A year later, in another article, they state that "indigenous beliefs and values have gained recognition and credibility among the world views that provide a reconceptualization of the universe and humanity's relationship to it. In social work this has opened avenues of acceptance toward Indigenous approaches to helping" (Gray, Coates & Hetherington, 2007, p. 60). Increasing environmental concerns and a renewed interest in spirituality within the social work field expressed by scholars in the dominant culture have perhaps resulted in greater openness to alternative world views. However, it is problematic that Indigenous world views and understandings about spirituality and the interconnectedness of all life, including the Earth, which have been a part of Aboriginal belief systems since creation, have been re-named "eco-spirituality" and have only now gained favour under the auspices of Western scholarship. The authors even go so far as to use the term "indigenous ecospiritual approaches" (Coates et al., 2006, p. 395).

I suggest that there is an alternative way to look at the significance of Indigenous world views and their connection to spirituality is within social work. Rather than insisting on adapting Indigenous knowledges, in attempts to make them fith with Western concepts, why not listen to what Indigenous peoples are saying and learn from them? Trying to force these knowledges into Western constructs can never work as this changes these knowledges into something they are not.

ASSESSING SPIRITUALITY

A fascinating approach is emerging within the area of spirituality and social work—methods that can be used to assess a person's spirituality. There are verbal models, spiritual histories, and visual tools such as spiritual life maps, spiritual genograms, spiritual eco-maps, and spiritual eco-grams (Hodge, 2005a, 2005b). These methods are used to assist service users in explaining their spiritual life journeys. Some of these methods are similar to art therapy and support creativity and self-expression, and facilitate the process of making meaning out of life experiences (Hodge, 2005a, 2005b). The methods are meant to explore spiritual resources and strengths.

I believe that including a person's spirituality in an assessment is a positive addition to the practice of social work. I have always found it confusing that as social workers we are expected to assess multiple areas of a service user's life, including whether a person has experienced physical and/or sexual abuse, yet we have shied away from exploring spiritual beliefs. Why is it easier to ask a person if she has been sexually abused than to ask if, for example, she believes in a Creator or God? If methods for spiritual assessments are helpful to social workers, I am in favour of them. Nevertheless, if we wish to send the message to service users that their spirituality is important in the helping process, why don't we simply ask them about their beliefs and practices? I believe that Indigenous methods of sincerely and respectfully inquiring about a person's spirituality can offer guidance to the profession of social work in this area. Ruth Koleszar-Green agrees:

Students are not taught to ask service users about their spiritual beliefs or even to ask if this is a space where an individual or family can draw strength in a time of struggle. There is spiritual space everywhere and students need to connect their spirituality with their practice. They need ways to ground themselves while practising social work; they need introspection to have an understanding of how their beliefs have been harmed or lessened.

Some clients want workers who practise spirituality. It can bring people from marginalized spaces together—we don't have to believe the same things—just believe. Students want spirituality in education. I found that in talking with my classmates, they had a desire to have a space where speaking about spirituality within the classroom was okay; that they shouldn't have to park their identities at the classroom door, but should be able to bring their whole selves in. (R. Koleszar-Green, personal communication, November 26, 2008)

A significant challenge in inquiring about a service user's or a social work student's spirituality may arise if spiritual beliefs are discriminatory. For example, how does a social work practitioner or educator respond to spiritual beliefs that are patriarchal or heterosexist? Both Indigenous world views and the profession of social work support values and practices of inclusion and respect for diversity. However, if some people are being harmed by others' spiritual beliefs, perhaps there needs to be limits to inclusion. This, in turn, leads to questions around who decides what beliefs ought to be included or excluded within social work education and practice. Such a discussion is valuable for educators, students, practitioners, and organizations that govern social work education and practice. Nevertheless, our profession, in all of its components, is supposed to be committed to social justice. It is social justice that guides our values and ethics. Therefore, as social workers, we must be prepared to take a stand against what creates injustice.

CONCLUSION

Research from around the globe tells us that a respect for life and an acknowledgement of the interconnectedness of all beings—everything on the Earth—and the Earth herself is central to Indigenous world views (Richardson & Blanchet-Cohen, 2000). Recognition of what the spirit can teach us through dreams and meditation, for example, are simply a part of natural life. Spiritual experiences, and the learning that comes from these experiences, are significant to each person's life journey.

The interpretation of spirituality as presented in this chapter, however, is not the sole domain of Indigenous peoples. We do not have a monopoly on spirituality. What we do have is a spirituality that is connected to place. Many of us would like to share this connection with *all* peoples of the Earth because without her, there is nothing.

There is absolutely no doubt that land-based spirituality can be lived by anyone regardless of one's perspective, adherence to a formalized religion, or one's belief in a God or Creator. Dennis Haubrich and the diverse people he met while on his pilgrimage shows us this. However, people need to find their own way in connecting to the land and to the spiritual aspect of themselves rather than imitating the specific ceremonies of Indigenous peoples. Certainly, guidance can come from the world views and knowledges of the Indigenous peoples of whatever land we are on, but specific practices in developing a relationship with the land and one's spirit are connected to one's own particular roots. There are many ways to meditate other than through fasting in a lodge made of willow branches in the bush. There are many ways to cleanse and purify other than smudging. There are many ways to heal one's spirit other than through the sweat lodge. Look inside yourself, find out who you are, and listen to your dreams and blood memories as these will lead you to your own practices of connection.

But, most importantly, please consider that if human beings continue to destroy our Mother the Earth, the colour of one's skin or the amount of money in one's bank account will not matter. If She dies, we all die. If there is only one thing that you learn about and decide to implement in your life after reading this book, let it be a belief in land-based spirituality, which, at the end of the day, is caring for the Earth and everything on Her.

REFERENCES

Anderson, K. (2000). *A recognition of being: Reconstructing Native womanhood.* Toronto: Second Story.

Baskin, C. (2002). Circles of resistance: Spirituality in social work practice, education, and transformative change. *Currents: New Scholarship in the Human Services.* Retrieved from http://www.ucalgary.ca/SW/currents/

Cajete, G. (1994). *Look to the mountain: An ecology of Indigenous education.* Durango: Kivaki Press.

Canda, E. (1988). Conceptualizing spirituality for social work: Insights from diverse perspectives. *Social Thought, 14*(1), 30–46.

Canda, E. (1989). Religious content in social work education: A comparative approach. *Journal of Social Work Education, 25*(1), 36–45.

Chossudovsky, M. (1998). *The globalisation of poverty.* Halifax: Fernwood.

Coates, J. (2003). Exploring the roots of the environmental crisis: Opportunity for social transformation. *Critical Social Work, 4*(1). Retrieved from http://www.uwindsor.ca/criticalsocialwork/

Coates, J. (2004). From ecology to spirituality and social justice. *Currents: New Scholarship in the Human Services, 3*(1). Retrieved from http://fsw.ucalgary.ca/currents/

Coates, J., Gray, M. & Hetherington, T. (2006). An "ecospiritual" perspective: Finally, a place for Indigenous approaches. *British Journal of Social Work, 36*(3), 381–399. doi: 10.1093/bjsw/bc1005

Deloria Jr., V. (1999). *For this land: Writings of religion in America.* New York: Routledge.

Drouin, H.A. (2002). Spirituality in social work practice. In F.J. Tuner (Ed.), *Social work practice: A Canadian perspective* (2nd ed.) (pp. 33–45). Toronto: Prentice-Hall.

Gause, R. & Coholic, D. (2007). *Spirituality—influenced social work practice: A descriptive overview of recent literature.* Unpublished manuscript, Laurentian University, Sudbury, ON.

Gilbert, M.C. (2000). Spirituality in social work groups: Practitioners speak out. *Social Work with Groups, 22*(4), 67–84. doi: 10.1300/J009v22n04_06

Graveline, F.J. (1998). *Circle works: Transforming Eurocentric consciousness.* Halifax: Fernwood Press.

Gray, M., Coates, J. & Hetherington, T. (2007). Hearing Indigenous voices in mainstream social work. *Families in Society, 88*(1), 55–66. doi: 10.1606/1044-3894.359

Hart, M. (2002). *Seeking mino-pimatisiwin: An Aboriginal approach to helping.* Halifax: Fernwood Press.

Hart, M.A. (2009). Anti-colonial Indigenous social work. In R. Sinclair, M.A. Hart & G. Bruyere (Eds.), *Wicihitowin: Aboriginal social work in Canada* (pp. 25–41). Winnipeg: Fernwood Publishing.

Hodge, D.R. (2005a). Developing a spiritual assessment toolbox: A discussion of the strengths and limitations of five different assessment methods. *Health and Social Work, 30*(4), 314–323. Retrieved from http://www.ingentaconnect.com

Hodge, D.R. (2005b). Spiritual lifemaps: A client-centered pictorial instrument for spiritual assessment, planning, and intervention. *Social Work, 50*(1), 77–87. Retrieved from http://www.ingentaconnect.com

Holmes, L. (1999). Heart knowledge, blood memory, and the voice of the land: Implications of research among Hawaiian elders. In G.J.S. Dei, B.L. Hall & D. Goldin Rosenberg (Eds.), *Indigenous knowledges in global contexts: Multiple readings of our world* (pp. 37–53). Toronto: University of Toronto Press.

Ingersoll, R.E. (1994). Spirituality, religion, and counseling: Dimensions and relationships. *Counseling and Values, 38*(2), 98–111. Retrieved from Psychology and Behavioral Sciences Collection database.

Jacobs, C. (1997). On spirituality and social work practice. *Smith College Studies in Social Work, 67*(2), 171–175.

McCormick, R. (1995). The fascination of healing for the First Nations people of British Columbia. *Canadian Journal of Native Education, 21*(2), 249–322.

Morrisseau, C. (1998). *Into the daylight: A wholistic approach to healing.* Toronto: University of Toronto Press.

O'Rouke, C. (1997). Listening for the sacred: Addressing spiritual issues in the group treatment of adults with mental illness. *Smith College Studies in Social Work, 67*(2), 177–195.

Oritz, L. & Smith, G. (1999). The role of spirituality in empowerment practice. In W. Shera & L.M. Wells (Eds.), *Empowerment practice in social work: Developing richer conceptual foundations* (pp. 307–319). Toronto: Canadian Scholars' Press Inc.

Peat, F.D. (1994). *Lighting the seventh fire: The spiritual ways, healing, and science of the Native American.* New York: Birch Lane Press.

Pellebon, D.A. & Anderson, S.C. (1999). Understanding the life issues of spiritually-based clients. *Families in Society, 80*(3), 229–239. doi: 10.1606/1044-3894.676

Richardson, C. & Blanchet-Cohen, N. (2000). *Survey of post-secondary education programs in Canada for Aboriginal Peoples.* For UNESCO: University of Victoria, Institute for Child Rights and Development, and First Nations Partnerships Program. Retrieved from http://www.nvit.ca

Spretnak, C. (1991). *States of grace: The recovery of meaning in the postmodern age.* New York: HarperCollins.

Titone, A.M. (1991). Spirituality and psychotherapy in social work practise. *Spirituality and Social Work Communication, 2*(1), 7–9.

Wackernagel, M. & Rees, W. (1995). *Our ecologist footprint: Reducing human impact on the earth.* Gabriola Island: New Society Publishers.

Zapf, M.K. (2005). The spiritual dimension of person and environment: Perspectives from social work and traditional knowledge. *International Social Work, 48*(5), 633–642. doi: 10.1177/0020872805055328

Chapter 9
Healing Justice

INTRODUCTION

Perhaps justice as seen through an Indigenous lens is one of the more well-known topics in Canadian mainstream society. Recognition of Indigenous forms of justice can be seen in the justice system's diversion programs for youth in conflict with the law and child welfare's family group conferencing as a way to come up with alternatives to state care of children. This chapter explores how Indigenous peoples and communities are leaders in restorative types of justice, and what others can learn from their knowledge and experience in this area.

THERE'S ALWAYS A STORY

I have been using the term "healing justice" for more than 15 years since I became interested in helping people who hurt others, particularly in family violence, including sexual abuse. At that time, I had worked with people who had survived violence for several years. There was one moment I remember clearly to this day that propelled me on the journey of learning about and practising how to help those who harm others. I had been working with a 13-year-old survivor of familial sexual abuse for a few months. One day, she said to me, "If what you are telling me is right—that I'm not responsible for what he did to me—then why am I in healing and he isn't?"

What I did first was approach some of the Elders and Traditional Teachers I knew to ask them what was historically done when people hurt others. They taught me about what they called *customary laws* or *natural laws*.

I spoke with Elders and Traditional Teachers (e.g., Rebecca Martel, Edna Manitowabi, Vera Martin, Lily and Paul Bourgeois, Gertie Beaucage, Jim Dumont, Eva Cardinal, Sylvia Maracle, Michael Thrasher, Herb Nabigon, and Jan Longboat) from a diversity of Nations, such as Anishnawbe, Haudenosaunee, Cree, and Métis, and found consistencies among their responses. They told me that prior to contact, violence within families and communities was rare due to a number of factors. For example, it was critical for people to get along as each person's survival depended on the others. Communities were small and people lived in close quarters, so co-operation was vital. Also, due to these living arrangements, plus the purpose of some of the clans—for example, the bear clan had the job of looking out for others and members of the fish clan were the mediators when problems arose—meant that many eyes and ears were on people.

I was also told that children were rarely alone with any adult. Instead, as children learned by observing and doing, girls, for example, tended to spend most of their time with the women of the community. In addition, since many Nations were matrilineal (e.g., Haudenosaunee, Mi'kmaq), through customary laws, women were the heads of their homes. This meant that if a man hurt his partner and she no longer wanted to be with him, he would have to leave the home. Any children would stay with her and he would continue to have the responsibility of providing for them.

Aside from practicalities, Aboriginal world views, as expressed through values and spiritual teachings, also played a crucial role in ensuring that harm to others was minimal. Such values and teachings have been discussed in earlier chapters, so I will simply mention them here: balance within and among people, harmony with all around them, children are gifts from the Creator, every person is valued as each has a role and purpose within the community, and everything one does has an impact on others.

It was explained to me that due to these practicalities and spiritual beliefs, incidence of harm was rare. If a person harmed another, it became a matter of community concern. The idea was to find out why the incident occurred and what harm was caused. Both the person who did the harm and the one who had been harmed were now seen as being out of balance, which impacted everyone in the community. Thus, balance needed to be restored by making the one who caused the harm accountable, providing compensation to the person who had been harmed, and conducting healing ceremonies. Once harmony within the community had been restored, everyone moved on.

For most Aboriginal peoples, the most severe consequence was being ostracized, which could occur if the harm caused was extreme. This was a powerful deterrent within customary law that no one would have wanted to face. Being ostracized by the community likely meant death as it would have been difficult to survive on one's own in such harsh environmental conditions.

All of the Elders and Traditional Teachers I spoke with were adamant that aspects of their customary laws are needed to be brought into today's world when harm occurs. They all spoke of ascribing to the same spiritual teachings and world views of their ancestors regarding balance and harmony. Each emphasized how out of balance those who harmed others were and how they needed to be accountable to the person they hurt, to that person's family, and to the community. They also emphasized healing for both the harmed person and the one who caused the harm. They consistently pointed out that situations such as woman and child abuse originated from the impacts of colonization through which violence had been learned and passed on from one generation to the next. Some of these Elders and Traditional Teachers were actively involved in restoring customary laws within their communities and Aboriginal agencies in urban centres. They were overwhelmingly supportive of me doing the same.

Then I turned to the literature, where I found little on the topic. However, I did find a report written in 1999 by A.C. Hamilton and Murray Sinclair, who is a traditional Anishnawbe man and who just happens to be a judge in Canada and presently a member of the Truth and Reconciliation Commission of Canada on the residential school system. Their report was based on an inquiry into Indigenous peoples and the criminal justice system in Manitoba. Not only did this report confirm what I already knew about racism in the system—as evidenced by over-policing of Indigenous peoples in urban centres, higher arrests, higher incarceration rates, longer sentences, higher denial of parole rates, and longer parole and probation sentences—it also echoed what the Elders and Traditional Teachers had shared with me about customary laws.

In the following sections I describe some key components of Indigenous justice, how they work in practice, and why many believe the principles can be applied to other populations.

VALUES BEHIND THE PRACTICES

As has been referred to in each chapter of this book, everything is related or connected within Indigenous world views. Everything is viewed through a relational lens. Thus, customary laws, natural laws, community-based justice, restorative justice, and alternative justice are all terms meant to describe processes that restore balance and harmony between people, communities, and all of creation.

When one person harms another, he has created an imbalance within people and communities. He has negatively impacted upon numerous relationships—between the harmed person and her sense of self, between him and his sense of self, among their family members and other community members. The person who has been harmed does not see herself in the same way. She may blame herself for what happened, lose confidence, and is often afraid. She no longer views her environment in the same way. Perhaps her home is no longer safe, she fears being out after dark, or cannot tolerate being alone. In other words, her relationships with all that she has been connected to have been damaged.

The person who has done the harm has likely been disconnected from himself, other people, and his community for some time because of the harms that have been done to him in the past. And the community may no longer trust him or they may shun him as they do not feel safe around him. The energy around all of the community is tense and can be felt among people and in the air; everyone and everything is out of sorts—all is out of balance.

Many processes can help at this point—Sentencing Circles, Healing Circles, ceremonies, one-to-one work with the people involved, Family Circles, and removing the person who has done the harm for a time. But if these methods do not centre on the restoration of balance for everyone from a relational lens, they likely will not heal. And healing is the overall goal of Indigenous world views of justice.

WHAT NEEDS TO BE LEARNED?

Many people—both professionals, such as social workers, and family members, such as partners—would agree that incarceration often further develops harmful behaviours rather than the opposite. Those returning home after spending time in jails or prisons are often more hardened, distanced from their emotions, violent, skilled in criminal behaviours, intimidating, and, at times, connected to drug-transportation networks.

Such a phenomenon is eloquently described by a Cree grandmother in northern Quebec, who asked Rupert Ross (2008) "What kinds of values they built relationships upon inside" jails (p. 11). According to Ross, this grandmother "then expressed her fear that being in jail might make it even harder for her community to teach those men, when they came back, how to live in relationships built on values and sharing instead" [of what they learned while incarcerated] (p. 11).

Living in relationships also invites us to see a person as separate from his or her behaviour. From this lens, a person is not an offender or perpetrator, but someone who has caused harm. Other examples of seeing people through this wholeness lens are a person who smokes crack rather than a "crackhead" or someone who is homeless rather than a "homeless guy." This can also be applied to those who have been harmed as well: Rather than calling someone "a victim," this is a person who has been victimized. In fact, I would say that most people who have been victimized prefer to be viewed as survivors over the long term rather than being identified as victims, which seems to be a label. My experiences in working with men who have hurt women and children through physical and sexual abuse has taught me that most of them have little understanding of the impact they have had as viewed through a relational lens. This seems to be because those who hurt others tend to have been hurt themselves in similar ways. They are not open to the others' pain because when they experienced their own pain, they learned how to shut down and turn off their feelings. They taught themselves to control, minimize, or deny what they were feeling when they were abused, and they do the same when they hurt others. Shutting down goes hand in hand with a deep sense of isolation, and they feel they have no purpose other than being used by others. Hence, people who were abused as children often grow up to abuse children themselves. They are behaving within the same sort of relationships they knew as children, except now they are the ones in positions of power.

Those who harm others, however, are capable of empathy. This is why the healing process with them must focus on ways that will chip away their layers of denial and minimization to eventually reach a place where empathetic connections can be accessed. No healing can begin until they understand that how they relate to other people is causing harm.

POWER OF THE CIRCLE

Bringing people together in a circle to look at how a person has been harmed, holding the one who did the harm accountable, and beginning a healing process for all the relationships involved is the foundation of Aboriginal justice.

Family members and friends of the person who has been hurt can make powerful contributions to raising the awareness of the one who has caused the harm and helping to create empathy within him. Because they are close to the one who has been harmed, they can offer first-hand stories of how she or he has been struggling to relate to others and the world around her or him since the harm occurred.

Within a circle, surrounded by those who love and support them, people who have been hurt can talk about the impacts they are now living with and ask questions of the one who hurt them. This is a remarkably different experience than sitting in a courtroom where unknown "experts," such as lawyers and judges, decide what is best for those involved based on intrusive questions, "evidence," and "the truth." As Ross (2009) wonders:

> When victims complain that the court has never really "heard" them, is it because neither the court nor the offender have ever defined the crime in the same way that victims experience it, as causing an enduring injury to central relationships in their lives? Are victims even able to articulate their injury in that way, or has our "thing-centred" way of looking at the world kept us from recognizing that what is truly injured by crime is our capacity for maintaining or creating healthy relationships?" (p. 6)

Family and friends of the person who has done harm are also present in the circle, not only to support him, but to offer relevant information about him. They may share their own experiences and insights as to how their relative came to do what he did. They may also share stories about their relationships with him and speak about him as a whole person rather than a one-dimensional person who has hurt another. On an emotional level, those family members and friends may feel pain for what their relative has done and wish to express remorse to the person harmed and her family.

Emotions are, in a large part, the essence of these circles. I was fortunate to meet and hear Robert Yazzie, chief justice of the Navajo Tribal Court, speak at a conference in 2009. He concisely explained: "Until I know how you feel and you know how I feel, we'll never move beyond those feelings." (R. Yazzie, personal communication, May 14, 2009) Is this not the beginning stage of healing for all involved?

My observation from being in these types of circles is that many significant questions are asked and answered for all who attend them. Family and friends of the person who has been hurt learn that the one who did the harm is not a monster or a psychopath, but a human being who is capable of empathy and remorse.

For those who have been harmed, perhaps the most important question is "Why me?" Unfortunately, this tends to lead to other self-blaming questions such as "Did I do something wrong?" "Was it because of the way I dressed or something I said?" "I shouldn't have been at that house party, right?" or "It was because I was drinking, wasn't it?" Of course, family, friends, and social workers will say repeatedly that it was not her fault, but this will never equal the impact of responsibility on the part of the one who did the harm when he says, for example, "You just happened to be there," "You were the first one I saw," "I was in a rage and wanted to hurt someone—anyone," or "I wanted to take my frustration out on you because I knew you wouldn't be able to stop me."

It is also remarkably helpful for both the one who did the harm and the person who has been harmed to hear the impact of what has been done. The harmed person needs to tell the one who hurt her what it feels like to be her right now. He needs to know what he has done to this person, and she may be the only one who can get him to understand.

There are times, however, when a harmed person does not want to participate in a circle of this kind. Perhaps she never wants to see the one who hurt her again; she is too afraid, angry, or intimidated or does not support the process. When this has been the case, I have held circles without her where her family, friends, and helpers speak on her behalf. This is not as powerful as having the harmed person present, but it still goes a long way in getting the one who has done the hurt to understand what he has done and helping both his and her family members and friends begin to heal.

RELATIONAL LENS

Viewing harmful acts through a Western lens means focusing on the acts alone, dealing with those referred to as "offenders" as individuals, and promoting the belief that "rehabilitation" will happen as long as these individuals choose to change themselves and their behaviour. I'm not sure it's that simple for the majority of people. Rather, I am certain that most will need help from others in their lives, so that making better choices becomes a group effort.

A relationship has formed between the person who has been harmed and the one responsible for it. Such a relationship has been forced on someone and inevitably involves violence or the threat of violence. The threat is always present as one wonders, "What will he do to me if I don't do what he says?" This relationship must be changed in order for both people to move forward. In particular, the harmed person will likely need to return to a place where she can have, once again, open and trusting relationships. This can happen if she is provided with the opportunity to ask the person who hurt her, face to face, the questions only he can answer and then decide for herself if he is sincere. As social workers and other helping professionals, we can tell hurt people over and over that what happened is not their fault, but this can never come close to hearing it from the person who hurt them. They can listen to defence lawyers and court workers talk about how sorry the person who hurt them is, but they need to hear it directly from him and decide this for themselves.

My work experience with those who have created harm has taught me that, for the most part, they tend to have a superficial understanding of the damage they have caused. They need to become aware, through a relational lens, that they have caused emotional, psychological, spiritual, and sometimes physical damage to the person they have hurt and all those who have a significant relationship with her. In order for them to be truly emotionally accountable for the harm caused, they need to move past the facade they show the world of being unfeeling or uncaring and feel someone else's pain. More often than not, they begin to feel another person's feelings only after they become conscious of their own. Through a relational lens, there is a focus on learning about the person who has created harm for others: Who are you? How do you identify yourself? How would you describe yourself? What was your childhood like? How do you deal with anger? How do you feel about yourself? By telling their story in this relational way, they can allow themselves to feel, and what they feel are usually the same emotions as those of the one they have hurt. This is a remarkably different experience from the one in a courtroom, where the focus is only on the facts and the process is over within minutes.

The healing process, through a relational lens, is not about trying to change someone, but about helping a person to relate differently to other people. What will help this person to see that he or she is not alone? That they can form relationships based on respect, and what will assist them in moving forward? I am convinced that if our aim is to help stop people from hurting others, then this is the most promising way to go. For those who have been hurt, listening to others who were once hurt in similar ways is a powerful tool for healing. They come to understand that their responses to being hurt—such as secrecy, shutting down, or abusing substances—are normal given what happened to them. They can hear the stories of others who also once thought that they would feel shame and fear forever, but were able to heal at their own pace and in their own ways, eventually developing new ways of seeing themselves and relating to others. Sometimes these stories come from one's own family members and friends. Other times they may come from the family and friends of the person who has caused the hurt and who were themselves once hurt in similar ways. Such stories are never intended as advice or what one should do. Rather, they are offered as encouragement and examples of what is possible.

In a similar way, it is helpful for those who have hurt others to participate in circles with people who once did the same, but who have been on their healing path for a long time. Their stories help to communicate that healing can occur and that one can learn to relate to other people in much healthier ways. Another important reason for having these men participate in processes where others are just beginning is because the former, more than any social worker regardless of experience, will be the fastest to catch the latter minimizing what they have done, coming up with excuses, or blaming others. I am deliberately naming men as those who harm others and women as the ones who are harmed. This is because even though women do harm other people, of course, the vast majority of reported physical and sexual assaults are committed by men upon women. According to Statistics Canada (2011), most victims of violence across the country are women who have been harmed by men and they experience more serious types of violence than men. Furthermore, the Canadian Research Institute for the Advancement of Women (2002) reports that half of Canadian women have survived at least one incident of sexual or physical violence and that 98% of sexual offenders are men with 82% of survivors being women and girls. In addition, the United Nations (2006) states that around the world, one in three women suffer serious violence at the hands of males.

Those who have been harmed and those who have created harm need to spend time with people who have been in similar situations. One of the most powerful ways in which this happens is when those who have had these experiences and have been through their particular healing journey wish to assist others by facilitating Healing Circles, or speaking at conferences, in social work classrooms, or in correctional institutions. These are incredible, brave, and unselfish acts on the part of both those who have been hurt and those who have caused the hurt. Their stories educate others, while at the same time, bring them closer to being free of the hold the experiences have on them.

ROLE OF THE HELPER

Interestingly enough, there seems to be little discussion in the literature or within social work education about the significant roles in advocacy and direct practice that social workers could have in the area of justice. I believe this is a serious gap in our education and practice.

Ultimately, it is the members of each group—whether they are a family, members of a Sentencing Circle, or participants of a Healing Circle—who come up with more positive and healthy ways of relating to one another, which, in turn, will be taken out into the rest of the world.

The helper, who is a social worker or other helping professional, is present as a guide who assists participants in creating respectful processes; identifying and releasing emotions such as fear, anger, and shame; relating to one another in open and honest ways; and exploring what led to hurtful behaviours in the first place. The helper provides a context in which all of these processes become possible.

THE COMMUNITY COUNCIL

Aboriginal Legal Services of Toronto (ALST) was established in 1990, following a needs assessment by the Native Canadian Centre of Toronto in the mid-1980s. The centre had been operating justice-related programs for Aboriginal peoples in Toronto, but concluded that an agency dedicated to this area was needed. ALST's mission is to strengthen the capacity of the Aboriginal community to deal with justice issues and provide Aboriginal-controlled, culture-based alternatives. Services offered at ALST include a court worker program, legal clinic, Gladue (Aboriginal person's court), community council program, test case litigation, and advocacy and law reform activities.

Rene Timleck, Anishnawbe and a member of Beausoleil First Nation, but born and raised in Toronto, has been an addictions counsellor for the past 25 years. She is the mother of five children, grandmother of 10, and great-grandmother of two. Rene has been a member of ALST's Community Council for Adults and Youth for over six years. A staff person at ALST whom she had known for a few years asked her if she would be interested in being a member of the Community Council. Rene agreed, motivated by the fact that she had a grandson who had been in and out of trouble with the law. A few years previously, he and another boy stole a car and were killed in an accident. She hoped that if she got involved in the council, she could help prevent another youth from a similar fate.

Rene's process of becoming a member included completing an application, going through an interview with existing council members and Elders of the community, attending an information session in which all aspects of the council were explained, and speaking with existing council members who shared their experiences with her. She then learned about the criteria for diversion, the history of Aboriginal peoples and the criminal justice system, the discrimination against Aboriginal peoples in Canada, and the objectives of the council.

Rene meets many diverse people through her involvement with the council—some who have been in as many as 22 foster homes, who were abused or neglected as children, who may be challenged by fetal alcohol syndrome, and who have never received care from others. Perhaps some of the participants are homeless and without families or other support systems. Rene sees that these community members have never had a chance, and she is touched by this. She hopes that those who come through the council as participants are touched by council members such as her, that they know others care about them, and that they don't have to be alone.

In my interview with Rene, I first asked her how the Community Council works. She explained:

> Participants coming before their own community members are facing their own people rather than strangers. This touches their emotions as it provides an environment where everyone sits together. Council members introduce themselves and give the participant some personal information about themselves, which is intended to show the participant that they are part of this community; we are their peers rather than an unknown judge. Council members ask not only about the charges that brought them to the hearing, but also about their lives and circumstances; about

their hopes and dreams. We try to assess the whole person; not just the crime, but the reasons behind it.

This is not about punishment, but rather the council tries to assist participants in changing some of the things that might have been contributing factors to committing the offence, such as lack of education or shelter or unresolved issues from the past. In other words, the council looks at what contributed to a participant ending up in the place of having to be at a hearing. (R. Timleck, personal communication, April 22, 2009)

I then invited Rene to share her thoughts on how the council process benefits participants. She was happy to oblige:

Participants have been shown (hopefully) that they are part of the community and not just a "case." We call on their pride and responsibility to deal with the problem at hand. I believe the process builds a relationship between council members and participants. Participants experience shame as they are in front of their community and truly have to face what they have done. After the shame comes pride because they have been able to go through this process of facing themselves and others. I can see that participants try not to disappoint or let down the council members.

Council members suggest ways of assisting participants, such as counselling, returning to school, entering apprenticeships, volunteering, writing a letter of apology, and [providing] financial compensation for what was stolen, for example. They can create paintings or sculptures if they have this talent, which helps them feel like they're a part of the community and that they're giving back to the community that is helping them. The art or other creative assignments have been donated to many different places in Toronto.

These suggestions for participants must be realistic: They need to know that they can meet the expectations that the council members suggest for them. If these expectations are too high, participants are set up for failure. There is a strong emphasis on finding a solution that can be accomplished, which involves taking into consideration all aspects of the information received and an exploration of the participant's capabilities, interests, and gifts.

Once the agreement is completed, it gives the participant a concrete circumstance under which they have accomplished something ... and maybe they can take another step. I believe if the justice system did more of this sort of intervention, there would be less reoffending. (R. Timleck, personal communication, April 22, 2009)

ALST also has a Community Council specifically for youth. It began in 2000 and serves youth 12–18 years old. This is how it works: A youth is charged; an Aboriginal court worker from ALST at the court talks to him or her about ALST's Community Council, explaining how all charges can be diverted except driving under the influence, domestic assault, and murder, and that the Crown attorney must agree to the diversion. The youth who is charged must admit responsibility, which is different from the mainstream justice system in which one can plead guilty and never take responsibility for what was done. With diversion to the council, a youth must take full responsibility, meaning "I did everything I am being charged with" or partial responsibility, which means "I was there and took part in some of the offence." If the young person takes responsibility, the charges are stayed or withdrawn according to the discretion of the judge in the case. Usually the Crown involved in the case will have a preference of the two, which is communicated to the judge.

A hearing date with the Community Council is set and the participant is given a hearing notice while still at the court with the date on it to serve as a reminder. Then an intake form is completed with the participant, and a synopsis is written about what happened regarding the incident.

If a person was harmed in the offence, the youth must also acknowledge the harm that was done to this person. There is a victim advocate at ALST who talks to the victim (if there is one) for his or her story of what happened, his or her feelings, and how the incident has impacted the victim. Victims can attend the hearing to have the opportunity to tell their stories to the council and explain how the crime impacted their lives.

I spoke with Colette Pagano, who is Anishnawbe, has a B.S.W., has been working at ALST since 2005, and is currently manager of the Community Council Program and High-Risk Youth Program. Colette specifically spoke about the council process for youth, which is much like the process for adults:

Two or three members of the Aboriginal community sit at each hearing; they are all volunteers representing a diverse group of Aboriginal people such as counsellors, bankers, Elders, and students. Any Aboriginal person is welcome to apply to be a member of the council; a criminal record will not prevent anyone from being on the council, but they must have a clean record for over one year.

Members hear the stories of the participant and find out if there are any addictions issues, if their parents or grandparents attended residential schools, or if there are any mental health issues. After this, the participant leaves the room while the members discuss the situation and come up with decisions as to what they think will be helpful for the participant. The youth returns to the room and hears the decisions of the council members.

Decisions can be artwork (the room where hearings are held is full of beautiful artwork created by people who went through the Community Council), community service, writing a letter of apology to the victim, or making restitution of some kind. Participants have input into the decisions. If the person doesn't want to do something that has been suggested, then they can negotiate this with the members.

Restoration is the aim: Members do not set up participants for failure or give the youth decisions that they cannot do. Rather, they help them access resources and assist them to get on the path to well-being—whatever that looks like for each youth. Often this experience is the first time that a youth has met Aboriginal community members in Toronto. (C. Pagano, personal communication, November 27, 2008)

LISTENING TO THE YOUTH

I knew it was important to have some of the youth who have been through the Community Council process represented in this chapter. With Colette's help, I held a Talking Circle with her and three youth who have experienced the process within the last few years. The youth identified themselves as:

- J.D., who is Anishnawbe, 18 years old, and originally from Sault Ste. Marie. He was homeless when he became involved with the Community Council.
- J.P., a 19-year-old Mohawk youth who was born and raised in the Toronto area. He, too, was homeless when he became involved with the Community Council.

- Midewin, who is Anishnawbe, 20 years old, and born and raised in Toronto. Like the other two, he was also homeless when he became involved with the Community Council.

These three youth came to ALST's Community Council with charges of unlawfully being in a dwelling, robbery, mischief, break-and-enter, and possession of burglary tools.

When I asked the youth if they would share with me a little about their lives when they came into contact with ALST and what the process was like for them within the Community Council, this is what they told me:

> *J.D.:* I wasn't doing much of anything before I got arrested, but once I got involved with the Community Council, I got help with finding housing and returning to school. Coming through the Community Council and continuing to get services at ALST prevents me from doing something wrong again. It keeps our Aboriginal cultures going; it helps me to calm down and stay that way. Before going through the Community Council, I didn't want anything to do with the Aboriginal community [in Toronto]. I believed Aboriginal people were all disrespected and disrespectful. I thought they would rob me or beat me up. (J.D., personal communication, November 27, 2008)

> *J.P.:* At ALST we got to experience the positive rather than the negative. Workers at ALST helped us do productive things. They smudged with us. They are people who care. I don't remember the police or judges I've had to deal with, but I remember and stay connected to the Community Council members, [the] staff at ALST, and all the other helpers who come my way. (J.P., personal communication, November 27, 2008)

> *Midewin:* The idea of the Community Council was introduced to me when I was in jail. I knew that trying this route was the best choice for me or I'd stay in jail. The council is important not only for averting jail, but to not have a criminal record, which is something that follows us forever.
>
> One of my decisions through the Community Council was to get help with my G1 [driving] licence. I told the members I wanted to get this and they asked me how it would help me. I told them it would be a piece of ID,

provide transportation, and help me get a job. The decision went through and ALST assisted me by paying for the licence.

Going through the council helped me understand how the past makes the present: We need to see what has happened in the past, which can lead to harmful behaviours in the present. If we understand this, we can begin to make positive changes. It also helped me to look at what we've overcome, not just what we've done that's not good.

In the past, I was ashamed to be Aboriginal because of what some other Aboriginal people did. It was also from what I saw on the news, which showed Aboriginal people committing bad stuff like sexual abuse, and stereotypes like being drunk, making trouble, and being poor. (Midewin, personal communication, November 27, 2008)

I then asked the young men if they would tell me a little about what they are doing now and how they are feeling. These are their responses:

J.P.: I come to ALST still. We can go to the YMCA for two hours a day to exercise, which is healthy and a stress reliever. We get help with resume-writing, anger management, workshops on job training. They have lawyers if we need them, such as for help dealing with landlords. Today I have housing, though. I also attend some of the circles [Drug and Alcohol Abuse Prevention Circle], offered by Colette. (J.P., personal communication, November 27, 2008)

J.D.: I have a problem with alcohol, so I'm involved in a harm-reduction program at ALST. This program helps me to drink less, not stop entirely. We look at areas such as admitting we have a problem, peer pressure, the impacts of colonization, anger, relationships, and traditional approaches to healing.

I have housing and am in school with the Native Learning Centre doing grades 9 and 10 work. Now I go to sweat lodge ceremonies and do fire-keeping sometimes. Now I'm into everything Aboriginal instead of how I was before, not wanting anything to do with it. I and the other youth don't want non-Aboriginal presenters coming into our circles to talk about their recovery stories, for example. We only want Aboriginal speakers. What do White people have to teach us? We can better relate to Aboriginal peoples who come to speak about their experiences—how

they got out of their destructive lives through their cultures and spirituality. We can learn from them; they're our role models. (J.D., personal
communication, November 27, 2008)

Midewin: Now I continue to attend services at ALST. I see the Medicine
People and Elders who come here, which is something I look forward to.
I attend the Drug and Alcohol Abuse Prevention Circle. I'm getting to
know my family who I never got along with in the past. I'm working on
getting my G2 licence. (Midewin, personal communication, November
27, 2008)

At the end of the circle, I gave each of the young men an honorarium of $50
to thank them for talking with me. J.P. repaid Colette $10 he owed her out of
his honorarium. J.D. said he was going to go buy cleaning supplies so he could
go home to clean his place. Midewin gave Colette $40 out of his money toward
the cost of his G2 test.

INTEREST IN INDIGENOUS APPROACHES

Interestingly enough, most of the literature on Indigenous approaches to
justice are written by White authors involved in the area of criminal justice
as lawyers or professors of criminology (Braithwaite, 2000; Hughes & Mossman, 2002; Pritchard, 2000; Roach, 2000; Roach & Rudin, 2000; Ross, 2008,
2009; Stenning & Roberts, 2001). These authors write about definitions of
justice; descriptions of specific processes such as the Gladue Court in Toronto;
reintegrative shaming, which is implemented in some non-Western societies;
the need for alternatives to the criminal justice system based on the needs of
Indigenous peoples; and both the effectiveness and the controversies of implementing these alternatives. These authors make some significant points, but
only Ross (2008, 2009) views Indigenous world views on justice through a
relational lens.

Bruce Johansen (2007), who may or may not be Indigenous, writes about the
historic ways in which diverse Indigenous Nations dealt with issues of justice.
He focuses on the strengths of the views he presents and provides examples of
concepts and legal customs that were taken up by dominant North American
society which originate in Indigenous world views. One of these is the idea of
"sleeping on it":

Nearly everyone knows the custom "sleeping on it" before making an important decision, allowing a night to pass so that all alternatives may be weighed in a balanced and rational fashion. Yet fewer people realize that this custom comes to us directly from the legal debating procedures of the Haudenosaunee (Iroquois) Confederacy. (p. 25)

As an aside, Johansen (2007) also notes that the original American Constitution and its policies were based on the teachings of the Haudenosaunee Confederacy.

Some writers, such as Roach (2000), believe that restorative justice historically existed in many parts of the world and "was rested in community practices that were eroded by industrialization and modernization" (p. 254). Roach (2000) provides examples of how restorative justice is becoming increasingly known today:

Restorative justice is most often used to describe informal and non-adjudicative forms of dispute resolution such as victim offender mediation, family conferences, and aboriginal forms of justice which give the victims, offenders, and the community decision-making power. At the same time, the rhetoric of restorative justice is also increasingly being used by police, legislators, judges and correctional officials. (p. 253)

It is also important to consider that the dominant justice system has been oppressive toward Indigenous peoples and other racialized populations. Although I do not agree that "systematic racism is not necessarily caused by intentional racism," I do agree that it includes "the disproportionate impact of standard operating procedures and increased surveillance of aboriginal people throughout the system by police and correctional officials" (Roach & Rudin, 2000, p. 370). Given the attention that police profiling of Black men in Toronto has been given in recent years, I know many who would agree with me. This statement also applies to racialized populations: "The court instructed sentencing judges to consider the systemic and background factors that bring aboriginal people before the criminal courts" (Roach & Rudin, 2000, p. 359). Of course, such statements do not only apply to Indigenous peoples and people of African and Caribbean descent in the city of Toronto; they apply to such people in urban and rural areas from New Zealand to South Africa to the United States.

Braithwaite (2000) writes about a specific type of restorative justice, known as reintegrative shaming. Braithwaite (2000) explains how this form of justice is not at all how shame is used in contemporary usage:

Reintegrative shaming communicates disapproval within a continuum of respect for the offender; the offender is treated as a good person who has done a bad deed. Stigmatization is disrespectful shaming; the offender is treated as a bad person. Stigmatization is unforgiving—the offender is left with the stigma permanently, whereas reintegrative shaming is forgiving.... (p. 282)

The First Nations of North America have strong traditions of restorative justice that are being revitalized through Healing Circles or Sentencing Circles. These circles put the problem, not the person, in the centre of the community discussion about crime (Melton, 1995 as cited in Braithwaite, 2000, p. 293).

Reintegrative shaming, according to the theory, will be more widespread in societies where communities are strong, where citizens are densely enmeshed in loving, trusting, or respectful relationships with others (p. 291).

In this way, shaming is in fact positive and can promote healing for the one who has been harmed, the one who has done the harm, and the community. Braithwaite (2000) cites several examples of societies that implement this concept of alternative justice and have low crime rates. According to him, "societies that are forgiving and respectful while taking crime seriously have low crime rates; societies that degrade and humiliate criminals have higher crime rates" (p. 282). He cites African societies, the Pushtoon of Afghanistan, and the country of Japan as using reintegrative shaming and having low crime rates. Braithwaite (2000) reports that Japan is the only nation where evidence indicates a sustained decline in the crime rate over the past 50 years, which is accompanied by a low imprisonment rate—37 out of 100,000 people as compared to over 500 in the U.S.

The Pushtoon, who are the largest ethnic group in Afghanistan, have a ceremony called Nanante, which takes place when someone has done harm to someone else (Braithwaite, 2000). In this ceremony, which is remarkably similar to processes of justice within Indigenous Nations in North America, the Pushtoon person who did the harm is responsible for bringing food for a community feast. The ceremony usually takes place at the home of the person who has been harmed and who participates in cooking the food that has been brought. Those who conduct the ceremony tell the one who has created harm that "You have done an injustice to this person [but] you are one of us and we accept you back among us" (Braithwaite, 2000, p. 282). The police and courts have no presence in communities that practise the Nanante.

The literature is consistent in the message that Indigenous forms of justice promote healing. Hughes and Mossman (2002), for example, explain why transformative justice is effective in meeting the needs of Indigenous peoples in Canada. These authors, as well as Braithwaite (2000), Johansen (2007), and Stenning and Roberts (2001), highlight the strengths of Indigenous forms of justice, but also point out that even though early research shows hopeful outcomes, there is a strong need for further research in the area. I agree.

I asked Rene Timleck, whose words of wisdom appear earlier in this chapter, if she thought that Indigenous forms of justice might be of assistance to other populations. She offered several points on why she believes it can be:

> First off, Community Councils could be a financial blessing to society as there are no court costs such as lawyer's fees or court clerk's pay, and all council members are volunteers. Plus, if the participant is successful in completing the agreement and does not reoffend, how much cost-saving is that for society?
>
> Next, for many people, being lost and alone has led them into trouble and the council process aims to change this. Feeling this way is not exclusive to Aboriginal people—many other people feel the same way. Participants are more likely to feel regret for the harm they have caused as they are facing their community and they are in an atmosphere that fosters the idea that they are important to it. They are less likely to have their armour on when in the hearings as they tend to when in the courtroom. The process of going through a hearing assists in breaking down that armour.
>
> Council hearings are much more personal and implement a human touch as compared to the court system. In a hearing, council members introduce themselves and say a little about who they are; then participants are invited to tell the members a little about themselves. This allows the council members to get to know more about the individual, which assists them in finding more concrete, viable solutions, which, in turn, may mean less chance of a participant reoffending.
>
> The process of the council focuses on restitution, recognizing what was wrongly done, and taking responsibility for it, which is not necessarily the

purpose of the criminal justice system. The court system is more about who can present better in the courtroom, which lawyer is the most eloquent—it isn't about what really happened.

By helping Toronto's Aboriginal community, this helps Toronto and the world. The council process would help people in other communities in the same way. The work is like a pebble in the pond—it is the atmosphere of community and belonging, which may initiate the urge to succeed. There are boxes of files at ALST of people who have completed their requirements and never reoffended. Can the criminal justice system make this claim? I know that all the work in the judicial system aims to assist; to help offenders to not repeat their mistakes, but, for the most part, this system never allows for the time to know the individual or what may be the most effective plan to assist him or her to not reoffend. Our work clearly shows that this is exactly what is needed. (R. Timleck, personal communication, April 22, 2009)

Colette and the young men who spoke with me also had a few ideas on non-Indigenous peoples in connection to Indigenous methods of justice. Colette told me that police officers involved in charging the youth who come to the council can attend the hearings, but separately from the participants. Colette notes that police officers have attended two hearings out of 70 in the past year. When I asked her why those officers came to the hearings, she replied, "They were curious about how the program works" (C. Pagano, personal communication, November 27, 2008).

According to J.P., some of the Aboriginal youth bring non-Aboriginal youth to the circles offered at ALST. He relayed that "the non-Aboriginal youth enjoyed being there. I can tell because they laugh with us and keep coming back" (J.P., personal communication, November 27, 2008). Midewin believes "It's a good idea to educate non-Aboriginal youth about Aboriginal people so they can tell others the truth and dispel stereotypes" (Midewin, personal communication, November 22, 2008). He also supports other people considering Aboriginal forms of justice for their young people: "The ways in which the Community Council helps Aboriginal youth could be helpful to youth from other populations. Other communities could have services that assist their youth like this rather than sending them to jail. They could help their youth instead of punishing them" (Midewin, personal communication, November 22, 2008).

NOT WITHOUT CONTROVERSY

Needless to say, in today's world, there is controversy about Indigenous culture-based forms of justice that come from both Indigenous and non-Indigenous communities. Thus, non-Indigenous social work students and practitioners may be particularly challenged or confused by these differing positions on the topic. One concern is about how Indigenous culture-based justice fits into the larger goal of self-government and decolonization. Authors such as Roach (2000), for example, speculate that problems will arise if funding is spent on criminal justice reforms rather than on economic development, including the settlement of land claims. Similarly, the majority of public inquiries in Canada involving Indigenous peoples have focused on justice issues rather than larger economic issues. Such a focus may deflect attention that could be devoted to what some people view as more urgent aspects of self-government, such as health care, unemployment, and poverty, in addition to land claims (Roach, 2000).

Hughes and Mossman (2002) raise several questions on the implementation of Indigenous forms of justice.

> I will briefly address what I see as the three most important areas of concern. One of these questions is about the definition of community: Even where we think the identification of community is easy, as in the case of Aboriginal circles, this may not be the case in urban rather than reserve settings. We need to establish more clearly the meaning and purpose of community in restorative justice initiatives (is the community always the same for purposes of reintegration and restoration, for example?) and develop ways of ensuring that there is some kind of organic connection between the offender and the community which makes the interaction between offender and community meaningful. (p. 46)

I hope that the experiences of some who have participated in the Community Council of Aboriginal Legal Services of Toronto, as shared in this chapter, will shed some light on there questions.

Another controversial area, in my opinion, is the implementation of Indigenous forms of justice in situations of family violence. I somewhat agree with Hughes and Mossman (2002), who state:

> In some [A]boriginal communities, however, flags have been raised about the treatment of wife abuse; concern about restoration of [A]boriginal

culture has often failed to take account of differential experiences in [A]
boriginal communities for women. One of the risks with restorative justice approaches is that while they may take into account the offender's
status, they may be less likely to understand the need to provide the victim
with the means of overcoming the cultural and patriarchal oppression
underlying wife abuse and the cultural norms which make it difficult for
them to demand redress for violence. (p. 47)

In response to this quote above, I would say that if the purpose is to restore
Indigenous cultures, but the voices and experiences of women have not been
at the forefront, then this, quite simply, is not restoring our cultures. If the
situation of the person who has done the harm is considered while that of the
harmed person is not, then, once again, this is not Indigenous justice. Lastly,
whose culture are the authors referring to when they mention overcoming cultural oppression and cultural norms that make redress difficult for women?

In cases of family violence, which includes sexual abuse, we must be cautious about bringing the one who has done the harm together with the one he
is responsible for hurting. Due to imbalances of power and safety issues, circles
with both of these people present may never be appropriate and must never
take place if the harmed one is not certain that that is what she wants. If they
do come together, perhaps it can happen only after separate healing processes
have taken place and everyone is seen as ready to go forward with this.

We must understand that in relationships of violence among family members
or with others a person is close to, there is always an imbalance of power and we
must not recreate this in a circle. Should we do so, those who have done the harm
will continue their manipulative behaviours, which may be evident only to the
harmed person. Those who have done harm will likely apologize profusely and
those who have been harmed will do exactly what they always do—feel sorry
for him and tell him it's okay; they accept the apology. Violence between people
who have relationships with one another is significantly different from stranger
violence. The stakes are much higher when violence comes from someone whom
a person loves or is connected to in some relevant way. It is not likely that the
harmed person will face the other once and then never have to see him again.
How can the harmed person feel safe enough to ask the questions she needs
answers to? How can she express her pain? These are some of the areas that must
be thoroughly explored before proceeding with such encounters.

This in no way means, however, that nothing can be done to assist those who have harmed others to learn about the pain they have created. In situations when the harmed one does not wish to participate in a circle, I have implemented other ways of attempting to teach empathy to those who have done harm to others. For example, I have brought in movies or letters or poems written by survivors. I have also brought in people who once experienced physical or sexual violence committed by someone close to them and who want to talk about it to help stop it for others. The purpose of this is to assist the person who has caused harm to see how his or her act has caused damage similar to that experienced by the person speaking about his or her own abuse. Although I do not support some of the language used (e.g., "offender" and "victim"), I agree with Rupert Ross (2009), who writes about this form of violence as well:

> I have seen several instances where an offender was brought together with a group of recovering victims of the same kind of crime. In some ways, these encounters with "surrogate victims" may be the most powerful way to begin. Surrogate victims are often able to provide excruciating detail about how their lives have been affected, perhaps because they are not facing their own assailant. At the same time, it seems easier for offenders to listen to such detail when it comes from strangers, to let it penetrate, perhaps because it is not their crime being discussed. When it does finally sink in that their crime must have caused almost identical damage, however, the impact is often significant—and the manifestation of an empathetic reaction is often sudden and extreme. (p. 16)

The third area of concern centres on aspects of power among the different people—the person who has done the harm, the person who has been harmed, and those who facilitate the process—involved in forms of Indigenous justice. According to Hughes and Mossman (2002):

> Much of the restorative justice literature glosses over differences in power between victims and offenders or between certain offenders and others, as well as the extent to which mediators or facilitators can pressure victims and (especially juvenile) offenders.... Requiring forgiveness may result in the victim ... being overwhelmed by pressure to forgive. This pressure on victims distorts the relationship between victim and offender in a way that is reminiscent of the re-victimization of the victim.... (p. 50)

These authors do not explicitly state that they are including Indigenous forms of justice under restorative justice in this quote, but these critiques do not seem to come across in the interviews I conducted with those involved with ALST's Community Council.

Hughes and Mossman's (2002) third concern, which I am including in this chapter, raises the bigger picture of structural oppression:

> ... restorative justice often seems "apolitical," failing to take into account structural inequality and imbalances of power between victims and offenders. ... [There is] an assumption that the individual relationship between the victim and the offender "transcends" the socio-structural relationship and ignores the social context. ... [O]ffenders may be poor or otherwise disadvantaged ... and it will be the offender who needs a better education, increased job training, and an improved living environment. (p. 50)

I think this is exactly what Indigenous forms of justice are trying to address.

CONCLUSION

The removal of people who hurt other people, who do not "conform," or who do not behave in acceptable ways taught by the dominant society begins early in countries such as Canada. It begins with children in an educational system that "expels" or removes children who fail to behave in ways that are acceptable to such systems. In the province of Ontario, for example, the vast majority of children and youth expelled from schools are Indigenous and African-Canadian (Ontario Human Rights Commission, 2004). It also occurs when White adoptive parents cut ties with their adopted Indigenous children because of their "acting out" behaviours (Richard, 2004).

Separating people from the community also takes place within the criminal justice system, which segregates those who break laws by incarcerating them in jails and prisons. As with the educational system and adoption breakdowns, the justice system in Canada segregates Indigenous peoples at much higher rates than it does others, closely followed by African-Canadians (Kroes, 2008; Rudin, 2006; Zinger, 2006). Perhaps this is because the dominant society does not want to deal with these particular groups of people—if we do not see them, then we do not have to do anything with them. We do not have to ask any of the tough questions, such as why certain people are not doing well, or consider the possibility that they are being targeted because they are members of certain populations. We do not have to consider whether the dominant society's rules, laws, and ways of dealing with those who do not conform are flawed and in need of examination and perhaps reform. We do not have to consider that society may have some responsibility for creating circumstances fostering personal, cultural, and structural factors that account for certain groups of people not doing well.

It is worth considering whether removing people from their families and communities is the only way to address their wrongdoing. Is it possible that society is sending people away when they most need to feel that they belong to something, when they most need to be connected to other people, rather than being excluded? Is it possible that being held directly accountable to the people they have harmed rather than to an anonymous criminal justice system might be more significant for both the harmed and the one who caused the harm?

These are the questions that supporters of Indigenous forms of justice strive to answer in practical and healing ways. Such an exploration is what we have to offer others who have been particularly targeted by the "just us" system as well. At the very least, I encourage readers, especially those in the helping professions, to engage in a dialogue that explores the application of values and concepts behind Indigenous forms of justice to all people.

REFERENCES

Baskin, C.(2002). Holistic healing and accountability: Indigenous restorative justice. *Child Care in Practice, 8*(2), 133–136. doi: 10.1080/13575270220148585

Baskin, C. (2010). The spirit of belonging: Indigenous cultural practices in conflict transformation. *Journal of Community Corrections, XIX*, 1–2, 9–14.

Braithwaite, J. (2000). Shame and criminal justice. *Canadian Journal of Criminology, 42*(3), 281–298. Retrieved from http://www.anu.edu.au

Canadian Research Institute for the Advancement of Women. (2002). Fact sheet on violence against women and girls. Retrieved from http://criaw-icref.ca/ViolenceagainstWomenandGirls.

Hamilton, A.C. & Sinclair, M. (1999). *Report of the Aboriginal justice inquiry of Manitoba.* Winnipeg: Aboriginal Justice Implementation Commission. Retrieved from http://www.ajic.mb.ca

Hughes, P. & Mossman, M. (2002). Re-thinking access to criminal justice in Canada:

A critical review of needs and responses. *Windsor Review of Legal and Social Issues, 13*, 1–132. Retrieved from http://www.heinonline.org

Johansen, B. (2007). Crimes and punishments: Justice in ancient America. *Native Peoples Magazine, 20*(2), 24 –27. Retrieved from http://www.nativepeoples.com/store/product.php?productid=16275&cat=283&page=1

Kroes, G. (2008). *Aboriginal youth in Canada: Emerging issues, research priorities, and policy implications.* Retrieved from http://www.policyresearch.gc.ca

Ontario Human Rights Commission. (2004). *Submission of the Ontario Human Rights Commission to the Toronto District School Board Safe and Compassionate Schools Task Force.* Retrieved from http://www.ohrc.on.ca

Pritchard, S. (2000). Between justice and law in Aotearoa New Zealand: Two case studies. *Law and Critique, 11*(3), 267–286. doi:10.1023/A:1008966226606

Richard, K. (2004). A commentary against Aboriginal to non-Aboriginal adoption. *First Peoples Child and Family Review, 1*(1), 101–109.

Roach, K. (2000). Changing punishment at the turn of the century: Restorative justice on the rise. *Canadian Journal of Criminology, 42*(3), 249–280.

Roach, K. & Rudin, J. (2000). Gladue: The judicial and political reception of a promising decision. *Canadian Journal of Criminology, 42*(3), 355–388.

Ross, R. (2008). *Colonization, complex PTSD, and Aboriginal healing: Exploring diagnoses and strategies for recovery.* Adult Custody Division Health Care Conference. Vancouver: Ministry of Public Safety and Solicitor General.

Ross, R. (2009). *Discussion paper: Exploring criminal justice and the Aboriginal healing paradigm.* Kenora: Ontario Ministry of the Attorney General.

Rudin, J. (2006). *Brief to the Standing Committee on Justice and Human Rights on bill C-10.* Retrieved from http://aboriginallegal.ca

Statistics Canada: Canadian Centre for Justice Statistics (2011). Family Violence in Canada: A statistical profile. Catalogue 85-224-x. Ottawa: Statistics Canada. Retrieved from http://www.statcan.gc.ca/daily-quotidien/110127/dq110127a-eng.htm

Stenning, P. & Roberts, J.V. (2001). Empty promises: Parliament, the Supreme Court, and the sentencing of Aboriginal offenders. *Saskatchewan Law Review, 64*(1) 137–168. Retrieved from http://www.heinonline.org

United Nations (2006). Ending violence against women: From words to action. Study of the Secretary General. Retrieved from www.un.org/womenwatch/daw/vaw/launch/english/v.a.w.-exeE-use.pdf

Zinger, I. (2006). *Report finds evidence of systemic discrimination against Aboriginal inmates in Canada's prisons.* Retrieved from http://www.oci-bec.gc.ca

Chapter 10
Caring for Families, Caring for Children

INTRODUCTION

Within provincial child welfare and practice standards, the principle of "the best interests of the child" guides how social workers work with children and their families. Everyone would agree that the protection of children is of paramount importance. Nevertheless, it is a principle based on a Eurocentric world view that may not be in alignment with the needs of the diverse populations of Canada. From an Indigenous world view, the guiding principle regarding child welfare would be oriented toward a values base that takes into account the best interests of the community, as this includes children, their families, and all other people around a child.

WHO SAID, "IT TAKES A VILLAGE TO RAISE A CHILD"?

In 1996, Hillary Rodham Clinton, then First Lady and wife of American President Bill Clinton, presented a talk on the importance of children and families in our lives and nations. When speaking about raising a happy, healthy, and hopeful child, Ms. Clinton stated, "It takes a village to raise a child" (1996, August). First Lady Clinton brought this saying to great prominence in her speech, but the statement was first coined by the people of the Igbo and Yoruba regions of Nigeria. The statement describes a belief held by numerous Indigenous peoples around the world since the beginning of time.

What does it mean and what does it look like for all members of a community to be involved in raising all children? It means that I, as an individual, have a contribution to make not only to my biological children, adopted children, nieces and nephews, children in my care at a particular time, but also to all children who live around me or who belong to whatever community I belong to. Such a community may or may not be based on geography and is defined by aspects described in earlier chapters about world views.

There are many Indigenous scholars who focus on research and writing about child welfare. Without a doubt, all these writers emphasize how children are part of families and communities, and must be viewed as such regardless of the struggles of their parents, as children do not learn or form their identities based solely on their contact with their parents. This is supported by Greenwood and de Leeuw (2007):

> Children, particularly young children, cannot of course be disentangled from the broader families, communities, and Nations that sustain them. Consequently, the process of reconnection with the Indigenous identity and associatively re-building cultural captivity might be understood as being connected to each of these potential learning sites (family, community, and Nation). (p. 51)

As all children learn from their families, communities, and nations or states, it seems reasonable that their well-being is connected to the support they receive from all of these groups. When we strengthen community life, we can begin to move family matters out of the courtroom and back into the capable hands of the community. This can be achieved through community members and service providers, such as social workers, creating strong environments that ensure the community's responsibility of caring for children. Indigenous communities around the globe are undertaking a gradual decolonization process by returning to beliefs such as "It takes a village to raise a child." One such program, located in northern Manitoba, called Meenoostahtan Minisiwin, meaning "pathways to peace" in Cree, "focuses on promoting families' strengths and capacities while exploring the best interests of children from a family and community prospective, away from the courts" (Pintarics & Sveinunggaard, 2005, p. 70).

Fortunately, a decolonization process is about going beyond raising awareness of how colonization has undermined our communities to care for our children. This process is about how we can go about creating positive changes in our communities. This is the work that is being done, so the literature needs to reflect this work by exploring, for example, the community strengths that help to make them stronger and exploring what social workers may need to understand about helping communities support the health of families and children.

THE STORY OF ANDREA AND CHARLENE

Much has been written about the devastation caused by the adoption of Indigenous children into White families (Blackstock, 2008, 2009; Carrière, 2005, 2006, 2008; Carrière & Scarth, 2007; Fournier & Crey, 1997; Hughes, 2006; Reid, 2005; Richardson & Nelson, 2007; Sinclair, 2007; Trocme, Knoke & Blackstock, 2004), which I will not go into here. Rather, I am offering the story of my good friend Charlene and her daughter Andrea, a story that, to me, represents a loving example of the joys and challenges of a White woman mothering an Indigenous child.

Charlene Avalos has practised social work with Indigenous peoples and communities for many years. From 1980 to 1984, she was working in Waglisla First Nation in B.C.; from 1985 to 1987 with the Nuu Chah Nulth Tribal Council in B.C.; and since 1989, she has worked at Native Child and Family Services of Toronto, where she is currently the acting director of services. Andrea Peers, Heiltsuk Nation, is a member of the Waglisla First Nation. Now a young adult, Andrea has two daughters, has worked at an Aboriginal agency for several years, and is now training to be a hairstylist.

The story of Charlene and Andrea began when Charlene was the partner of one of Andrea's uncles, and worked as the band social worker in Waglisla. Charlene met Andrea when she was four months old, as she and her partner would babysit her. A short time later, Andrea's mother was struggling and having difficulty caring for Andrea. Andrea's mother was splitting up with Andrea's father and trying to figure out how to do that and where to go. She decided to leave her First Nation community and went to Vancouver to take a break. It was then that Andrea came to stay with Charlene and her partner on a full-time basis. Later on, one of Andrea's aunts wanted to care for the child, but it was clear that Andrea did not want to leave Charlene and her uncle. Charlene called Andrea's mother to ask where she wanted Andrea to live. She replied, "I would love it if you kept her" (C. Avalos, personal communication, February 3, 2009).

In Waglisla it is common for children to live with relatives other than their parents. Everyone knows the circumstances, and it is an accepted practice. Many traditional adoptions occur as well. Elders will approach young women to see if they need others to help care for their children, and adoption happens when needed. According to Charlene, "this was the way it was done in the past and is based on the Aboriginal world view that it takes a village to raise a child" (C. Avalos, personal communication, February 3, 2009).

Andrea's great-grandfather, a hereditary chief, was well respected and listened to by everyone in Waglisla. There was no child welfare involvement in child care. All decisions were made by the family. This was the traditional way of doing things and was considered natural. The family was co-operative and supportive of this arrangement, so child welfare did not have to be involved. Charlene states matter of factly, "I think if child welfare had been involved, it would have complicated the process" (C. Avalos, personal communication, February 3, 2009). The great-grandfather and hereditary chief instructed Charlene that if she was to keep Andrea with her, then she was not to take her for only a short time and then pass her on to others. At the time, although there was no traditional ceremony to adopt Andrea because potlatches were only just being reintroduced into Aboriginal communities after being banned under the Indian Act for many years, it was decided that Andrea, then 18 months old, would stay with Charlene and her uncle permanently. About one year later, Andrea's father and his girlfriend wanted to take Andrea to live with them, but Andrea's great-grandfather said no, that Andrea was to stay with Charlene and her uncle.

When Andrea was five years old, she moved with Charlene and her uncle to Vancouver so that Charlene could attend university to get her Master of Social Work degree. They lived in Vancouver for one year and during this time Andrea had visits with her mother and visits to her home community. When Andrea was six, she and Charlene moved to Toronto, where Charlene is originally from. All of Andrea's family were in agreement with this. However, Charlene needed to get legal guardianship at this point, so she could travel with Andrea. Both of Andrea's parents came to the courthouse to sign the documents. Charlene was viewed as Andrea's aunt as she had been in a relationship with Andrea's uncle for many years. The family knew that Charlene would not disappear with Andrea. They knew they would see Andrea while she was growing up, and they knew that this was important to them.

Andrea talks about a childhood that combined living with Charlene in Toronto during the school year and living with her family in Waglisla during the summer:

> I was always attached to Charlene and always saw her as my mother. When I visited with my biological mother, I felt kind of uncomfortable or it felt strange to call her "Mom," like I was betraying Charlene when I called her that. It felt confusing. The visits with my mother were regular. Sometimes I saw my father, but not as often. I had fun with my mother, but I never felt close to her. We never talked about why I was living in Toronto rather than with her. Usually, I'd be a little afraid each time it got close to me leaving for a visit to Waglisla, but after being with them for awhile, I'd get attached and want to stay there rather than go back to Toronto. (A. Peers, personal communication, February 3, 2009)

This desire to stay in both places reflects what Charlene was also experiencing during these years:

> I wanted to ensure that Andrea knew her family and community, which is why I sent her to visit there every summer. But it was emotionally hard on me because each time Andrea visited Waglisla, I worried that she would decide to stay there, rather than return to me. (C. Avalos, personal communication, February 3, 2009)

Life was different for Andrea living in both Waglisla and Toronto:

My family lived traditionally, so when I was in Waglisla during the summer, what I remember most is food. My family hunted, fished, and canned what they caught during that time of the year. They lived off the land. It was during other times of the year that they attended potlatches and other ceremonies.

In Toronto, Charlene's family made me feel loved and accepted and I felt like a part of the Aboriginal community there. But I always had a sense of not quite belonging, for example, I looked so different from Charlene and her family. It was the same at school. Other kids would tell me I didn't look like my mother Charlene. It went fine, though, when I told them I was adopted. As far as I know, I was the only Aboriginal kid at my school and, at times, I was referred to as Chinese, Japanese, or Mexican, which I didn't like. But I did appreciate being different from other kids because once teachers knew I was Aboriginal, I seemed to get a lot of positive attention.

I went to lots of ceremonies and culture camps with Charlene while growing up. I would often tell my friends that my mother was more traditional than I was. I never felt that connected to Aboriginal culture either in Toronto or Waglisla. I just wasn't sure how I fit in with either of them and felt confused. What was taught in Toronto were the teachings of the Ojibway and Cree people, which didn't really interest me. There isn't much information in Toronto about Aboriginal people from B.C. (A. Peers, personal communication, February 3, 2009)

Charlene is adamant that Andrea would have struggled much more as a young adult if she had not spent time with her family and community while growing up. Charlene always felt it was important for Andrea to know where she came from, where her roots were, and what contributed to her identity as an Aboriginal person, even if she felt confusion at times. She has always felt it was the best choice for Andrea.

Andrea continues to wonder if going back for visits to B.C. was the best for her because her family there did not talk about why she was not living with her biological mother or father. She now thinks it might have been better for her if she had started going for visits when she was a little older, maybe at 10 years old, so that she might have had more of an understanding about her situation. However, Charlene points out that Andrea had seven years of visits with her mother, whereas if she had only begun to visit her at the age of 10, she would have had only three years of visits because, tragically, Andrea's mother was murdered when the girl was only 13 years old. Charlene emphasizes that "Andrea wouldn't have gotten to know her mother if she hadn't gone out to visit in the summers when she was a young child" (C. Avalos, personal communication, February 3, 2009). Charlene and Andrea do agree that Andrea may have grown up to be more confused and angry if she had not known her mother, who her family is, where she comes from, where her roots are, and what her cultural affiliation is.

Charlene and Andrea have a great deal to teach social workers about caring for families and children. Andrea suggests that everyone involved with children who are not living with their biological parents should tell these children why they cannot live with their parents at a particular time. Charlene believes that this approach is much better than silence, which leaves a child wondering, confused, and perhaps blaming herself or himself because they are unable to be with their parents, or they may feel they are not wanted by their families.

As Andrea explains:

> I know it would have helped me if my mother told me why I wasn't with her, if she had shared her feelings with me. If not her, then someone else in my family [should have told me]. I know my family was affected by residential schools, which likely had a lot to do with why they had difficulty talking, sharing feelings, and connecting, but knowing this while growing up would have helped me to understand. (A. Peers, personal communication, February 3, 2009)

Charlene expands on these thoughts using a broader perspective:

> Adoption always has an element of loss and grief to it and people need to recognize this, but not get stuck in it. Open adoptions require maturity on the part of all involved. In mainstream society, there continues to be more of a position of ownership of a child, but not so in traditional Aboriginal communities. This makes a large difference on how open adoptions operate.
>
> Aboriginal world views embrace self-reflection and healing, which is so important in adoption arrangements. Adoptive parents need to work on their own issues and accept the fact that adoptees will have their issues, too. If this is accepted from the beginning, then room is available

for the biological parents to be involved in some way. Aboriginal communities also recognize the value of raising a child collectively. The idea that it takes a community to raise a child is embedded in the Aboriginal value system and world view. This idea is valuable to all peoples of the world. (C. Avalos, personal communication, February, 3, 2009)

Both Andrea and Charlene now believe it would have been helpful if there had been a Family Circle when Andrea was a child. That would have allowed the family to talk openly about what happened and why. They believe this would have helped everyone to express their emotions. Andrea and Charlene think having circles for adoptees, biological parents, and adoptive parents would also be helpful because circles could assist people to understand that they are not alone and that what they are experiencing is okay.

Both Andrea and Charlene caution, however, that every situation is unique and needs to be considered on its own. Not all situations are the same, so not all solutions will be the same. There cannot be one way for everyone when it comes to families and children. Both Andrea and Charlene strongly encourage social workers to look closely at the values of mainstream society and the profession in terms of how they view the caring and raising of children. They agree that it is important not to view children living with others, rather than their biological parents, as a negative situation.

ELIMINATING THE CHILD VS. THE FAMILY DICHOTOMY

The notion of state authority over children needs to be revisited when it comes to child welfare, particularly for Indigenous and African/Caribbean peoples living in Western countries such as Canada, the United States, and Australia. History needs to inform how child welfare legislation, policies, and practices are created and implemented. It is critically important that bureaucracy not be allowed to harm communities, families, and children any longer. Instead, the world views and identities of these communities need to direct policies and practices on how children are raised and cared for. Resources need to be focused on whatever is needed to keep children within their families and communities, and on supporting families in their personal growth, healing, and empowerment. I agree with Greenwood and de Leeuw (2007), who argue that "through fostering Indigeneity in Aboriginal mothers, there exists the potential to counteract the state's ongoing child welfare intervention into Aboriginal mothers' families" (p. 180).

We need to pay attention to what research is telling us about how children need to be a part of their families and communities. According to Richardson and Nelson (2007), "youth in the child welfare system tend to move back to their birth family as soon as they are cut loose from the child welfare authorities—that is if their familial connections were not completely severed by social work practice" (p. 76). Babb (1996), in writing for the American Adoption Congress, reports that 65 percent of adopted adolescents wanted to meet their birth families. Courtney and Piliavin (1998) found that after leaving foster care, one-third of youth returned to live with their families. Furthermore, Grotevant, Dunbar, Kohler, and Esau (2000) challenged the notion that adoption policies, such as confidentiality and cutting ties to birth families, promote greater attachment to adoptive families. Grotevant et al. (2000) refuted the assumption that adoptive parents can replace birth parents by eliminating information about the birth parents. It is important to note that the above studies were conducted not only with Indigenous groups of adolescents and youth, but with other diverse groups as well.

Who is to say, then, that openness in adoption would not have a positive impact on children and youth in terms of, for example, the crucial issue of identity formation? Growing up in the homes of a few extended family members is not necessarily a sign of instability or harm, but can be understood as a way to provide multiple supports and positive social relationships for children and youth.

In my work and research with Indigenous social workers in child welfare, I have found similar findings to those of Michelle Reid (2005), a member of the Heiltsuk Nation, who writes that Indigenous child welfare social work practitioners "discussed the 'pressure' and the 'pain' of working under delegated models within their communities that are dealing with the ongoing 'impacts of colonization'. These practitioners do not want to be seen as 'perpetrators of colonialism' within their own people" (p. 30). These concerns are supported by Cindy Blackstock (2009), of the Gitksan Nation and director of First Peoples Child and Family Caring Society, who states that "the concept that we can do harm or even do evil rarely appears on the optical radar screen of professional training, legislation or practice in anything other than a tangential way through procedural mechanisms such as codes of ethics" (pp. 31–32).

As social workers, we do not want to discuss, let alone hear, that our work may be causing harm to others, particularly children. After all, aren't we supposed to be the good people? Blackstock (2009) wisely points out, however, that making positive change means "understanding the harm from those who experienced it, it means setting aside the instinct to rationalize it or to turn away from it because it is too difficult to hear" (p. 36).

These voices of Indigenous women in Aboriginal child welfare are crucial to hear. I also wanted to hear from a non-Indigenous voice in mainstream child welfare. I thought it would be interesting to talk with a social worker who had worked with Indigenous peoples in this area to see what her or his experiences and perceptions were. I spoke with Carolyn Ussher, who has worked for 17 years in child welfare and who is currently a child welfare supervisor at the Children's Aid Society of Toronto. I knew Carolyn from my years at an aboriginal family services agency when we worked with some of the same families.

This is how Carolyn perceives the ways that family problems are dealt with through mainstream, state-controlled child welfare:

> Mainstream society personalizes and individualises problems. There is an emphasis on the person to deal with whatever the problem is. Families tend to be isolated and living in silos—isolated and cut off from resources and supports, formal or informal on their own, not connected. Mainstream child welfare tends to simply look at the fact that there is a problem with the parents or mother. The child is the client by law, yet the work has to occur with the parents or mother. Someone did not get into a particular difficult situation just because. Rather, there have been many factors involved that have contributed to the situation. The person cannot get out of their difficult situation just because child welfare tells them to or a judge says they have to if they want their children back. (C. Ussher, personal communication, March 10, 2009)

Carolyn thinks that those who work in mainstream child welfare believe that people do not want to reach out to others because parents who are struggling do not want others to know they are having difficulty caring for their children. However, she also believes that "this is an assumption. It's more authentic, natural, real, to get many people to help rather than not doing so" (C. Ussher, personal communication, March 10, 2009). A thoughtful Carolyn then went on to explain what she saw and learned from having the privilege of speaking with Indigenous Elders and Traditional Teachers who taught her about their ways of looking at the world and helping people:

Aboriginal people pull all kinds of people in to support the family, which validates people and acknowledges how grandparents, for example, can take responsibility for caring for their grandchildren.

In Aboriginal ways of helping, there is a widening of the circle of care for families and children. There are more eyes to see what the family is experiencing and this leads to how others can help. The community is opened up to care for children, rather than the responsibility being only on parent(s) to do so.

Indigenous people look at the extended family, the community, the family's ancestors, where the child comes from, and the meanings of all of this when trying to assist those who are struggling. Their ways of helping see the bigger picture. A client is more than just a client; she or he is not just a parent who has abused his or her child, for example. There is so much more to people; they are part of a community, a circle, a past, and a future.

Indigenous ways of caring for families and children provides hope for everyone as parents can see themselves as much more than "a problem." These ways also look at the strengths, skills, and gifts of people and assures them they are not alone because they are part of a whole. They teach that everyone has a job, purpose, role; that everyone is worthwhile and everyone's life experiences are valued. (C. Ussher, personal communication, March 10, 2009)

As a self-reflexive social worker, Carolyn is able to critique some child welfare practices that she does not see as helpful, such as determining where children are allowed to live:

Mainstream child welfare puts too much emphasis on a certain kind of home where children should live. There can be rigid versions of what an "appropriate" home is. But there can be homes for children that are not with their biological parents but are warm and caring. The extended family and the community can provide these homes for children so they have a continued connection to their parents.

Mainstream child welfare rules people out for caring for children because they do not have a Eurocentric way of seeing the family, like the two-parent, middle-class family. We continue to be judgmental about variations of what families look like.

But Indigenous ways emphasize that it is not important what material possessions a person has, but rather that he or she can see that they are connected to other people and everything around him or her. This is good for all people—to feel a connection to others and to place. (C. Ussher, personal communication, March 10, 2009)

Carolyn also critiques the rigidity of child welfare, which often requires parents to participate in programs and services, in order to keep their children or have their children returned to them:

Mainstream child welfare directs clients to attend all sorts of services, but maybe the person just needs to sit with their situation and think about what will help. We can't always direct clients to services without helping them to incorporate the learning, knowledge, and change that come with this. When we overwhelm people with services, it's just checking off a little box to say they went without really incorporating the learning. People need time to change and sitting with things, with supports, can help, I think. Give people some space and time, which is another teaching from Indigenous people. (C. Ussher, personal communication, March 10, 2009)

CUSTOMARY LAW AND CARE

Obviously, Indigenous peoples around the globe cared for their children for centuries according to Indigenous values prior to colonization. Indigenous peoples had ways of caring for children that we are now working collectively to bring back. There are alternatives to the enormously costly and adversarial court processes when it comes to the care of children and preservation of families. Much time, effort, and money is expended when families are required to attend court for child-protection issues. In addition, the adversarial nature of the court system usually has a negative impact on the relationship between the child-protection worker and the family. Instead of working together to protect the best interests of the child, child-protection workers and families are fighting to win. Since the process is so intrusive, rigid, and impersonal, effective communication and trust are unlikely.

Some Indigenous peoples, like me, believe that ideas for alternatives to the court system—such as child-protection mediation, kinship care, and family group conferencing—originate within Indigenous world views. Some of these initiatives appear promising. For example, child-protection mediation that is separate from existing child-protection bodies has proven to be effective in Manitoba and Ontario (Crush, 2005).

The overrepresentation of Indigenous children in the care of the Children's Aid Society in northern Ontario caused Nishnawbe-Aski Legal Services in Thunder Bay, Ontario, to implement an initiative called the Talking Together Program (TTP) in 2001. The program offers an alternative to court proceedings in child-protection matters. The program holds Talking Circles with families, social service workers, and Elders to explore creative solutions in a non-judgmental environment. These solutions are then implemented as the Plan of Care for the child. In 2005, 135 children remained in their community following involvement with TTP, and 218 remained in their community in 2006 (Mishibinijima, 2006). The participation of families and community members in the process is the cornerstone of TTP and allows for more innovative and appropriate solutions for the care of children, as opposed to the usual and often ineffective addiction and anger management treatment options (Mishibinijima, 2006). In some areas, the TTP has been so effective that it has evolved into a prevention program rather than a crisis intervention service. This means the program is able to address concerns so that child-protection services do not have to become involved.

British Columbia operates a Child-Protection Mediation Program (CPMP), which brings together families and child-protection workers to negotiate their disputes with the assistance of a neutral third party. Since 1997, 70 percent of participants in CPMP were able to completely or partially resolve their child-protection issues out of court (Ministry of Attorney General, 2006).

Another effective alternative to the court system is the Meenoostahtan Minisiwin: First Nations Family Justice Program (MM: FNFJP) in Manitoba. This program, developed by a mandated Indigenous child-protection agency, brings families, community members, and service providers together to resolve child-protection matters. The idea is to reach solutions that will address the long-term protection of children by getting at the roots of the family concerns. The process is based on Indigenous traditions of peacemaking, and all participants must be fully informed volunteers. Since 2000, MM: FNFJP has serviced approximately 200 families per year.

In a 2004 evaluation of MM: FNFJP, 100 percent of the participants cited satisfaction with the services, while 81 percent stated that they were very satisfied (Pintarics & Sveinunggaard, 2005). Participants stated that the program ensures that their voices are heard; that there is clear communication; and that a safe, comfortable environment is provided for families. Ninety percent of service providers who made referrals to the program stated that there were less children going into care, and there was more effective planning when a child was required to go into care (Pintarics & Sveinunggaard, 2005). Service providers also noted that the process improved collaborative working relationships with everyone involved, and that the process helped keep families together. Finally, 95 percent of service providers identified that a family-oriented approach made a positive difference in the service provided, and was preferable to the child-oriented focus traditionally taken by child-protection agencies (Pintarics & Sveinunggaard, 2005).

KINSHIP STRUCTURES AND FAMILY GROUP CONFERENCING

Indigenous values about children and families are understood and practised in many areas of the world, particularly when there are child-protection concerns. These methods are being implemented in similar and diverse ways by Indigenous peoples in countries such as the United States, Australia, and New Zealand. I have personally witnessed these approaches being used in countries such as Jamaica, Brazil, Peru, Guatemala, Mozambique, and Ghana, although these approaches may not be formalized or implemented through social service structures.

One of these processes that has gained greater attention is the Family Circle, which has come to be known as the Family Group Conference (FGC) in New Zealand. It was in Aotearoa/New Zealand, where FGC originated following the legislation of Children, Young Persons, and Their Families Act in 1989 (Connolly, 2004; Mishibinijima, 2006). FGC evolved over time, beginning as a part of legislation in the late 1970s when several reports were issued revealing the structural and institutional racism experienced by the Maori, who are the Indigenous people of this area (Connolly, 2004). Not surprisingly, Maori children and families were experiencing the same difficulties with child-protection agencies as Indigenous children and families in Canada, including overrepresentation in child-protection services, alienation from their families and communities, and difficulties with a system that failed to provide long-term security for children. In the early 1980s, the New Zealand government, in partnership with Maori tribal societies, launched Maatua Whangai, which implements "Kinship structures within a fostering framework to care for Maori children, its objectives being to release Maori children from institutional placements and place them into the care of their family and tribal groups" (Connelly, 2004, p. 1).

As with efforts in Canada, FGC is intended to involve families in decisions about children, include extended family members in kinship care, and support their empowerment by adopting a less intrusive approach. The FGC "became the legal mechanism through which the dual principles of child protection and the strengthening and maintenance of families would be formally addressed" (Connolly, 2004, p. 2).

Today, versions of FGC show up in other Western countries' child-protection agencies, including Canada. Carolyn Ussher has much to say on this topic:

> Mainstream child welfare has co-opted kinship care and family group conferencing from Indigenous peoples. However, family case conferencing, which is not the same as family group conferencing, is the procedure in child welfare now. Thirty days after a case is opened, the workers bring people together to widen the circle of care and help create a plan to move forward.
>
> Mainstream child welfare puts a lot of rules on this method. It's more of a structure on how to invite people, how to share the decisions, who will lead the conference, how will people communicate. Conferencing is happening more now and [is] seen as how to implement shared responsibility for children. There is more input from the family on what will help and support them now.
>
> But mainstream child welfare is not thinking creatively about conferencing. Workers only view immediate and extended family as caring for children while Indigenous people involve the entire community, which is seen as able to care for children. Mainstream needs to look at how workers translate what conferencing is, for example, are they allowing families to direct the process? Is the process more client-focused? If so, there ought to be more agreement amongst all involved.
>
> Something else that I think is really important is I'm certain that Indigenous ways of supporting families makes it much easier for people to disclose the difficulties they are experiencing, like a mother feeling comfortable enough to say, "I'm afraid I'm going to use [substances]." Workers do not tend to hear this from people as they are afraid of what the child welfare workers will then do. Yet this can be such a helpful and

successful way to work with families. I view parents being able to disclose their fears and realities as making so much sense to the helping process, and conferencing creates more safety for greater openness for this. The more information a child welfare worker has, the better, as it helps them to make more creative decisions with a family.

Conferencing is a different way of communicating for mainstream child welfare workers. It means not talking to people in silos or individually, but bringing them together to think creatively instead.

Looking at widening the circle of care for families and children can be powerful for child welfare workers because when they do so, they are not the only ones responsible for child protection and safety. Widening the circle means workers can feel that there is a sharing of this responsibility. This is a much more supportive way for workers. (C. Ussher, personal communication, March 10, 2009)

Carolyn finished her conversation with me with a caution to non-Indigenous social workers who want to incorporate Indigenous ways of helping:

Do not co-opt Indigenous ways of helping. Give credit where it is due. When we co-opt something, it feels like we take a great idea and tweak it to look like it's our idea. Instead, we need to give credit to where ideas and practices come from, such as kinship care and family group conferencing.

Try to learn from Indigenous world views as I have and see if you connect to the values. Mainstream ways teach everyone to want something else, which is whatever we do not have now, but Indigenous teachings help people to focus, stay in the moment, and ground us, which are so much more fulfilling than always wanting something else.

All people can connect on a human level. We all need to go to this place, begin there, and see where it takes us. (C. Ussher, personal communication, March 10, 2009)

Several studies have been conducted on the effectiveness of FGCs with a number of diverse groups, such as African-American, Cherokee, and Latino communities in the southeastern United States. Within this region in the United States, there was a history of enslavement and segregation of African-Americans; the forced removal of the Cherokee, known as the "Trail of Tears"; and high numbers of undocumented Mexican people who continue to be treated punitively by U.S. police immigration officials. Research has shown that, within all three groups, participants agreed that FGC provided a respectful way for child welfare to involve them in decision-making that was congruent with their cultural beliefs (Pennell, 2007a, 2007b). It has also been demonstrated that FGCs are partly effective in countering institutional or structural racism, and that they have been associated with a decline in the numbers of children entering state care (Edwards & Tinworth, 2006; Merkel-Holguin, Nixon & Burford, 2003; Texas Department of Family and Protective Services, 2006).

The question of whether or not FGCs should be implemented in situations of family violence is often raised. Social workers and others who work in this area are often fearful that children and women will be harmed by family group conferencing, or that violence will occur after the conference. Although the research is limited on FGCs in the area of family violence, what research there is shows promising results. For example, a Canadian study did not find that any violence occurred during or after the meetings (Pennell & Burford, 2000). This research also found that there were reductions in indicators of child maltreatment and woman abuse for families who participated in family group conferences, while indicators of violence rose for families who did not participate in FGCs (Pennell, 2007a).

Of course, FGCs require thorough preparation and follow-up, especially where family violence has occurred, so that all family members can feel safe. I agree with Pennell (2007a), who states that "given the benefits of FGCs to children and their families from diverse populations, prohibiting its application in all instances where there is a history of domestic violence would be problematic" (p. 6).

CHILD WELFARE COMMUNITY COUNCIL

State intervention in the relationship between parents and children is justified only when a parent is placing the child in jeopardy. Within a more mainstream perspective, when a child is viewed as being in need of protection, typically fault is attributed to the parents. Within Indigenous world views, the focus is not on finding fault with the parents, but on healing. Since fault does not need to be established, parents do not have to feel that they have failed if they are able to call upon a broader community for assistance. Looking at the needs of children means exploring what children need in order to thrive, and finding the resources to ensure that this happens. When all of a child's needs cannot be met by a parent, this does not mean that the child must be taken from that parent. However, it does mean that the unmet needs of a child need to be addressed.

Aboriginal Legal Services of Toronto's (ALST) Child Welfare Community Council (CWCC) is the only council of its kind in the world. Like FGC, its concept is not new, but rather rests on an Indigenous understanding and practice that the responsibility for raising children rests with the community rather than only with the parents. The CWCC falls within the scope of an alternative dispute resolution process under the Child and Family Services Act of Ontario:

> The CWCC process can occur at two stages. For families who are at risk of having children apprehended there is the Talking Circle—a process that occurs with a view to preventing an apprehension from taking place. The Talking Circle process can take place when Native Child and Family Services of Toronto, which is the mandated child protection agency for Indigenous families in Toronto, believes that if the relationship between them and a family that they are involved with does not improve, then apprehension will likely occur. A Talking Circle is a body external to NCFST that attempts to help open or re-open the lines of communication between the family and the agency, so that progress can be made with the apprehension of a child averted. A Talking Circle would involve the family, NCFST, a facilitator from the CWCC members and an Elder.
>
> Community Council hearing takes place following the apprehension of a child by NCFST. The hearing can only occur if both the parents and NCFST agree. NCFST will consider participating in a Council hearing where they believe there are circumstances under which they might agree, at some point, to have the child either returned to the parent or to another caregiver suggested by the parent. If NCFST and one parent agree to have the matter heard by the CWCC and one parent does not agree, the hearing will take place with the one parent.
>
> Council hearings will take place as soon as possible following the first appearance of the matter before the court. Council hearings cannot usurp the role of the Court in determining what is in the best interests of the child. However, a Council hearing, as an alternative dispute resolution forum, may arrive at a plan for the child more quickly, and with greater participation from the parties, than the Court process.

All parties with an interest in the matter will be invited to attend the hearing. This will include the parents, a representative from NCFST, the child (if he or she is over 12 years of age), a representative from the child's First Nation or Aboriginal community, and any other individuals who may have something to contribute to the discussion.

An Auntie will be chosen in advance of the hearing from among the CWCC members. The role of the Auntie is to represent the interests of the child. In order to do this, the Auntie meets the child on at least one occasion prior to the council hearing. At the hearing, the Auntie's role is to ensure that the child's interests remain a priority. The Auntie meets with the child if the child will be attending the hearing, or if the child is too young to speak.

The council members decide how the hearing will be governed. After hearing from everyone and satisfying themselves that they have all the information they require, the council members, along with the Elder, determine an appropriate plan for the child. If an agreement is reached, then everyone signs the written plan. If an agreement is not achieved through this process, the matter will be dealt with through the court system, whereby the council's plan is presented to a judge for his or her consideration (ALST, 2007).

Rene Timleck was introduced to readers in Chapter 9. She is a member of the CCWC and, at times, takes on the role of the Auntie. She sees the purpose of the CCWC Council as "a process that helps to heal families while protecting children." Rene openly shares that she grew up with neglect and substance abuse in her family of origin. As an adult, her own children went into the care of the Children's Aid Society due to neglect and abuse. Today, she wonders why no one did anything to help her when she or her children were growing up. Rene believes that since she was once in a similar position as the parents who come through the council process, she is able to assist these families:

> My own experiences not only give me insight into many aspects of the cases, but also help me recognize pitfalls or dangers that might not be apparent to others. I understand the fear the parents feel in their dealings with Native Child and Family Services of Toronto. It is almost an inevitable position of being at loggerheads when it comes to the relationship between families and those that have the power to take or keep their children away from them. I also understand the responsibility that the agency's workers feel in keeping the children safe. (R. Timleck, personal communication, April 22, 2009)

Rene explains that it tends to be the parents who ask for a hearing with the council. She states that there tends to be much more emotion involved in these kinds of hearings, as compared to hearings that concern youth and adults, because the process concerns a child. Parents are often fearful, which makes it more difficult for them to open up. At times there are outbursts. There may be anger directed at the NCFST's workers or the agency itself. There may be crying. As Rene explains, "these are deeply personal cases. People's lives are and may be deeply affected by what happens on the day of the hearing, so there may be a whole gamut of emotions that participants experience" (R. Timleck, personal communication, April 22, 2009).

Rene notes that a participant at a hearing may at first be opposed to others' suggestions for a plan for the child and family, but during the hearing process, the participant's perspective will often change, whereby an agreement can be achieved in the end. Rene hopes that "when consensus is achieved and everyone signs the agreement, each party feels heard and that they have truly participated in the process" (R. Timleck, personal communication, April 22, 2009).

The council hearings may determine that the child can return home, or the family may get more access to the child through visits and gradually increased overnight stays, or there is always the possibility that the child may be made a Crown ward without parental access. According to Rene, "nothing is set in stone except that the child's best interests are met and that the child be safe" (R. Timleck, personal communication, April 22, 2009).

Rene believes that this council has great potential for all people as "each community could take care of its own children, allowing for more personal responsibility. It would allow for more people to be involved in the safe-keeping of the children in their communities." Rene also notes that in the mainstream system, judges are burdened with the sole responsibility of making decisions regarding children and their families, but "with the Council, decisions are made by a collective, so the onus of responsibility is spread out amongst several people rather than on only one" (R. Timleck, personal communication, April 22, 2009).

Rene also supports alternatives to state child welfare, such as the council, for all people because:

> Much is revealed in a day-long hearing. Everyone involved comes closer
> to the truth than when they are in a courtroom. There is less chance of
> losing sight of the real issues in the Council process. In court proceed-

ings, it is often how knowledgeable the lawyers are and who presents their case the most eloquently, rather than the real issues at hand—whether it be criminal or family proceedings. The council process allows for the problem to be dealt with on a more personal level with the people involved being a part of the process. I believe that such councils could be a very effective tool in assisting people of any culture and, therefore, in all society. (R. Timleck, personal communication, April 22, 2009)

CONCLUSION

Perhaps no practices embody the values of a society more than how a society views and treats its children. Indigenous practices of caring for children from a collective, communal perspective are spreading across international boundaries and into the West. Systems of child welfare are beginning to adopt our practices, such as kinship care and family group conferencing, in ways that suit their particular beliefs and needs. Are Indigenous practices regarding families and children being co-opted or appropriated by dominant forms of child welfare? Or is the West beginning to learn from us that sharing power with families and communities helps to serve the best interests of children?

My answer to these questions is that both may be the case, but what I know to be much more important comes from two other authors since I cannot say it any more eloquently than they can: "Sharing good ideas is an essential human endeavour. As we share our gifts, we contribute to the knowledge basket of all who work with children and families" (Connolly, 2004, p. 3). In a broader perspective, Richardson and Nelson (2007) summarize what truly matters:

When we look deeply, we see that we are at a crisis point in the way we are living on the Earth. Most critically, we need to move from a culture of problem solving to one of visioning and creating the world we want....

Through "cleaning up" our practice and working in ways that actually preserve and strengthen extended families and communities, we help families to help themselves. With increased wellness and improved White/Aboriginal relations (free of racism, Euro-centrism and economic marginalization) true collaborations may emerge. Under improved conditions, all individuals will begin to care for the young ones, as well as the Earth, in a loving and thoughtful way. On a spiritual level, separation is the cause of much of our planetary grief; solutions will not come from

continuing to separate children from their families, from their community and from their lands, traditions and spiritual practice. (p. 81)

This chapter, and the words of wisdom above, suggest that separating children
from their families and communities may not necessarily be in the best interests of the child. This in no way applies only to Indigenous children; it applies
to *all* children.

REFERENCES

Aboriginal Legal Services of Toronto. (2007). *Aboriginal Legal Services of Toronto's Child Welfare Community Council*. Toronto: Aboriginal Legal Services of Toronto.

Babb, L.A. (1996). Statistics on U.S. adoption. The Decree, American Adoption Congress.

Blackstock, C. (2008, February). *The breath of life: When everything matters in child welfare*. Paper presented to University of Victoria Aboriginal Child Welfare Research Symposium, Victoria, B.C.

Blackstock, C. (2009). The occasional evil of angels: Learning from the experiences of Aboriginal peoples and social work. *First Peoples Child & Family Review, 4*(1), 28–37. Retrieved from http://www.fncfcs.ca

Carrière, J. (2005). *Connectedness and health for First Nation adoptees*. Doctoral dissertation. Retrieved from Proquest Dissertations & Theses (AAT NR08619)

Carrière, J. (2006). Promising practices for maintaining identities in First Nation adoption. *First Peoples Child and Family Review, 3*(1), 46–64. Retrieved from http://www.fncfcs.ca

Carrière, J. (2008). Maintaining identities: The soul work of adoption and Aboriginal children. *Pimatisiwin: A Journal of Aboriginal and Indigenous Community Health, 6*(1), 61–80. Retrieved from http://www.pimatisiwin.com/online/

Carrière, J. & Scarth, S. (2007). Aboriginal children: Maintaining connections in adoption. In I. Brown, F. Chaze, D. Fuches, J. Lafrance, S. McKay & S. Thomas Prokop (Eds.), *Putting a human face on child welfare: Voices from the prairies* (pp. 205–223). Prairie Child Welfare Consortium, Centre of Excellence for Child Welfare. Retrieved from www.cecw-cepb.ca

Connelly, M. (2004). A perspective on the origins of family group conferencing. Englewood: American Humane Association FGDM issues in brief.

Courtney, M. & Piliavin, I. (1998). *Foster youth transitions to adulthood: Outcomes 12 to 18 months after leaving out-of-home care*. Madison: University of Wisconsin.

Crush, L. (2005). The state of child protection mediation in Canada. *Canadian Family Law Quarterly, 24*(2), 191–219. Retrieved from http://ezproxy.lib.ryerson.ca/login?url=http://proquest.umi.com.ezproxy.lib.ryerson.ca/pqdweb?did=90458756 1&sid=1&fmt=1&clientld=10120&rqt=309&vname=pqd

Edwards, M. & Tinworth, K. (with Burford, G. & Pennell, J.) (2006). *Family team meeting (FTM) process, outcome, and impact evaluation: Phase II report.* Englewood: American Humane Association.

Fournier, S. & Crey, E. (1997). *Stolen from our embrace.* Vancouver: Douglas & McIntyre.

Greenwood, M. & de Leeuw, S. (2007). Teachings from the land: Indigenous people, our health, our land, our children. *Canadian Journal of Native Education, 30*(1), 48–53.

Grotevant, H.D., Dunbar, N., Kohler, J.K. & Esau, A.M.L. (2000). Adoptive identity: How contexts within and beyond the family shape developmental pathways. *Family Relations, 49*(4), 379–387. Retrieved from http://www.jstor.org

Hughes, T. (2006). *B.C. Children and youth review: An independent review of B.C.'s child protection system.* Retrieved from http://www.mcf.gov.bc.ca

Merkel-Holguin, L., Nixon, P. & Burford, G. (2003). Promising results: Potential new directions: International FGDM research and evaluation in child welfare. *Protecting Children, 18*(1–2), 2–11.

Ministry of Attorney General. (2006). *Child protection mediation program.* Retrieved from http://www.ag.gov.bc.ca

Mishibinijima, L. (2006). *Aboriginal child protection alternative dispute resolution: Environmental scan.* Toronto: Aboriginal Legal Services of Toronto.

Pennell, J. (2007). Safeguarding all family member–FGC and family violence. *Social Work Now: The Practice Journal of Child, Youth, and Family,* 37, 4–8. Retrieved from http://www.cyf.govt.nz/documents/about-us/publications/social-work-now/social-work-now-37-Sept07.pdf.

Richardson, C. & Nelson, B. (2007). A change to residence: Government schools and foster homes as sites of forced Aboriginal assimilation—A paper designed to provoke thought and systemic change. *The First Peoples Child & Family Review, 3*(2), 75–83. Retrieved from http://www.fncfcs.ca

Rodham Clinton, H. (1996, August). Speech presented at the Democratic National Convention, Chicago, IL.

Sinclair, R. (2007). Identities lost and found: Lessons from the sixties scoop. *The First Peoples Child & Family Review, 13*(1), 65–82. Retrieved from http://www.fncfcs.ca

Texas Department of Family and Protective Services. (2006, October). *Family group decision-making: Final evaluation.* Retrieved from http://www.dfps.state.tx.us

Trocme, N., Knoke, D. & Blackstock, C. (2004). Pathways to the overrepresentation of Aboriginal children in Canada's child welfare system. *Social Services Review, 78*(4), 578–599. Retrieved from http://www.jstor.org

Chapter 11
Pedagogy

INTRODUCTION

Chapter 11 focuses on a discussion about teaching and how crucial it is to include multiple knowledges within our classrooms. Both Indigenous educators and students share some of their experiences and perspectives on how to make social work education more inclusive for Indigenous and other marginalized learners. Contributions from non-Indigenous students and educators are also highlighted in terms of how they value and incorporate Indigenous pedagogy. The message of this chapter is that education can be healing and decolonizing for both Indigenous and non-Indigenous learners and educators.

HOW I TEACH

Fortunately, with a spirit name, in both Mi'kmaq and Anishnawbe, that means something like "The Woman Who Passes on the Teachings," I love being an educator. I enjoy opening doors for learners and watching them walk through on their journeys of self-discovery. I take pride in helping students gain new understandings, seeing their eyes light up, their heads nod, hearing their questions, and engaging in critical discussions with them. It is a privilege to walk with learners as they transform into critical, caring thinkers over the time they are in the classroom. However, along with this privilege comes responsibility.

As an educator, I must be mindful of what and how I teach. It is no easy task to teach about colonization and oppression, nor is it easy to teach about decolonization and anti-oppression. Learners are looking for solutions, and I do not necessarily have any since I am on this search as well. The challenge is to teach these topics with integrity, so that nothing is watered down, without shaming learners for their privileges or their lack of knowledge. Walking the journey of teaching with integrity and caring is founded upon an Indigenous world view and values that I live by. I carry these values with me at all times and the classroom is no exception, regardless if I am teaching "Aboriginal Approaches to Social Work" or "Strategies for Conflict Resolution" or "Advanced Social Work Theory and Practice." Over the years, I have been honoured to hear students share with me that I do not make them feel ignorant about what they do not know. My words offer encouragement, without shaming, to students to help them think more deeply about their work, and my down-to-earth style makes learning fun.

All of my classrooms are set up in a circle, so that everyone can see everyone else. There is no seat in the circle that represents a place of power. There are often no desks between me and the learners, which creates an egalitarian energy in the circle. Such a classroom set-up sends out messages that are remarkably different from one in which the teacher stands at the front of the room or behind a podium and learners sit in rows, looking at the backs of those in front of them.

I have also held some classes outdoors, weather permitting. During a recent one-week intensive course, the learners and I sat outdoors the entire time. We tend to share food in my classrooms, along with personal experiences and lots of humour. Laughter lightens the heaviness of some of the material, material that focuses on colonization and oppression. Telling the stories of real people makes the information come alive for learners.

I am a teacher who discloses personal stories to learners. I tell students about my background, where I am from, what I believe in, why I'm in the academy, and the community I am a part of. I include these stories in my talks about Indigenous world views and the impacts of colonization. I allow learners to see how these world views and their impacts are not only written about in journals or books, but also relate to the lives of real people. Sometimes I also share about my struggles with mental illnesses, past drug addiction, and attempted suicides. I do this because I know there are learners in my classrooms who have similar stories, and I want them to believe that they belong in the classroom.

Previous chapters, such as "Centring All Helping Approaches," "Holistic or Wholistic Approach," and "The Answers Are in the Community," emphasized that there are many diverse ways of looking at the world, and all are equally valid. Bringing multiple knowledges into the academy is crucial. I believe that it is harmful and irresponsible of educators to assume that Western ideas and their associated values are universal. Embracing multiple knowledges is particularly important to the helping professions as those we seek to assist and those who come into our classrooms come from diverse backgrounds. As educators and practitioners striving to change the world, we need all the help we can get from all multiple knowledges available to us.

As educators, we have a responsibility to ensure that what we are teaching and how we are teaching it are relevant to learners and the communities in which these learners live and work. Our world is constantly changing, and social work is not the profession it was 20 years ago. Our job as educators is to keep up with these changes, including making ourselves aware of the multiple knowledges that we may be privileged to know something about.

LEARNING THROUGH STORY

One way to practise inclusive education is to teach through storytelling. It is an important aspect of Indigenous world views as it embodies life's lessons and shows how knowledge is transmitted to all. Stories are not one-dimensional, but are told in order to convey several different lessons depending on when and where they are told and by whom (Cruikshank, 1999). Storytelling is a powerful medium of life instruction and a means of conveying values. Stories also serve as important links to the past and provide a means of surviving into the future.

Anishnawbe writer Esther Jacko (1992) explains that stories teach ... in a way that is warm, entertaining and lots of fun! Storytelling improves speaking skills and listening skills, and provides a novel way to learn. I think people can learn more from something if they are able to enjoy what they are learning, as well as participate in it. Storytelling allows listeners to participate by asking questions and by contributing their personal interpretation of what they have heard afterwards. (p. 42)

According to Cree educator Charles Lanigan (1998), storytelling is the oldest art and is universal to all people:

It is the basis of all other arts—drama, art, dance and music. It has been and is an important part of every culture. It can be a starting point from moving away from assimilationist to liberationist education. Stories provide the communication of essential ideas. Stories have many layers of meaning, giving the listener the responsibility to listen, reflect and then interpret the message. Stories incorporate several possible explanations for phenomena, allowing listeners to creatively expand their thinking processes so that each problem they encounter in life can be viewed from a variety of angles before a solution is reached. (p. 113)

Storytelling is a powerful technique that can be used to teach young children about life and reciprocity. Thus, stories often do not have a conclusion, but are told in ways that help develop critical thinking skills. This allows learners to interpret their own truths and arrive at their own conclusions, which allows learners to see that one way is not the only way.

Storytelling in a classroom setting combines the teachings of the past and adds a new dimension to the political, cultural, and environmental challenges faced by our world today. Everyone has a story, and honouring stories can not only provide an important healing dimension to our lives, but can also inform the formal learning process, especially when people have been deeply impacted by social, political, and economic marginalization.

Storytelling, through music, can also focus on social problems, as well as social justice. Music can also build bridges between Aboriginal and non-Aboriginal communities.

By building bridges, contemporary Aboriginal music also serves as a healing mechanism in several ways. By building bridges between Aboriginal society and the dominant society—that is, by facilitating an understanding through the telling of stories about history, traditions, spirituality, and problems— contemporary music attempts (intentionally or otherwise) to heal the rift of misunderstanding, mistrust, and negative stereotypes (Ladner, 1996, as cited in Settee, 2007, p. 97).

A caution to incorporating many ways of seeing the world is needed. Educators must be aware that if multiple knowledges are to be incorporated in social work education, it is not enough to present *parts* of multiple world views in order to support Western views of social work because once these knowledges become disassembled, they no longer retain their meaning. Thus, learning about multiple world views, values, and ways of helping must be explained within a particular context. In terms of education, this means that multiple knowledges need to be considered and taught as complete approaches in and of themselves, not as information that is secondary to Western knowledges and added to "sensitize" people who are learning about social work. Incorporating multiple world views in education also means that educators need to be careful not to use Western social work theories to legitimize diverse world views.

The knowledges of diverse peoples need to be included in all aspects of social work education. This means incorporating multiple knowledges about social policy development and analysis, about research methodologies, and about direct social work practice. The inclusion of diverse world views in each of these areas of interest influences each area, and these world views are all interconnected, influencing both social workers and the people with whom social workers interact.

TEACHING IN CONTEXT

In ancient times it was the ability to connect knowledge to the world that marked a scholar—not the letter grade given for the production of a text. Text too easily becomes a map that preceded the territory it represents and promotes the notion that knowledge can stand apart from contexts, relationships and living things. (Baudrillard as cited in Dumbrill & Green, 2008, p. 495)

Knowledge comes to us from watching, learning, and doing. Since educators hold power in the academy, they have a responsibility to promote positive change. This may include how learning is evaluated. There is an assumption within the academy that learning must be proven in specified and limited ways, such as by writing papers or memorizing information for an exam. Each learner is individually evaluated and given a letter grade. I often wonder what's more important to students: what they have learned that helps them to make positive changes in the world, or the letter grade that they are awarded? I have heard some students say that in forming groups for presentations, they seek out other students they believe will work for an A grade, and they inform their peers that this will be the focus. This is not the fault of students, however. It is the academy that has set up an evaluation system that extends from elementary school to Ph.D. programs, which engenders this kind of competitive attitude.

From an Indigenous perspective, knowledge does not focus on writing, but on making live connections within complex, multifaceted contexts and relations. Such connections, I believe, are what we are trying to help social work learners understand. It is unfortunate that text-based knowledge is privileged over other forms of knowledge as there is much wisdom that can be learned from people's stories, including students' experiences.

Leona Wright, of the Gitanmaxx First Nation and a recent B.S.W. graduate, explains how Indigenous pedagogy contextualizes knowledge:

> Eurocentric education is like opening up one's head and having professors put information in it. Aboriginal education is about learning through hands-on experience, never judging and understanding that it is the spiritual aspect that keeps helpers grounded. Learning happens through the whole person, according to Aboriginal education, not just through the mind. Education has a ripple effect in that it not only helps the individual, but it has an effect on families and communities. Perhaps most importantly, there is a healing of the mental, physical, spiritual, and emotional aspects of the individual through learning. Since each individual is unique and no one is better than the next person, we learn from each other and are willing to share our life experiences with one another as a way of teaching others. (L. Wright, personal communication, December 4, 2008)

Leona also contextualizes her social work education in terms of her past life and the person she is today:

I witnessed changes in myself while in social work education. Before I started I just accepted things for the way they were. Now I question things, learn what not to do, and am passionate about my work, especially when I really believe in something. I'm no longer the quiet one. Now I have a better understanding of injustices people face in today's society and want to give back to people because of the opportunities that were given to me. By trying to provide opportunities to others, standing beside them, and supporting them when they need it, I can be a part of how they empower themselves. (L. Wright, personal communication, December 4, 2008)

Leona's years in a social work program fostered her resourcefulness in how she was able to translate what she was learning into an Indigenous context:

I had to work much harder than most students due to having to translate everything from a Eurocentric world view, which is taught in social work education, into an Aboriginal world view. This is similar to language translation. I did diagrams for course outlines, circles rather than boxes, visual representations were helpful.

My mind heads right to circles all the time when I'm trying to figure a concept out. This is how I attempt to make sense of information. I need to be able to make what I learn my own understanding of what is being taught to me and find ways of being able to use it for myself in the context of an Aboriginal perspective. (L. Wright, personal communication, December 4, 2008)

I wonder how many students, Indigenous or not, also have to undertake knowledge translation during their education. I further wonder how educators and students might be able to eliminate, or at least decrease, the necessity of this translation by incorporating multiple knowledges and ways of learning into classroom teaching.

Lynn Lavallée, Anishnawbe/Métis associate professor in the School of Social Work at Ryerson University, acknowledges that multiple knowledges are needed in the academy in order to contextualize a learner's world views. Lynn explains simply that "the way I teach has come from Aboriginal world views because that's who I am" (L. Lavallée, personal communication, December 4, 2008). She believes that:

... discussing Aboriginal world views can be used as examples of how there are other ways of seeing things. I often bring Aboriginal examples into all the classes I teach to help explain theories, for example. I use circle diagrams to explain concepts such as interconnectedness. Values can be a grey area in terms of teaching them as they are influenced by world views, yet it's important to bring other values into the classroom because social work education is so Western and those are the only values that get taught. For instance, in explaining certain Indigenous cultural practices (not in detail), it may help other students to bring in or think about examples from their own communities. This is valuable in allowing students to have experiential experiences in the classroom. (L. Lavallée, personal communication, December 4, 2008)

As a White working-class woman, Jennifer Ajandi has much to contribute about how she has come to critical consciousness about education and the need for diverse world views and diverse approaches to pedagogy. She shared some experiences from her childhood and how she later came to see these experiences through gaining an understanding of her privilege:

I grew up in a low-income neighbourhood in St. Catharines: poor White people and poor Aboriginal people. I had many Aboriginal friends and didn't see any differences between myself and them. They were all heavily policed, had CAS [Children's Aid Society] involvement, were living with alcoholism, and were often involved with the criminal justice system. I had a young single mother, was left alone a lot, got into shoplifting and was caught at the age of 12. All that happened was [that] the police officer told me I was bad at shoplifting. He didn't charge me. He brought me home in the police car to my mother, who was devastated and grounded me.

As an adult I look back and can now see racism, which I didn't see while growing up. I believe I was privileged not to see it. I think because at the time I didn't see any differences. I just thought we all grew up with these things like alcoholism, violence, young pregnancies, overpolicing. It wasn't until I was in university that I saw that because of colonialism these experiences were experienced differently in that I grew up with "resilience factors" that my friends did not have because of racism.

For example, I had supportive White teachers who believed and supported me and [I] was able to access paid employment without fear of racial discrimination. I had strong teachers in school who were role models, but Aboriginal friends didn't have Aboriginal teachers as role models. I began to think about what got me to where I was in university while my Aboriginal friends didn't make it there. (J. Ajandi, personal communication, December 8, 2008)

Jenn goes on to tell her story of how experiencing Indigenous world views in the academy positively impacted her education:

I took your [Cyndy Baskin's] elective ["Strong Helpers' Teachings"] in 2005 and found it to be taught differently from other courses. Everyone was encouraged to learn from one another. There was little hierarchy, everyone's thoughts were appreciated. Attending to the whole person and including spirituality were present in the classroom. Students were encouraged to bring their own experiences into the classroom, and all parts of them and their lives were recognised. You also attended to students' differences without outing them by, for example, not having mandatory attendance which accounted for student absences due to mental health issues or the fact that they were single mothers with many responsibilities. Students tended to feel valued and respected in the class. Reflexivity was central in that the teaching was always connected to the students' personal situation or location and their social work practice. Learning about the processes and analysing colonization and its impacts helped me put my own experiences of childhood and youth into context.

I then deliberately selected courses based on the fact that they included some Aboriginal content. I had an Aboriginal faculty for my practice course in social work, took a course in graduate education on "Philosophical Foundations in Women's Studies," which had readings by Aboriginal scholars, such as Patricia Monture-Angus and Jean Fyre Graveline, and took a Ph.D. course on spirituality, which included materials and guest speakers on Indigenous spirituality. (J. Ajandi, personal communication, December 8, 2008)

Now, as an instructor, Jenn incorporates what she learned in her own education into her pedagogy. A true ally, she is a wonderful example of how a non-Indigenous scholar can take up the responsibility of ensuring that diverse perspectives can be taught regardless of one's subjectivity:

Much of what I learned about teaching comes from the class I took with you [Cyndy Baskin]. I ensure that I include Aboriginal content into every course I teach, look at the whole student, and encourage them to bring their experiences into the classroom. These are the principles that provide a general framework for my pedagogy. I also strive to help students feel valued and respected in my classes. I notice that marginalized students, in particular those who are queer or have disabilities, feel comfortable in my classes. I notice that these students would spend a lot of time with me after classes, they speak in class, discuss their feelings in the critical reflection assignments, tell me after the fact that they learned so much in the class—more than other classes. They would state this in their course evaluations of me. There have also been a few Black students who would stay with me after class and disclose how they experienced racial discrimination within the academy, and we would talk about strategies to address this. Sometimes they would raise this in class. (J. Ajandi, personal communication, December, 8, 2008)

I use storytelling in the class that Jenn took, and one of the novels, *In Search of April Raintree* by Beatrice Culleton-Mosionier (1999), which was about child welfare, impacted her so much that she used it in a child and youth course that she taught at Brock University in 2008. Students told her they loved this book and could not put it down once they started reading it. Jenn appreciates how instructive and meaningful it can be to bring storytelling, narrative, and novels into a course because these narratives are written by authors who have had the experiences they are writing about. This helps students make links to their own lives and make the links to the lives of those with whom they will be practising social work. These are the kind of readings that impact students because they help students to understand the structural issues facing marginalized peoples.

Jenn partners with Aboriginal peoples in the academy who can come into her classrooms to teach on subjects. For example, in a class that she taught on ethics in social work, she brought in someone to do a teaching on Aboriginal ethics because "it's important to look at ethics from many perspectives." She also encourages alternative assignments for students and pushes them "to contribute to knowledge in the classroom as I can't include everything and of course I don't know all of the different perspectives" (J. Ajandi, personal communication, December 8, 2008).

WHO TEACHES WHOM?

From an Indigenous perspective, educators, students, and community members teach one another and learn from each other. Indigenous values of humility and reciprocity are emphasized in the classroom "through recognition of the validity of students' knowledges and experience and through the development of authentic relationships exemplified by acknowledgment that everyone has something to learn" (Harris, 2006, p. 127).

Such classrooms depend on recognizing the wealth of information and experience that learners bring with them. In classrooms there needs to be an emphasis on co-operation rather than competition. These classrooms need to include educators who acknowledge their own lack of knowledge or expertise, and who are open to trusting the process that unfolds. As Lynn Lavallée states, "the teacher is always a learner in the classroom. Students teach me and they teach each other" (L. Lavallée, personal communication, December 4, 2008).

The academy must also meaningfully engage the communities that will receive the services to be delivered by social workers and other helping professionals. This means that the visions and goals of communities must be reflected in all areas of education programs. One way to accomplish this, as Lynn Lavallée states, is "to bring community into the classroom and the classroom into the community" (L. Lavallée, personal communication, December 4, 2008).

Consultation between community members and teaching staff can be achieved through community advisory committees, which can guide program curriculum and help develop strategies for learning that are relevant, empowering, and transformative. Such guidance "foster[s] a sense of responsibility as students, but also as community members" (Harris, 2006, p. 123), and this kind of consultation helps to link the needs and abilities of learners with the needs of communities.

Meaningful community involvement also ensures that there is a place where members can raise concrete concerns about programs and have these concerns satisfactorily addressed. This requires educators

> ... to be especially flexible in their own role as educators ... [T]hey must learn to see themselves as being in partnership with community members and as being students as well as teachers. ... These ideas may represent a radical shift in thought—perhaps too radical to accept. Nevertheless, this kind of humanity and this willingness to use one's professional abilities

in the service of others is at the heart of community-based programming. (Alcoze & Mawhiney, 1988, p. 37)

It would appear that even though this statement was made 23 years ago, university/community partnerships are still seen, for the most as part, as too radical to accept. I would say the fact that we do not have more university/ community partnerships is likely due to the academy's senior administration's resistance. Although helpful and influential, committees made up of university and community members have no real decision-making powers, which means that partnerships between the community and the academy are often unequal as the academy retains the power to make decisions. However, if we were to move toward a politics of post-colonialism, and adopt practices that support the kinds of transformational processes that are needed within a post-colonial framework, power-sharing would be addressed in the relationship between communities and the academy.

In addressing post-colonialism and the concerns related to practices within a post-colonial framework, new debates on anti-oppression in social work theory and practice are being raised. Cree/Assiniboine/Saulteaux scholar Raven Sinclair (2004) offers the following critique of anti-oppressive theory and practice:

> ... anti-oppressive practice has an inherent danger. The danger lies in proclaiming an anti-oppressive stance, while doing little or nothing to address the reality of oppression. As a profession, social work can do many things with "awareness" of critical issues such as racism including nothing. "Awareness itself lacks political substance and is sociologically naive" (Dominelli, 1998, p. 13). Awareness without legitimate action is a cognitive play that risks passing for anti-oppressive and anti-racist peda- gogy and practice in social work. It contributes to silence and inactivity about tangible issues of racism and oppression in the field of social work and in society. Contemporary anti-oppressive pedagogy does not address the culture of silence because it does not require anything beyond a theoretical grasping of issues. Neither the personal involvement nor the commitment of the social work student or practitioner is requested or required. Social workers risk falling into the trap of believing that just because they are social workers they are, therefore, non-racist and non- oppressive because the profession has a Code of Ethics to guide practice

and because social work institutions proclaim they are committed to this ideology. (p. 36)

Sinclair's critique is well taken. Insight alone doesn't change anything. Knowledge must lead to action. Her analysis comes at an important time when both social work programs and social services agencies are proclaiming anti-oppressive approaches. However, a plaque on the reception area's wall, a two-day training workshop, and a statement on a program's website does not make for anti-oppressive social work. Such superficiality is merely co-optation. What is required is a common phrase often cited by Indigenous peoples: "Walk the talk."

Post-colonial thought may have something to add to a pedagogy that centres the importance of turning knowledge into practice. Post-colonialism involves a critical analysis of history, thereby contextualizing colonization. It also teaches about valuing Indigenous healing and helping approaches, which is part of the decolonization process for all people. Post-colonial practice also has the ability to integrate Indigenous knowledge and therapies with Euro-American models of therapy (Duran, Duran & Yellow Horse Braveheart, 1998, p. 70). And, as Sinclair (2004) adds, "Aboriginal social work education ... is charged with the task of impacting this knowledge to students in order that they can effectively work in a decolonized context" (p. 40). I would add, however, that such a task belongs to *all* social work educators, not just Aboriginal educators.

Jennifer Ajandi believes that Indigenous world views have much to teach social work students, practitioners, and educators about practising anti-oppression:

> Let's consider ethics: self-determination has always been a part of Abo-riginal world views and is now an important part of social work's code of ethics as well. There is also being non-judgemental, linking individual issues with structural causes or contributions, that behaviour is learned and can be changed, that there are many different paths a person can take, that there is no ONE right answer, options depend on the person, family, and their community at the particular time.
>
> Aboriginal languages tend to be non-judgemental. There is much more of an equalizing dynamic between people. There is a strong emphasis on building relationships with those seeking help rather than mechanically running through a list of questions. "Intakes" and "assessments" are

discussions rather than standardized forms to complete; trust building happens before talking about personal issues.

The Seven Grandfathers Teachings are ethics as well. Love is one of these, but it has a different connotation than a more typical mainstream society or social work definition. Love is about connectedness. In my experience, I found that students can relate to this concept of love within social work practice and are able to discuss it. I found that when this concept is presented to different classes, students seem to respond to this concept, acknowledging that important relationships are built between social workers and service users, and that it is okay for social workers to care about the people they are working with. The feminist Ethics of Care Model emphasizes the interconnectedness of people, connections between people, between people and the Earth. This model emphasizes that building relationships can be "therapeutic," and it is important to recognize that all of these ideas have been an important part of Aboriginal world views since the beginning of time. (J. Ajandi, personal communication, December 8, 2008)

HEALING IN THE CLASSROOM

Education was a horrible tool of colonization for Indigenous peoples across the globe. Therefore, it is education that needs to take on a role of positive change for today and for the future. Decolonization must include healing, and must also take into account the ways that people learn with their entire beings, rather than with only their minds. As the Dalai Lama noted in a visit to Vancouver, B.C., to give a talk on "balancing educating the mind with educating the heart," "too much energy in your country is developing the mind instead of the heart. Develop the heart" (University of British Columbia, 2004 as quoted in Harris, 2006, pp. 125–126).

Robina Thomas practises what the Dalai Lama notes about education in Canada. She states:

> ... we ask whether all students are learning to be proud of all aspects of their identities, we question whether they are gaining their own vision and are developing an understanding of why they wish to become social workers. Ultimately, we evaluate whether students are connecting the knowledge entering their heads to the feeling in their heart. (Dumbrill & Green, 2008, p. 496)

Decolonization and healing can occur in the classroom as Barbara Harris (2006), a Dene professor emeritus of the School of Social Work, University of Victoria, states:

> ... reconciliation occurs in a holistic learning environment that attends to the emotional effect of the content being addressed. In this sense, the talking circle has been an effective strategy in the classroom, as everyone shares his or her own knowledge and experience.... (p. 128)

Michael Kim Zapf, a White social work scholar at the University of Calgary, recounts his experience of decolonization, healing, and reconciliation through the Talking Circle. Zapf was co-teaching a social work course with an Aboriginal educator. All of the learners in the class were Aboriginal. Without Zapf present, they held a circle to discuss internalized colonization. The following day, they held another circle with Zapf in attendance. He relates that:

> Many students had spent the night agonizing over the buried issues that had now been made conscious. It was not enough that I was the only non-Native in the room; I was now a white male authority figure, an easy target....
>
> With Apella's [the co-teacher] support I moved past my initial defensive reactions. I could see that this was not a personal attack; the students needed a target for their new rage. How I would react would be critical for the future of our work together.... This was a slow and very difficult sharing process, with hesitation and tears on both sides. I was involved with this class, with our process, with an immediacy that I had never experienced through prepared lectures, lab exercises or class discussion.... We came to a realization, probably the most powerful and crucial insight to come out of the entire course. If their anger forced them to shut me out and dismiss me, or if my guilt sent me back to the city where I could comfortably ignore the issue, then we would waste a special opportunity to build a bridge that we both needed. (Zapf as cited in Harris, 2006, p. 125)

Leona Wright shared similar experiences of decolonization and healing in the second-year mandatory course in the School of Social Work at Ryerson University:

Much of what I learned in this course was about me and my experiences and what these have to do with how I practice social work or helping. I learned about how non-Aboriginal students see Aboriginal peoples. This is what I got out of the course; this was the purpose for me to take it. It was as though I was looking through non-Aboriginal students' eyes and thinking what they think.

The assumptions non-Aboriginal students have came out through the presentations they did in the classroom and through some of the remarks they made. But I watched them grow in this class. I saw that some students were upset in the beginning having to take a course that they felt wasn't important to them and some felt there was favouritism towards Aboriginal people because this was a mandatory class. Some students felt their cultures and traditions were being left out. But as the class continued and they started to get an understanding of what Aboriginal people went through, they came to see the resilience of Aboriginal people in dealing with the struggles and the healing journeys that they are now taking. They soon lost those assumptions that society often portrays about Aboriginal people, and they began to heal themselves through tears in the classroom.

This class was held in a circle. It took a while for some students to get used to this. But it eventually became a safe place for all of them to share their feelings. It became a safe place for them by the teachings they received on the sacredness of the circle to Aboriginal people, how no one is higher within the circle and what is said in the circle remains in the circle. Students learned to share their own experiences when they could relate to some of the experiences of Aboriginal people. They learned to respect what they were learning and come to understand the importance of sharing. (L. Wright, personal communication, December 4, 2008)

Interestingly enough, the instructor who taught the section of the course that Leona speaks about is White. As mentioned earlier in this book, there are people inside and outside the academy who stand against non-Indigenous peoples teaching and practising Indigenous methods of helping. There are others who accept this. I believe the answer to this situation is contextual. If a non-Indigenous person has meaningfully experienced Indigenous teachings and healing, and is accepted by the Indigenous community, which includes sincere relationships with individuals in the community, as well as recognition from those they work with, and this person reflects Indigenous world views through their actions, then why not? Leona further shared her experiences with her instructor, which support this position:

> Having a non-Aboriginal person as an instructor was hard at first. I was disappointed that I had a non-Aboriginal instructor for such a course. I felt that she was just a "wanna be" [a person who romanticizes being Aboriginal and tries to act like one], but as the course went on, I gained respect for this instructor and the way she presented the information. I saw that she did not take credit for what she was teaching, but respected the knowledge that was passed on to her through the Aboriginal community. I saw her as an ally working from the inside out within the Aboriginal community. She was sincere and passionate about wanting all the students to learn about Aboriginal world views. I say chi meegwetch [many thanks in Anishnawbe] to this instructor for such a wonderful learning experience. (L. Wright, personal communication, December 4, 2008)

CONCLUSION

This chapter shows that multiple knowledges and ways of learning are needed and welcomed in the social work classroom if all involved are willing to walk the talk of anti-oppression and decolonization. The journey is at times painful, but the rewards are well worth it. Leona Wright explains this beautifully:

> Aboriginal world views ought to be taught to all students. Non-Aboriginal people must learn about Aboriginal people as it is the only way to stop racism and stereotypes. We [Aboriginal people] need to share our ways of understanding and seeing the world to assist non-Aboriginal students to see the great value in our world views, which can help all peoples. The Seven Grandfathers Teachings, which are the Anishnawbe people's code of ethics, speaks for itself as it talks about wisdom, love, respect, bravery, honesty, humility, and truth—all peoples believe in these, what else is there? (L. Wright, personal communication, December 4, 2008)

More often than not, students come into the helping professions because they want to help people. I see this as a good reason to go into such professions. As educators, our work is to assist students in exploring what help means and how it can be carried out, which means, in part, creating classrooms that welcome diverse world views of how to do so. Constantly listening to, and learning from, the students who enter our programs will assist us in accomplishing such inclusion. Incorporating the Seven Grandfathers/Grandmothers Teachings, as mentioned by Leona in the quote above, into our pedagogy may be a useful foundation from which to begin.

REFERENCES

Alcoze, T. & Mawhiney, A.M. (1988). *Returning home: A report on a community-based Native human services project.* Sudbury: Laurentian University Press.

Cruikshank, J. (1999). Editing on the page and in performance. In L.J. Murray & K. Rice (Eds.), *Talking on the page: Editing Aboriginal oral texts* (pp. 97–119). Toronto: University of Toronto Press. C

Culleton-Mosionier, B. (1999). In search of April Raintree. Winnipeg, MN: Portage and Main Press.

Dumbrill, G. & Green, J. (2008). Indigenous knowledge in the social work academy. *Social Work Education, 27*(5), 489–503. doi: 10.1080/02615470701379891

Duran, B., Duran, E. & Yellow Horse Braveheart, M. (1998). Native Americans and the trauma of history. In M. Battiste & J. Barman (Eds.), *First Nations education in Canada: The circle unfolds* (pp. 60–76). Vancouver: UBC Press.

Harris, B. (2006). What can we learn from traditional Aboriginal education? Transforming social work education delivered in First Nations communities. *Canadian Journal of Native Education, 29*(1), 117–134.

Jacko, E. (1992). Traditional Ojibway storytelling. In L. Jaine & D. Hayden Taylor (Eds.), *Being Native in Canada* (pp. 40–51). Saskatoon: University of Saskatchewan, Extension Division.

Lanigan, M. (1998). Indigenous pedagogy: Storytelling. In L.A. Stiffarm (Ed.), *As we see... Indigenous pedagogy* (pp. 103–120). Saskatoon: University of Saskatchewan Press.

Settee, P. (2007). *Pimatisiwin: Indigenous knowledge systems, our time has come.* Doctoral dissertation. Retrieved from Proquest Dissertations and Theses Database (AAT NR31078).

Sinclair, R. (2004). Aboriginal social work education in Canada: Decolonizing pedagogy for the seventh generation. *First Peoples Child & Family Review, 1*(1), 49–61. Retrieved from http://www.fncfcs.ca

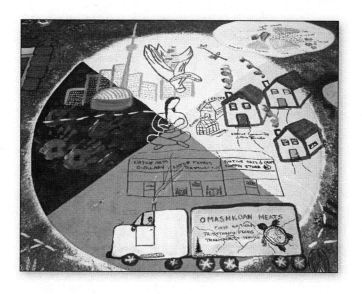

Chapter 12
Research

INTRODUCTION

"I spent several weeks going through books, articles and journals trying to find one good definition of Indigenous research methodology, and in the end I realized that I would not find a specific answer" (Steinhauer, 2002, p. 69). This statement remains true despite the explosion of literature in recent years on the topic of Indigenous scholars' research methodologies. This is not surprising given that there are numerous Indigenous Nations and cultures, so there will be many research methodologies. What works well in one community may not work in another. However, as with world views, there are foundational values and ways of knowing contained within these research methodologies.

SELF-IDENTIFICATION

Indigenous researchers tend to identify themselves within their research projects and publications (Anderson, 2004; Baker, 2008; Baskin, 2005; Green, 2009; Hart, 2007; Martin, 2001; Smith, 1999; Tupuola, 2006; Weber- Pillwax, 2001; Wilson, 2001). This is intended so that we can situate ourselves within the research and show why it is important to us. This practice is also meant to legitimate projects in which we are reclaiming our knowledges and ways of conducting research. Historically, research has been *done to* Indigenous populations with often harmful results (First Nations Centre, 2007; Steinhauer, 2002). According to a report published by the National Aboriginal Health Organization, "past research processes were often disrespectful, damaging and stigmatizing to First Nations people" (First Nations Centre, 2007, p. 3).

Western approaches to research tend to focus on the research participants, with little or no attention paid to the researcher, other than to her or his academic qualifications. In Indigenous research, not identifying oneself or stating why one is conducting a particular research project is problematic. The issue of insider-outsider researcher status also needs to be taken into consideration. In other words, who should conduct research with Indigenous people? Only Indigenous researchers, or only non-Indigenous researchers, or both? Standing Rock Sioux academic Vine Deloria Jr. (1997) positions himself by writing:

> Even with tribal peoples now entering academic fields, there is bias, and most academics deeply believe that an Indian, or any other non-Western person, cannot be an accurate observer of his or her own traditions because that individual is personally involved. (p. 34)

I agree with what Deloria Jr. says about Indigenous researchers often being personally involved in their projects, and how other academics often see us as not being objective when we conduct research with our own communities. I also agree with his assertion that *everyone*, whether Western or non-Western, who conducts research has biases. As human beings, how could it possibly be any other way?

I also believe that there are advantages to biases and we ought to acknowledge them as such rather than pretending that they do not exist. When Indigenous peoples conduct research with Indigenous communities, it is less likely that these communities will be exploited and more likely that they will benefit from the research findings. When an Indigenous researcher chooses projects within her or his community, the researcher is not only grounded geographically, culturally, and experientially in that community, but is also personally invested in the research findings because the results may have impacts on her or his family as much as on the research participants. Thus, when a researcher is personally involved in the research process and its outcomes because the project matters to him or her as a community member, rather than as a person whose agenda is to advance his or her career, the integrity of the work may be of a higher calibre.

Another area of tension for Indigenous researchers using Indigenous research methodologies occurs when we present our findings. Often the academy criticizes Indigenous writing as subjective, emotional, and personal, rather than adhering to the accepted Eurocentric value of objectivity in presenting research findings. In my own research projects, my findings are presented in a subjective way, without apology. I have deliberately chosen to write in this way as it, too, is a part of Indigenous research methodologies. My voice is embedded throughout my writing. In addition, I take the position that there is no such thing as objectivity. A lens and value base through which one views the world is inherent in every written work. It is just that some of us are upfront about this, while others pretend that this value base does not exist.

HOLISTIC AND RECIPROCAL

Indigenous research methodologies, like Indigenous world views, are intrinsically holistic. As Shawn Wilson (2001), of the Opaskwayak Cree from northern Manitoba, states:

> Knowledge is shared with all of creation. It is not just interpersonal relationships, not just with the research subjects I may be working with, but is the relationship with all of creation. It is with the animals, with the plants, with the earth that we share this knowledge. (pp. 176–177)

Communities give researchers the gift of being able to conduct research projects in their spaces, and participants give the gift of their knowledge. What gifts do researchers give to communities and participants? Within Indigenous world views, it is widely understood that one never takes without giving something back. This applies to research as much as it does to food and relationships. "Engaging in reciprocity allows community members and researchers to remain equal partners. If researchers make use of participants' ideas and time, they must give back by providing resources, skills, employment, and/or training" (Caldwell et al., 2005, p. 9). Capacity-building, as described here, is one form of reciprocity that has always been practised by Indigenous peoples. Many Indigenous scholars write about this value (Bartlett, Iwasaki, Gottlieb, Hall & Mannell, 2007; Caldwell et al., 2005; Jones, Crengle & McCreanor, 2006; Porsanger, 2004; Smith, 1999; Weber-Pillwax, 2001). As part of this reciprocal capacity-building, community members may be hired as research assistants and project coordinators. Elders may be called in for their wisdom and guidance, and community groups may be involved to provide catering services. I have been involved in projects in which storytellers and visual artists were hired to help develop research tools and methods of dissemination. It is also crucial to hire research assistants who are part of the population being researched. For example, if youth are the focus of the project, then youth need to be hired as research assistants.

The research group somewhat resembles an extended family. Members spend time together in order to get to know each other; they make consensus-based decisions. Each group member supports the others, everyone's input is respected, and hospitality is an expected norm. Hence, research projects need to focus on mutual purposes and outcomes for both the researcher and participants. As Maori scholar Russell Bishop (1998) notes within Indigenous research relationships, "there is common understanding and a common basis for such an understanding, where the concerns, interests, and agendas of the researcher become the concerns, interests, and agendas of the researched and vice versa" (p. 203). Non-Indigenous students and researchers in Western countries, such as Canada, Australia, and New Zealand, may be challenged by the amount of time it can take to develop relationships with research participants and reach decisions through consensus. Rigid timelines can interfere with such processes, so this needs to be taken into consideration when planning research projects.

I agree that in a "collective action way of making knowledge, emotional bonding with particular others is what generates new insights and knowledge" (Apffel-Marglin, 1998, p. 20).

Apffel-Marglin explains that in Indigenous research, "knowledge is not separated from emotion" (1998, p. 20). This is another significant component of Indigenous world views. Our holistic way of seeing an individual means that all four aspects of a person—spiritual, emotional, psychological, and physical—are included and these aspects are understood to be connected. It is important to relate to others on all these levels. Indeed, intellect and emotion cannot be artificially separated, nor can the spirit and the body. I would argue that knowledge comes out of all of these aspects because none of them can be separated.

I believe that research needs to be more than participatory. I agree with Bishop (1998) that it needs to be participant-driven, meaning that it is the community members who come up with the research questions, the design, the distribution of findings, etc. The researcher is one of the participants in this process. It is not a relationship of "I" and "them." It is a relationship based on "us" as we work together. This focus on the collective will and collective interests helps researchers avoid the danger of generating research that does not represent Indigenous communities, and "producing research that exists in the context of an ideology of individualism that Europeans claim as a virtue of their culture" (Lattas, 1993, p. 253). Furthermore, "this individualist, passion-less, factual expert professional knowledge reproduces existing social, political and economic orders" (Apffel-Marglin, 1998, p. 20).

More respectful types of research relationships reposition researchers "in such a way as to no longer seek to *give voice to others*, to *empower* others, to *emancipate* others, to refer to others as *subjugated voices*, but rather to listen to and participate with those traditionally 'othered' as constructors of meanings of their own experiences and agents of knowledge" (Bishop, 1998, p. 207). This is a crucial message for researchers in the helping professions as it is important to understand that it is not possible for us to empower anyone. The only person I can empower is myself. However, helping professionals as researchers can use their privileges to assist community members to empower themselves through the research projects we choose to take on and the research methodologies that we implement.

CONTROL AND OWNERSHIP

Having control and ownership of research is consistently emphasized by Indigenous scholars (Bartlett et al., 2007; Caldwell et al., 2005; Ermine, Sinclair & Jeffery, 2004; First Nations Centre, 2007; Hart, 2007; Jones et al., 2006; Martin, 2001; Smith, 1999). I see ownership of research as part of the political project. As explained by the First Nations Centre (2007):

First Nations need to protect all information concerning themselves, their traditional knowledge and culture, including information resulting from research. The Principles of Ownership, Control, Access, and Possession (OCAP) enables self-determination over all research concerning First Nations. It offers a way for First Nations to make decisions regarding what research will be done, for what purpose information or data will be used, where the information or data will be used, where the information will be physically stored, and who will have access. (p. 1)

Karen Martin (2001), of the Noonuccal people of Quandamooka, Australia, also wrote about Indigenous control of Indigenous research, which she describes as a process of reclaiming:

To reclaim research is to take control of our lives and our lands to benefit us in issues of importance for our self-determination. It is to liberate and emancipate by decolonization and privileging the voices, experiences and lives of Aboriginal people and Aboriginal lands so that research frameworks are reflective of this. To reframe research is to focus on matters of importance as we identify these. It is to respect our ways and honour our rights and social mores as essential processes, through which we live, act and learn. (p. 2)

This perspective is taken up by Indigenous scholars globally. "Indigenous scholars from Australia, Aotearoa-New Zealand, the U.S. and Canada have brought to academic discussions the indigenous peoples' project of reclaiming control over indigenous ways of knowing and being, a project that implies better control over research on indigenous issues" (Porsanger, 2004, pp. 108–109). Thus, a primary guideline is that research with Indigenous peoples needs to be community-based and community-controlled. This primary guideline has several directives that say research and research findings should:

- be the intellectual property of the community;
- be of direct benefit to families and communities;
- transfer skills;
- include mechanisms for continued gains/work;
- be reviewed to ensure accuracy; and
- include community members as co-authors in publications (Porsanger, 2004, p. 117)

Research that is community-based and controlled, first and foremost, involves work on areas that are of interest and concern to the local community that is approached. Ideally, the community itself identifies the areas and initiates the projects. Community-based work also means ensuring that a multiplicity of viewpoints are fairly represented. It means eliminating or at least reducing barriers to community members' participation in the project.

Community control means establishing "collaborative procedures to enable community representatives to participate in the planning, execution, and evaluation of research results" (Battiste & Youngblood Henderson, 2000, p. 137). It also means hiring community members for paid positions, such as research assistants, within the research project. Self-determination can be facilitated in many ways, including providing financial remuneration and helping people gain new skills, which are of benefit to the community. All too often, Indigenous peoples' knowledge and work are used, and people are never compensated. Instead, paid positions are given to non-Indigenous peoples. Not only is this unfair, but it is terribly disrespectful. A shift in thinking could mean that the ongoing work of research can be taken up by community members themselves. I also believe that it is important to include community participants as co-authors of published research.

TELLING STORIES

Storytelling has a long history among Indigenous communities around the world, and it stands on its own as a research methodology. Some of the literature regarding research with Indigenous peoples refers to qualitative research, narrative approaches, and participatory action research as methodologies that will capture the experiential knowledge of Indigenous peoples (McKenzie, Seidl & Bone, 1995). Such authors also suggest that participatory research, which is a combination of education, research, and action, contributes to the empowerment of Indigenous peoples. The problem with such statements is that these research methodologies are viewed as novel in conducting research with Indigenous peoples and other populations, which is not the case. Story-telling methodologies existed long before narrative approaches and participatory action methods were developed. In fact, I would say that these research methodologies are based on Indigenous ones, such as storytelling circles. Some other Indigenous scholars who agree include Jenny Lee (2009), of the Maori Nation, who describes Maori narratives as being revived today within research, which implies that these are traditional Indigenous approaches or methodologies rather than new ones. She uses narrative terminology and discusses the traditional role of narratives or storytelling within Maori world views. In her 2009 book, *Indigenous Methodologies: Characteristics, Conversations, and Contexts*, Cree educator Maggie Kovach writes that storytelling is not unique to Indigenous knowledge systems alone, but is used in various qualitative methodologies, including narrative inquiry (p. 96). She emphasizes how stories were an intrinsic part of Indigenous oral societies long before the rise of Western education and academic research (p. 27). Interestingly enough, non-Indigenous academics Roxanne Struthers and Cynthia Peden-McAlpine (2005) directly correlate Indigenous storytelling and oral histories or narratives as a premise to phenomenological research, which uses in-depth narrative accounts and methods.

Storytelling is a vibrant component of Indigenous research methodologies and exists in all cultures. Cree educator Mary Anne Lanigan (1998) suggests that storytelling:

> ... can be a starting point for moving away from assimilationist to liberationist education. ... Stories have many layers of meaning, giving the listener the responsibility to listen, reflect and then interpret the message. Stories incorporate several possible explanations for phenomena, allowing listeners to creatively expand their thinking process so that each problem they encounter in life can be viewed from a variety of angles before a solution is reached. (p. 113)

To me, storytelling as a methodology fits beautifully with research, as indicated in this quote. It includes responsibility on the part of the listener/researcher, interpretation/analysis, room for many explanations of the phenomena being researched, a creative search for solutions, and a political act of liberation/self determination.

I agree with Chickasaw scholar Eber Hampton (1995), who sees storytelling as encouraging for research participants because it ensures a reflective discussion that enables all participants, including the researcher, to build knowledge together. I believe this is the key to Indigenous research methodology—building knowledge collectively by focusing on the community in order to create richer understandings.

Storytelling also makes room for healing within the research process. As has already been noted, Indigenous world views centre on the notion of holism, which addresses all four dimensions of a human being. From my perspective, it is inevitable that many research topics will elicit strong emotions from participants. Since, as Indigenous peoples, we have decolonizing aims, we acknowledge our history and our current situations on the journey toward self-determination and our future. There is much pain woven into our stories, and the circle and its protocols are designed to welcome and address anger and hurt, should these emotions emerge. I agree that in an Indigenous research framework, a "collective action way of making knowledge, and emotional bonding with particular others is what generates new insights and knowledge. Knowledge here is not separated from emotion" (Apffel-Marglin, 1998, p. 20).

Researchers need to be prepared for strong emotions that participants in a storytelling circle may experience. Although these emotions may not intentionally be invited, doorways may be opened for participants in terms of memories, insights, feelings, and spiritual encounters. In my own research work with Indigenous peoples, I have explained to participants beforehand that emotions may come up through storytelling in order to encourage them to assist one another and ask for support outside of the project.

BENEFITS

If my work as an Indigenous scholar cannot or does not lead to action, it is useless to me or anyone else. I cannot be involved in research and scholarly discourse unless I know that such work will lead to some change out there in that community, in my community. (Weber-Pillwax, 2001, p. 169)

I completely agree with this statement. Why conduct research that does not originate out of the interests and needs of the community? What is the point of research that is not meaningful or of some benefit to the community? Data collected through research projects have the potential to change social policies for the better, which is one of the ways in which educational institutions can help to create positive change for Indigenous peoples and other marginalized communities.

Completing a research project does not mean ending the relationships established during the research process. Rather, the next phase of the research process requires ongoing relationships among participants to continue. I believe that it is the responsibility of the researcher to ensure that the positive and meaningful intentions of the research project can continue, which means that participants are then potentially able to put their new knowledge into action. An additional responsibility of researchers and writers is taken up by Maori scholar Linda Smith (1999), who refers to a process that she calls "researching back." She states that "researching back, like writing back, is partly about talking back to the West … and partly about talking to ourselves" (p. 204).

Indigenous research is also especially pertinent to social work practice and other helping professions. The research conducted by Indigenous researchers proves time and again the competency, capability, and valuable knowledge that is held by Indigenous peoples and communities (Anderson, 2003; Baker, 2008; Bartlett et al., 2007; Baskin, 2005; Caldwell et al., 2005; First Nations Centre, 2007; Hart, 2007, 2009; Jones et al., 2006; Lavallée, 2008, 2009; Martin, 2001; Porsanger, 2004; Sinclair, 2004; Smith, 1999; Steinhauer, 2002; Tupuola, 2006; Weber- Pillwax, 2001; Wilson, 2001). Indigenous research produces knowledge that schools of social work use to inform their teaching. It is important for both Indigenous and non-Indigenous students to have access to Indigenous knowledges. Indigenous research methodologies assist populations of over-researched and exploited Indigenous peoples to empower themselves. These methodologies can also help to inform the next generation of social work students/researchers who wish to work with other historically marginalized and racialized communities.

COLLABORATION

Some of the literature on Indigenous research is written by research teams made up of both Indigenous and non-Indigenous scholars. The work of Bartlett et al. (2007) was conducted by two Métis and three non-Indigenous academics. The study by Jones et al. (2006) was done by one British and two Maori scholars. I have been involved in a number of collaborative research teams made up of both Indigenous and non-Indigenous researchers in areas such as food security, homelessness, child welfare, and addictions.

In the literature on collaborative research projects, the favoured research methodologies of choice appear to be combinations of community-based and participatory action research, as seen in the quote below by a group of non-Indigenous researchers:

Community-based, collaborative, and participatory research makes tribal people full partners, benefits the communities studied, and empowers people to define and address the issues that affect their lives; in the process, community members set the agenda of research that affects them. Scientists and community members must share equally in the research planning, implementation, evaluation, and results dissemination phases, as well as in any resulting benefits. (Caldwell et al., 2005, p. 7)

Many Indigenous writers (Hoare, Levy & Robinson, 1993; Kovach, 2005; Loppie, 2007) agree that participatory action research (PAR) is an ally of Indigenous research methodologies. Some go a bit further to suggest that PAR may actually be based on some of the concepts of Indigenous world views. For example, Maori authors Lynne Harata Te Aika and Janinka Greenwood (2009) state how, for Western researchers, PAR is a relatively "recent" engagement; however, for Maori traditions, "it is embedded" by way of their *marae*, the people's communal house, where issues are debated and investigated within and by the community (p. 59). Cree/Métis academic Weber-Pillwax (2009) discusses PAR as a research methodology that supports "the intellectual and spiritual revolution of Indigenous peoples" (p. 48). She does not exactly state that PAR is derived from Indigenous methods; however, she alludes to this when she states how "fully complementary" it is with the research process of "ancient" Indigenous knowledges and peoples. She also cites other Indigenous authors as having said that PAR processes are "particularly derived and intrinsically connected to the original sources of their own Indigeneity" (p. 48).

Some Indigenous researchers also use a number of different research frameworks in combination. For example, one project by Tupuola (2006) used "three different cultural methodological frameworks: indigenous, cross-cultural and trans-national. These different cultural designs reflect my shifting positions as an insider researcher during these individual studies as well as the diverse cultural identities of the young people with whom I collaborated" (p. 293).

I have consistently used Indigenous research methodologies in all of the research projects I have been involved in. In some of these projects, I have been the only principal investigator, while in others I have collaborated with Indigenous and non-Indigenous researchers. Here I will write about two successful collaborative research projects that I have been involved in.

Upon the completion of a research project with young Indigenous mothers on food security in Toronto, I was invited to participate in a collaborative research project with seven other groups. The invitation came from social work educator and project co-ordinator, Izumi Sakamoto, because my work had been noticed by groups that were implementing community-based, arts-informed research methodologies. These projects focused on homelessness and/or the threat of becoming homeless, but the researchers did not have a specific Indigenous project in mind. Since my work was closely connected to the issue of homelessness (I had previously conducted research on homelessness with Indigenous peoples in Toronto), since I implemented Indigenous research methodologies, and since the women who participated in the food security project had created a mural of their depiction of a food-secure Indigenous community in Toronto, my work seemed to fit with theirs. However, I did not simply join this group because they asked me to. I first needed to find out more about the people who were involved, and I needed to have many questions answered, such as the following:

- What was the perspective of the groups that I would be working with? Were the researchers anti-oppressive?
- What did the researchers know about Indigenous peoples in Toronto? Were Indigenous participants working with any of them in their projects?
- How would my project be represented? Would it be given the same amount of space as other projects?
- Would I and the young Indigenous mothers who worked with me have real input into the overall project or would we just be the "token Indians"?

After a few meetings with the group, my questions were answered in ways that showed me these researchers had a sincere desire to include Indigenous peoples in the research project in meaningful ways. They heard me when I emphasized that homelessness is different for Indigenous peoples as it is connected to colonization, which has led to the kinds of social, economic, and political conditions that have seriously disadvantaged Indigenous peoples. The group seemed to understand my comment that it is particularly ironic that Indigenous peoples are homeless in their homeland. We began to build relationships that were necessary in order for us to do this work together.

I liked the group's idea of using community-based, arts-informed, participatory research methodologies to conduct projects in the area of homelessness because of the ways I felt I could make connections between these research methodologies and Indigenous ones. The funding application for the project read as follows:

Homelessness is an enormous issue that must be pursued from different perspectives considering the intersections of gender, race, Aboriginal heritage, disability, and other differences. These factors contextualize the diverse experiences of people who are homeless. Yet, research on homelessness has typically focused on men who are on the street or in shelters (Sakamoto et al., 2007). To the extent we lack information on these different sub-groups of the homeless, it is imperative to develop a ground-up approach to reflect the diversity of experiences while exploring commonalities of such experiences. Community-based participatory research and arts-informed research value these experiences and provide mechanisms to articulate how different groups of individuals experience homelessness and how they themselves envision solutions to homelessness.

Arts-informed research allows those directly affected by the issue (i.e., homeless people) to document and express their concerns and their worldviews effectively (Finley, 2005). The exclusive use of words limits the audience's grasp of the multifaceted realities that homeless people experience. Alternatively, arts-informed research offers more than one interpretive method for understanding research participants' lives, challenges, and resiliencies. Furthermore, the creative "works" resulting from arts informed research (e.g., film, photography, multimedia exhibits) likely have a far greater potential to move people to action than words in conventional position papers and journal articles (e.g., Wang & Burris, 1997).

Within the homeless community, our respective arts-informed studies have provided project participants an opportunity to use art to capture and express their daily experiences and challenges as they related to health, poverty, social exclusion, and other day-to-day struggles, as well as to their hope, vision, and resiliency. Homeless citizens have found arts-informed research useful in order to think critically about problems and solutions from the community's perspective, and to work towards social change (Davis, Halifax et al., under review; Sakamoto et al., 2007). The arts used in research projects herein elaborate, contextualize and expand upon what has escaped broader social attention: the strengths of people who are homeless. Community-based participatory research methods (CBR/CBPR) came out of the reflection that traditional social research based in academic institutions does not directly benefit marginalized communities which are often "the researched" in traditional forms of research (Flicker & Savan, 2006; Israel et al., 1998; Minkler & Wallerstein, 2004). Rather, CBR/CBPR recognizes the strengths of the community as the core of the research endeavours, and promotes the equitable involvement of all partners in the research process including academic researchers, community agencies and community members, to make the research more relevant to the community with which they work (Community Partnership for Health, 2007). (Sakamoto, 2009, p. 10)

These participatory and emancipatory approaches can sit alongside an anti-colonial research framework that centres emancipatory aims within the research process. An anti-colonial framework is about community control over decision-making, over the research agenda, over how resources will be distributed, and over ethical practices. It includes a focus on critical questions such as the following:

1. What research is important and worthwhile to carry out?
2. Who will conduct the research?
3. How will it be carried out?
4. Who will own the research?
5. Who will the research benefit and what positive differences will it make?
6. How does conventional research support local capacity to undertake research?

Within an anti-colonial framework, when a research project is undertaken, it must be endorsed by the community, and credit needs to be given to those community members who participate in the research process. Relationship is critical, as Dakota academic Angela Cavender Wilson (1998) writes:

The scholar must understand the internal mechanisms Native people have for determining within their own communities whether they have information relevant to a scholar's study, whether they feel a scholar is respectful enough of their culture to share their valuable insights, who within the community is authorized and informed enough to share the information, and what information is appropriate to share. (p. 26)

Other Indigenous scholars, such as Cecil King (1997), raise the notion of creativity within research projects, which, of course, is complemented by arts-informed methodologies:

> Creative approaches must be discussed and debated by aboriginal communities, academic institutions, and individual researchers to reach a working relationship that neither constricts the advancement of knowledge nor denigrates the aboriginal communities' legitimate authority over the integrity of their own intellectual traditions. (p. 118)

Furthermore, an agenda for research with Indigenous peoples must focus on the goals and processes of decolonization and self-determination. If a research project does not contribute in some way to these objectives, then it is not worth doing. Such a research agenda:

> ... becomes a goal of social justice which is expressed through and across a wide range of psychological, social, cultural and economic terrains. It necessarily involves the processes of transformation, of decolonization, of healing and of mobilization as peoples. (Smith, 1999, p. 116)

Community-based participatory research also aims to benefit and mobilize marginalized populations.

The rationale for a collaboration of eight research projects to come together was explained in a way that emphasized that, despite the diversity amongst us,

> these studies validate the relevance of community-based, arts-informed, participatory action research especially when such diverse projects have all arrived at similar policy and practice recommendations. These projects represent homeless people as the "experts" in their life experiences who know the solutions to mediate their life circumstances. In addition, such research gives voice to a highly stigmatized population that is generally framed in negative, "deficit" based terms. Community-based, arts-informed and participatory research can thus break and disturb the fixed stereotypes surrounding homeless people in our society and allow for a dialogue about solutions to poverty and homelessness to begin with people most directly impacted.

Although the informed projects in this Collaborative employed different arts-based research methods and worked with people with different identities and experiences of homelessness, they came to many of the same conclusions. A consensus was reached across all eight projects on the recommendations about what needs to be done to address homelessness in Toronto, challenged many of the assumptions that exist about homeless peoples' lives and confirmed the power of CBR/CBPR as a tool for social change (Sakamoto, 2009, p. 11).

Upon completion of the eight research projects, we held a five-day exhibit of our work at Metro Hall in Toronto. Indigenous world views guided the set-up of the exhibit. We chose to organize our projects according to one of the versions of the teachings of the Medicine Wheel of the Anishnawbe people. We recognized that there are many versions of the Medicine Wheel across several Indigenous Nations in Canada, and our intention was not to value any particular version over another. Our decision to implement this particular version of the Medicine Wheel was based on our commitment to acknowledge and honour those peoples whose original territory we were on. This idea was initiated by the project I led, which focused exclusively on Indigenous peoples in Toronto. The idea was then supported by the Indigenous peoples who participated in the various projects of the collaborative endeavour.

We came to the agreement that the Medicine Wheel symbolized a good fit among all of our projects as it represents unity. The Medicine Wheel symbolizes bringing people together and, in seeking to find solutions to homelessness, this initiative brought together people with experiences of homelessness, as well as community agencies and academics. Implementing the Medicine Wheel as a symbol of our collaborative work also seemed appropriate because Indigenous peoples are overrepresented among those with experiences of homelessness due to historical and contemporary forces of colonization, and because many of the people actively involved in many aspects of our collaborative and individual research projects identified themselves as Indigenous.

Another successful collaborative research project I was recently involved in focused on developing collaborative relationships between pregnant/parenting Indigenous women with substance-use problems and drug and alcohol treatment counsellors and child welfare workers. For this project, the team of researchers worked from an anti-colonial theoretical framework, which "recognizes the importance of locally produced knowledge emanating from cultural history and daily human experiences and social interactions and it sees marginalized groups as subjects of their own experiences and histories" (Dei & Asgharzadeh, 2001, p. 300). This framework promotes powerful Indigenous peoples' discourses, such as storytelling, and guides researchers to use Indigenous concepts and cultural frames of references in our work.

For some time now, a paradigm shift has been emerging whereby several studies "agree that a significant element of the solution" to the costs of social problems facing Indigenous peoples "is the need to shift the research paradigm from one in which outsiders seek solutions to the 'Indian problem' to one in which Indigenous people conduct research and facilitate solutions themselves," which highlights Indigenous knowledge traditions and research methodologies (Saskatchewan Indian Federated College, 2002, p. 1). We chose to implement Talking Circles with the women who decided to participate in our projects. As Cree scholar Laara Fitznor (1998) suggests, we understood that:

> ... sharing circles embrace such concepts as learning from what is said, gaining information and knowledge to incorporate into one's life, honouring and respecting what is heard, honouring the confidentiality of who said what, sharing the joy and pain of others, recognizing that what each person says is placed on an equal footing (no one person's voice is more important than another's), and the willingness to share information about one's experiences in light of personal growth and development. Sharing circles promote personal well-being and the well-being of Aboriginal peoples. They reflect the traditional concept of interconnectedness. (p. 34)

Hosting and taking care of people, whether they are guests or research participants, is also of great importance within Indigenous world views. Those who share their knowledges with a researcher must be given food, drink, honoraria, and gifts of thanks. These exchanges are as natural as breathing, and are also expected. To not carry out these protocols of reciprocity would be considered disrespectful and could even jeopardize the research project and, more importantly, possibly damage relationships.

Within this research project, as in the others I have been involved in, the team did not ask any direct questions of the participants. Rather, we introduced the research topic to the women, explained why we wanted to do this work, introduced ourselves, and invited them to share their stories about their experiences regarding the topic. Direct questioning can be viewed as intrusive or disrespectful within Indigenous world views. In addition, I tend to view direct questions, particularly within a research framework, as potentially leading participants in the direction that the researcher wants to go. However, inviting participants to share whatever is important to them and allowing each to take as much time to speak as he or she wishes expresses respect and caring for the speaker and what the person has to say.

We suggested topics for discussion to the women in this particular research project such as:

- What comes to mind when you think about women who are pregnant or have kids and are in substance use treatment programs?
- How do substance use treatment programs help these women?
- How do these programs recognize the spiritual, physical, emotional, and mental aspects of a woman?
- How are women impacted by their involvement in substance use treatment programs and child welfare services at the same time?

The team for this research project was made up of Indigenous and non-Indigenous women. One was a university professor, another was a full-time research scientist. There were women who worked in the areas of child welfare and addictions, and there were students. Some of the team members worked at huge institutions, while others were employed in grassroots agencies. Some had personal experiences of child welfare involvement and addictions, while others worked directly with women who did. A female Elder, also a member of the team, was involved in all aspects of the project from planning, to participation in circles, to analyzing the information that was shared with us.

As with the previous research project mentioned in this chapter, the team members worked together in a respectful partnership in which Indigenous world views and research methodologies were privileged. The non-Indigenous co-principal investigator generally stood back, listened more often than she spoke, offered the resources of her workplace such as space, supported the leadership of the Indigenous co-principal investigator, and followed the protocols specified by the Elder involved in the project. She also politely declined when asked to represent or present information about the project, instead referring the enquirer to me. She did, however, join us in representing the project when we asked her to. In addition, all members of the research team were acknowledged in our publications.

Again, this was a research project whereby those involved asked me to participate as a co-principal investigator not only because I am an Indigenous researcher, but because they wanted someone who worked from an Indigenous world view and used Indigenous research methodologies. I consistently felt welcomed, appreciated, and respected, and I believe all of the other Indigenous team members did as well.

WHAT NON-INDIGENOUS RESEARCHERS CAN LEARN FROM US

All people and everything else in our world is dependent upon and shares in the work and growth of everyone and everything else. When there is a healthy interconnected web linking individuals, communities, and all of nature, everyone prospers because we are aligned with our Mother the Earth.

Every decision that each of us makes and everything we do affects all around us, not only our families and communities, but the animals, plants, water, the air we breathe, and the earth we walk on. We are completely dependent on everything else around us. In all that we do, including research, we have relational responsibilities. The following quote by Forbes (1992) applies to all peoples, Indigenous and non-Indigenous alike:

> I can lose my hands, and still live. I can lose my legs and still live. I can lose my eyes and still live. I can lose my hair, eyebrows, nose, arms, and many other things and still live. But if I lose the air I die. If I lose the sun I die. If I lose the earth I die. If I lose the water I die. If I lose the plants and animals I die. All of these things are more a part of me, more essential to my every breath, than is my so-called body. (pp. 145–146)

Gaining knowledge through research, then, is not an abstract pursuit but is meant to lead to transformative action in all of our relationships.

Another important aspect to consider within Indigenous research methodologies is how knowledge comes to people. Knowledge can come through dreams, intuition, and cellular memories, memories that are stored in our cells and blood, as much as through interviews, Talking Circles, and observation. Once again, all people dream and carry memories within their blood and bodies.

Relational responsibilities and transformative action are often not part of dominant research paradigms. Rather, dominant paradigms follow the belief that knowledge is individual; a researcher searches for knowledge; she or he gains the knowledge and, therefore, owns it. An Indigenous paradigm recognizes that knowledge is relational. Knowledge is meant for everyone and everything. What is the point of acquiring knowledge if it is not shared for the benefit of all?

A researcher's honesty is another component in an Indigenous paradigm. Research is never objective and there is always a motive for conducting it. This is assertively articulated by Hampton (1995), who writes that the motive is

> ... emotional because we feel. We feel because we are hungry, cold, afraid, brave, loving, or hateful. We do what we do for reasons. That is the gift of the Creator of life. Life feels. ... Feeling is connected to our intellect and we ignore, hide from, disguise, or suppress that feeling at our peril and at the peril of those around us. Emotionless, passionless, abstract, intellectual, academic research is a goddamn lie, it does not exist. It is a lie to other people. Humans—feeling, living, breathing, thinking humans—do research. When we try to cut ourselves off at the neck and pretend an objectifying that does not exist in the human world, we become dangerous, to ourselves first, and then to people around us. (p. 52)

Every researcher brings her or his own cultural expectations, values, and biases to the research process, and these expectations, values, and biases influence the ways that research questions are created, influence the choice of methods, data interpretation, and research recommendations. Thus, it can only be beneficial to all involved that researchers clearly and honestly discuss their emotional reasons for wanting to conduct any research project.

CONCLUSION

There is no such thing as one Indigenous research methodology. Rather, there are many and we create them as we go about conducting our research projects. They become Indigenous research methodologies as long as they follow Indigenous world views, which are the key foundational values and beliefs of our Nations. These values and beliefs, such as a holistic approach, relationship-building, and connection to everything around us, apply to everything we do. Research is not exempt from these values and beliefs.

It is not Indigenous research methodologies that I believe can be valuable to the world. Rather, it is the values and reasons behind Indigenous methodologies that can be valuable. When Indigenous and non-Indigenous researchers work together with Indigenous participants or communities, it is the cultural protocols and specific methodologies of those involved that need to be taken up. But the values of self-identification, reciprocity, benefits, control and ownership, and hearing people's stories can be applied to all peoples of the world. This is particularly the case in the helping professions, such as social work, a profession that seeks, through research, to make the world a better place for all.

REFERENCES

Anderson, K. (2003). Vital signs: Reading colonialism in contemporary adolescent family planning. In K. Anderson & B. Lawrence (Eds.), *Strong women stories* (pp. 173–190). Toronto: Sumach Press.

Anderson, K. (2004). Speaking from the heart: Everyday storytelling and adult learning. *Canadian Journal of Native Education, 28*(1/2), 123–129.

Apffel-Marglin, F. (1998). *The spirit of regeneration: Andean culture confronting Western notions of development.* London: Zed Books.

Baker, E. (2008). Locating ourselves in the place of creation: The academy as Kitsu'lt melkiko'tin. *Canadian Woman Studies, 26*(3/4), 15–20.

Bartlett, J.G., Iwasaki, Y., Gottlieb, B., Hall, D. & Mannell, R. (2007). Framework for Aboriginal-guided decolonizing research involving Métis and First Nations persons with diabetes. *Social Science & Medicine, 65*, 2371–2382. doi:10.1016/j.socscimed.2007.06.011

Baskin, C. (2005). Storytelling circles: Reflections of Aboriginal protocols in research. *Social Work Review, 22*(2), 171–187.

Battiste, M. & Youngblood Henderson, J. (2000). *Protecting Indigenous knowledge and heritage: A global challenge.* Saskatoon: Purich Press.

Bishop, R. (1998). Freeing ourselves from neo-colonial domination in research: A Maori approach to creating knowledge. *International Journal of Qualitative Studies in Education, 11*(2), 199–210. doi: 10.1080/095183998236674

Caldwell, J.Y., Davis, J.D., Du Bois, B., Echo-Hawk, H., Shephard Erickson, J., Stone, J.B. (2005). Culturally competent research with American Indians and Alaska Natives: Findings and recommendations of the first symposium of the work group on American Indian research and program evaluation. *American Indian and Alaska Native Mental Health Research, 12*(1), 1–21. Retrieved from http://www98.griffith.edu.au

Cavender Wilson, A. (1998). American Indian history or non-Indian perceptions of American Indian history? In D.A. Mihesuah (Ed.), *Natives and academics: Discussions on researching and writing about American Indians* (pp. 23–26). Lincoln: University of Nebraska Press.

Dei, G. & Asgharzadeh, A. (2001). The power of social theory: The educational discursive framework. *Journal of Educational Thought, 35*(3), 297–323. Retrieved from http://vnweb.hwwilsonweb.com

Deloria Jr., V. (1997). *Red earth white lies, Native Americans and the myth of scientific fact.* Denver: Fulcrum Publishing.

Ermine, W., Sinclair, R. & Jeffery, B. (2004). *The ethics of research involving Indigenous peoples.* Retrieved from http://www.iphrc.ca

First Nations Centre. (2007) *OCAP: Ownership, control, access, and possession.* Sanctioned by the First Nations Information Governance Committee, Assembly of First Nations. Ottawa: National Aboriginal Health Organization.

Fitznor, L. (1998). The circle of life: Affirming Aboriginal philosophies in everyday living. In D. McCane (Ed.), *Life ethics in world religions* (pp. 21–40). Winnipeg: University of Manitoba Press.

Forbes, J.D. (1992). *Columbus and other cannibals: The Wetiko disease of exploitation, imperialism, and terrorism.* Brooklyn: Autonomedia.

Green, J. (2009). Gyawaglaab (Helping one another): Approaches to best practices through teachings of Oolichan fishing. In R. Sinclair, M.A. Hart & G. Bruyere (Eds.), *Wicihitowin: Aboriginal social work in Canada* (pp. 222–233). Winnipeg: Fernwood Publishing.

Hampton, E. (1995). Memory comes before knowledge: Research may improve if researchers remember their motives. *Canadian Journal of Native Education, 21,* 46–54.

Harata Te Aika, L. & Greenwood, J. (2009). Ko tatou te rangahau, ko te rangahau, ko tatou: A Maori approach to participatory action research. In D. Kapoor & S. Jordan (Eds.), *Education, participatory action research, and social change: International perspectives* (pp. 59–72). New York: Palgrave Macmillan.

Hart, M. (2007). Indigenous knowledge and research: The mikiwahp as a symbol for reclaiming our knowledge and ways of knowing. *The First Peoples Child & Family Review, 3*(1), 83–90. Retrieved from http://www.fncfcs.ca

Hart, M.A. (2009). For Indigenous people, by Indigenous people, with Indigenous people. In R. Sinclair, M.A. Hart & G. Bruyere (Eds.), *Wicihitowin: Aboriginal social work in Canada* (pp. 153–169). Winnipeg: Fernwood Publishing.

Hoare, T., Levy, C. & Robinson, M.P. (1993). Participatory action research in Native communities: Cultural opportunities and legal implications. *Canadian Journal of Native Studies, 13*(1), 43–68. Retrieved from http://www2.brandonu.ca

Jones, R., Crengle, S. & McCreanor, T. (2006). How tikanga guides and protects the research process: Insights from the hauora tane project. *Social Policy Journal of New Zealand, 29*, 60–77. Retrieved from https://www.msd.govt.nz

King, C. (1997). Here come the anthros. In I. Biolsi & L.J. Zimmerman (Eds.), *Indians and anthropologists: Vine Deloria Jr. and the critique of anthropology* (pp. 115–119). Phoenix: The University of Arizona Press.

Kovach, M. (2005). Emerging from the margins: Indigenous methodologies. In L. Brown & S. Stretga (Eds.), *Research as resistance* (pp. 19–36). Toronto: Canadian Scholars' Press Inc.

Kovach, M. (2009). *Indigenous methodologies: Characteristics, conversations, and contexts.* Toronto: University of Toronto Press.

Lanigan, M. (1998). Indigenous pedagogy: Storytelling. In L.A. Stiffarm (Ed.), *As we see... Indigenous pedagogy* (pp. 103–120). Saskatoon: University of Saskatchewan Press.

Lattas, A. (1993). Essentialism, memory, and resistance: Aboriginality and the politics of authenticity. *Oceania, 63*(2), 24–267.

Lavallée, L. (2008). Balancing the medicine wheel through physical activity. *Journal of Aboriginal Health*, 64–71. Retrieved from http://www.naho.ca

Lavallée, L. (2009). Practical application of an Indigenous research framework and two qualitative Indigenous research methods: Sharing circles and Anishnaabe symbol-based reflection. *International Journal of Qualitative Methods, 8*(1), 21–40. Retrieved from http://ejournals.library.ualberta.ca

Lee, J. (2009). Decolonising Maori narratives: Purakau as a method. *MAI Review, 2*, 1–12. Retrieved from http://ojs.review.mai.ac.nz

Loppie, C. (2007). Learning from the grandmothers: Incorporating Indigenous principles into qualitative research. *Qualitative Health Research, 17*(2), 276–284. doi: 10.1177/1049732306297905

Martin, K. (2001). *Aboriginal people, Aboriginal lands, and Indigenist research: A discussion of re-search pasts and neo-colonial research futures.* Paper submitted to School of Indigenous Studies, Master's Program, James Cook University, Australia.

McKenzie, B., Seidl, E. & Bone, N. (1995). Child and family service standards in First Nations: An action research project. *Child Welfare, 74*(3), 633–654.

Porsanger, J. (2004). *An essay about Indigenous methodology.* Retrieved from http://www.ub.uit.no

Sakamoto, I. (2009). *SSHRC funding application: Mobilizing and leveraging knowledge on homelessness through arts-informed, community-based research.* Toronto: University of Toronto.

Saskatchewan Indian Federated College. (2002). *A brief to propose a national Indigenous research agenda*. Submitted to the Social Science and Humanities Research Council. Retrieved from http://old.fedcan.ca

Sinclair, R. (2004). Aboriginal social work education: Decolonizing pedagogy for the seventh generation. *First Peoples Child & Family Review, 1*(1), 49–61. Retrieved from http://www.fncfcs.ca

Smith, L.T. (1999). *Decolonizing methodologies: Research and Indigenous peoples.* Dunedin, NZ: University of Otago Press.

Steinhauer, E. (2002). Thoughts on an Indigenous research methodology. *Canadian Journal of Native Education, 26*(2), 69–81.

Struthers, R. & Peden-McAlpine, C. (2005). Phenomenological research among Canadian and United States Indigenous populations: Oral tradition and quintessence of time. *Qualitative Health Research, 15*(9), 1264–1276. doi: 10.1177/1049732305281329

Tupuola, A. (2006). Participatory research, culture, and youth identities: An exploration of Indigenous, cross-cultural, and trans-national methods. *Children, Youth, and Environments 16*(2), 291–316. Retrieved from http://www.colorado.edu/journals/cye/16_2/index.htm#australia

Weber-Pillwax, C. (2001). Coming to an understanding: A panel presentation: What is Indigenous research? *Canadian Journal of Native Education, 25*(2), 166–174.

Weber-Pillwax, C. (2009). When research becomes a revolution: Participatory action research with Indigenous peoples. In D. Kapoor & S. Jordan (Eds.), *Education, participatory action research, and social change: International perspectives* (pp. 46–58). New York: Palgrave Macmillan.

Wilson, S. (2001). What is an Indigenous research methodology? *Canadian Journal of Native Education, 2*(2), 175–179.

Chapter 13
We Are All Related

INTRODUCTION

Peggy Wilson (2001) relates a story about how, before the Exxon Valdez Oil Spill, one of her students in Alaska had a dream in which everything was black, and how she felt like she was being strangled by this black mass. The student was moved and shocked into action by this experience because it was the day before the oil spill, and she wondered if anyone else in the world had had that warning. So she placed an ad in a number of newspapers throughout the world. She received responses from as far away as England and Africa with people describing similar dreams before that monumental disaster. She referred to this experience as the collective unconscious (Steinhauer, 2002, pp. 75–76).

Experiences such as this one send a clear message: We are all connected. Regardless of how we explain such phenomena, whether we refer to it as the collective unconscious or spirituality, the Earth ties us together.

CONNECTED THROUGH WORLD VIEWS

As an awareness of global colonization and Indigenous world views gradually become a part of social work education in Canada, it is helpful to consider why this might be so. I believe this acceptance is due to a number of positive events around us. One of these is the fact that Canada is a country of many people who are represented in social work classrooms. Many of these learners are Indigenous to other parts of the world, and they bring with them world views that are remarkably similar to those of Indigenous peoples here.

Another reason is likely due to the increasing prevalence of literature on spirituality in social work practice and the interest that some educators have shown in discussing spirituality in their classrooms. The growing awareness of the destruction of the Earth and all that lives on Her is a third reason for the growing interest and inclusion of Indigenous knowledges in social work education.

These three events—a similarity in world views, spirituality, and a concern for the world around us—are impacting social work education and practice. Spirituality is viewed as a celebration of diversity that promotes inclusion and, in a similar way, eco-social work draws our attention to our collective interest in protecting our spirituality and our world (Gray, Coates & Hetherington, 2007). These concepts of interdependence and relatedness to Mother Earth come from global Indigenous world views. By embracing interdependence and relatedness, "we end up with multiple forms of interventions," as stated by Gray et al. (2007, p. 57), although I would use the term "helping" rather than "interventions."

In combating the ever increasing and ongoing destruction of the Earth and its effects on the Earth's peoples, we need to look toward our commonalities and focus on how we can work together to address these potentially life-threatening problems. We need to embark on a journey together to search for alternative ways to live rather than continuing to embrace ongoing Western development without questioning its effects. The world's Indigenous peoples may hold the world views that will help to heal and protect our Earth and everything on Her.

In conducting the research for this book, I found countless examples of commonalities among the world views of Indigenous peoples on Turtle Island, New Zealand, Tibet, and the continent of Africa, to name a few. I have also learned about these similarities from relatives, friends, and students, and by taking classes for my Ph.D. program at OISE/UT. My brother-in-law, who is originally from Mozambique, and I have shared many stories about our world views. Our world views are similar in their focus on community values rather than individual interests, and in their focus on the importance of ceremony for one's well-being. We have similar understandings about the drum, language, and the healing properties of plants, even though we grew up on opposite sides of the world.

In my class discussions with Dr. George Dei and other learners while at OISE, I was amazed at what I heard about Indigenous knowledges from around the world. My classmates were from many countries throughout Africa, Asia, and South America, but when they spoke about their world views, I understood what they were saying. I was able to relate to how they lived their world views. For the first time in my education, I participated in class discussions in which what I had to say was met with understanding and interest, rather than uncomprehending silence and dismissal. In the class, there was both a diverse range of individual perspectives and also a sense of connection through our Indigenous knowledges and identities.

The literature from Indigenous scholars around the world also recognizes commonalities within world views. For example, in the area of research, Maori scholar Jelena Porsanger (2004) writes:

> The Maori concept of *whanaungatanga* has been proposed as a methodological frame for research. As a concept, *whanaungatanga* has a great array of meanings, which may be translated as "relationships," primarily those between kin, the extended family (*whanau*), individuals, ancestors, spirits, the environment and many other aspects of the holistic Maori understandings of connectedness. (p. 111)

Afrocentricity is described as relying on spirituality, appreciating the connectedness of all on the planet and in the cosmos, emphasizing the collective rather than the individual, and promoting harmony among all (Mazama, 2002). African-American scholar Mambo Ama Mazama (2002) writes that within African forms of spirituality, "special rituals take place before cutting trees down" (p. 220), which is exactly what happens on Turtle Island as well. Mazama speaks of the connection between human beings and the spirit world, noting that "the ancestors provide guidance; they will send us messages about how we operate in this life, in this world, if we honor them" (p. 222). We are more alike than we are different!

The use of the circle is also prominent in the helping and healing practices of Indigenous peoples throughout Africa and North America. Mazama (2002) states that the circle "is the African symbol par excellence" (p. 221). Two examples of African-based approaches that focus on the spiritual energy of the circle are the story circle technique (Williams-Clay, Olatunji & Cooley, 2001 as cited in Garrett, Brubaker, Torres-Rivera, West-Olatunji & Conwill, 2008) and the dance of the ring (Spencer, 2001 as cited in Garrett et al., 2008). These approaches offer support to the members of the circle through connectedness and belonging. Similar to the methods of many Indigenous groups on Turtle Island, these approaches help participants to connect with themselves, the world around them, and the ancestors who came before them (Garrett et al., 2008).

Like other African scholars, Odora Hoppers (2002) states that there is a need to instill Indigenous knowledge systems as a tool to rebuild democratic values, ethics, sustainable development, and human liberation, free from all forms of oppression. Black scholars, such as hooks (1984), Davis (1974), and Dei (2000), claim that only when intellectual production is de-racialized and Black intelligentsia is fuelled by African values will an African renaissance truly take place. Similar thoughts are expressed by Indigenous writers in other parts of the world as well as with respect to Indigenous values.

Similarities in world views also extend to spirituality. Kabat-Zinn (2005) explains why mindfulness meditation has spread across the planet:

> The systematic cultivation of mindfulness has been called the heart of Buddhist meditation. It has flourished over the past 2500 years in both monastic and secular settings in many Asian countries. In recent years the practice of this kind of meditation has become widespread in the world. This has been due in part to the Chinese invasion of Tibet and the continual war in Southeast Asia, both of which made exiles of many Bud-

dhist monks and teachers; in part to young Westerners who went to Asia to learn and practice mediation in monasteries and then become teachers in the West; and in part to Zen masters and other meditation teachers who have come to the West to visit and teach, drawn by the remarkable interest in this country in meditative practices.

Although at this time mindfulness meditation is most commonly taught and practiced within the context of Buddhism, its essence is universal. Mindfulness is basically just a particular way of paying attention. It is just a way of looking deeply into oneself in the spirit of self-inquiry and self-understanding. (p. 12)

Another significant component of global Indigenous world views is how Elders are viewed. Everyone I spoke to and all that I have read describe Elders as older people who are sought by their communities for their knowledge and spiritual leadership. Each Elder has something different to offer since each has his or her own unique experiences, personalities, and knowledge. Through their accumulation of knowledge and experience, Elders can talk to people and help them in ways that contribute to their well-being. Their knowledge and experience is acknowledged and respected by community members who go to Elders to receive teachings and assistance.

Elders can play a role in any or all of the following practices: counselling, teaching, conducting ceremonies, healing, advising, resolving conflicts, facilitating group problem-solving and decision-making, and acting as role models (Stiegelbauer, 1996). Elders also tend to be talented storytellers:

The ability of an elder is to be able to tell a story in such a way that it's meaningful to you and that's almost an art, and to complement that fashion to relate to that person and at the same time, not take it out of the broader framework of the whole picture. (Stiegelbauer, 1996, p. 48)

This general view of Elders is also written about by diverse Indigenous scholars, such as George Dei (2000) from Ghana, Leilani Holmes (2000) from Hawaii, Njoki Nathani Wane (2000) of Kenya, and Laara Fitznor (1998) of the Cree Nation. Similar views of Elders have also been recorded by Elders themselves around the globe, such as Flordemayo, Mayan Nation of Nicaragua; Rita Pitka Blumenstein, Yupik Nation of Alaska; and Mona Polacca, Hopi Havasupai/Tewa of Arizona (Schaefer, 2006). Thus, throughout the world:

Elders are important for their symbolic connection to the past and for their knowledge of traditional ways, teachings, stories and ceremonies. It is very common for respected Elders to be called upon to help communities with decisions regarding everything from health issues, to community development, to governmental negotiations regarding land and self-government. (Stiegelbauer, 1996, p. 39)

I would add that Indigenous Elders are also crucial to our collective endeavour to heal the Earth and all that lives on Her.

Indigenous Elders in the Kimberley region of Australia have a cultural practice that links "the physical movement of walking (often vast distances) with the process of maintaining spiritual, economic and familial ties to country" (Palmer et al., 2006, p. 321). During these walks, the Elders, and the youth they bring with them, conduct ceremonies, carry out land management practices such as burning areas of land, harvest plants, and build knowledge (Palmer et al., 2006). These journeys of walking across parts of the country are one of the ways in which the Elders pass on Indigenous knowledges to the youth. It is also considered that "the act of walking on country [is] also the act of looking after it" or "to fail to walk on country is to neglect it" (Palmer et al., 2006, p. 325).

Walking on country helps to clean up the Earth these groups are walking on. It helps to divert youth away from social problems, reduces substance abuse, and addresses the high incidence of suicide (Palmer et al., 2006). Elders encourage youth to stand up and prepare for leadership by building their strength in physical and spiritual ways. As the authors suggest, although enlisting youth participation through the typical youth forums, consultations, and committees are beneficial, they "have young people taking time away from active pursuits and adopting the rather sedentary posture of 'sitting' on committees" (Palmer et al., 2006, p. 332).

These Elders and many others around the world have been passing on knowledges to younger generations through doing rather than sitting since the beginning of time (Baskin, 2008; Battiste, 2000; Schaefer, 2006). Much of my own education has come about while doing physical labour for the Elders who have taught me, while picking and preparing medicines, and preparing for ceremonies. Learning from Elders through doing seems to be a commonality among Indigenous peoples globally that may also be useful to other peoples on the Earth.

I came across another journal article from Schiff and Moore (2006) that discussed healing through the sweat lodge ceremony of Turtle Island, but that also discussed how similar practices have occurred in many other places around the world:

> The process of sweating for cleansing and healing has a history that extends around the world and goes back for millennia. Both the ancient Greeks and the Romans used hot baths and sweating techniques to draw out bad humors and as a general form of relaxation and social gathering. Likewise, Finnish saunas promoted cleanliness, healing, and renewed strength. Russians used a bania, which combined steam and hot air to create a humid, healing environment, while Turkish hammans and Japanese hot tubs are widely used in their respective countries (Aaland, 1978). Sweating cleanses the body of toxic elements and boosts the immune system (Smoley, 1992).
>
> While heat and water are universal in these various manifestations of cleansing processes, only a few cultures have incorporated them into a carefully prescribed ceremony which emphasizes the spiritual element in addition to the physical healing and cleansing that are universally acknowledged. Indigenous North Americans are among those people for whom the sweating experience is a traditional ceremony that aims to purify, cleanse, and heal the body, mind, emotions, and spirit. (p. 49)

CONNECTED THROUGH COLONIZATION AND GLOBALIZATION

Global Indigenous peoples are also connected through the history of colonization and its present-day impacts. No Indigenous population on the planet has escaped the destruction of colonization, the genocide that murdered millions of people, raped the land, and did everything it could to wipe out the knowledges of Indigenous peoples. The same systems that were used to colonize the Indigenous peoples of Turtle Island were also used against other Indigenous peoples around the world, including the imposition of religion, education, and child welfare. Mazama (2002) refers to Christianity as "one of the pillars of Western supremacy" and "part and parcel of the White supremacy project" (p. 223). Given the role of Christian religions in the colonization of Indigenous peoples worldwide, I agree with Mazama (2002) that Christianity is "responsible for more misery and suffering than any other religion" (p. 223). Throughout both Africa and Turtle Island, Christianity reduced our Indigenous spiritualities to superstitions, played a role in genocide and enslavement, and created schools that demonized our cultural practices, physically and sexually abused our children, and forbade our children to speak their own languages (Mazama, 2002).

Sami culture in northern Europe, which is distinct from the Nordic culture that surrounds it, was also historically attacked through educational systems. Education was used to oppress the Sami people and "outlawed Sami language, clothing and music" (Hicks & Somby, 2005, p. 280). In the 20th century, the Sami people have focused on protecting their communities, reducing the prejudice against them, and addressing economic hardships. According to Hicks and Somby (2005), "prior to the end of the Second World War many Sami hid their Sami identity in order to save themselves and their families from persecution" (p. 276). They faced "racist policies" in their "attempt to reduce the poverty level" for their communities (p. 277).

Child welfare in New Zealand has also implemented racist policies with regard to Indigenous children. Historically, in New Zealand a disproportionate number of Maori children are represented in both foster and institutionalized care (Ernst, 2001). Many Maori children were lost forever to their families and communities when they were placed in European homes, which meant that their cultural and spiritual needs were not met (Ernst, 2001). In addition, social workers within child welfare services "sometimes ignore the wishes of a child's parents in seeking family connections from both sides of the child's family" (Ernst, 2001, p. 171).

We, as Indigenous peoples around the globe, have more similarities regarding the history of colonization and its current impacts than we have differences. It is this horrific history, along with our world views, that bind us together and that will potentially help us take a stand in the future.

Today's impacts of this colonial history include extreme poverty, stolen land, and languages that have been wiped out. Colonization, however, was not completely successful. Indigenous peoples and our knowledges have survived, which speaks to our incredible strength and spirit. And through our survival, all peoples of the world can benefit. In the past the colonizers needed Indigenous peoples in order to survive, and now the descendants of the colonizers need Indigenous peoples to help them survive into the future.

Social work has functioned as an arm of colonization, and this has been written about by many Indigenous scholars across the globe from Hart (2002) in Canada, to Ling (2003) in Asia, to Nagpaul (1993) in India. Social work exists as a modernist Western creation that has gained influence in many parts of the world. Despite its aims to support and assist people, however, social work has also historically been used to silence Indigenous peoples in the name of helping. Notions of international social work, which seek to delineate a universal definition for the profession and create universal educational standards, can be seen as a modern form of colonization. Trends to professionalize social work in many parts of the world may be due to the profession's historical and ongoing inferiority complex. Historically, in order to address this inferiority complex, the profession has sought to gain status in the eyes of other helping professions and within society as a whole through standardization of practices and "professionalization."

Within the social work profession, there is an inherent contradiction between a desire to incorporate Indigenous ways of helping in order to provide services that are in alignment with the values and needs of diverse peoples and communities, and the push to standardize social work practices according to Western values and Western models. The answer is not to try to make Indigenous ways of helping fit within Western social work models, but to take complete direction from Indigenous communities. Only in this way can social work avoid becoming part of colonialist globalization projects.

Leadership in all areas that affect Indigenous peoples must come from Indigenous peoples themselves as they are the ones who know what they need. I agree with Gray, Coates, and Hetherington (2007), who write:

> Indigenous movements usually involve people collectively asserting their rights for self-determination since Indigenous people recognize that political, economic, educational, and health benefits and privileges cannot occur as long as the entire population is disenfranchised. Self-determination for Indigenous people has greater meaning in the sense that it concerns the empowerment of entire populations. The self-directing potential of individuals cannot be increased without considering historical, social, cultural, economical and political realities. (p. 56)

As Indigenous peoples are on a natural journey of deconstructing Western hegemony, which includes social work education and practice, they can learn from one another as they share their histories and struggles and rebuild their communities based on their world views. As Dei (2000) states, "Local input must be from the grassroots.... [It] should be ecologically sound, and should tap the diverse views, opinions, resources, and interest manifested in the cultural values and norms of local communities" (p. 73). Once again, however, this wisdom applies to more than Indigenous peoples. Such wisdom is also relevant to any people who live on the land, who are farmers, who have concerns about food security, or who care about the future of our Earth.

MY RELATIVES IN BRAZIL

I have a story that I would like to share with you about the connections between colonization and world views among Indigenous peoples globally.

In 2005, I was approached by Ryerson University's Centre for Studies in Food Security (CSFS) to become part of the centre to conduct research and write about food security and Indigenous peoples. I agreed, as food is not only a structural determinant of health, but also has cultural and spiritual meanings for Indigenous peoples worldwide. In the spring of 2006, the centre invited me to visit the interior of Brazil, where the centre's team was involved in a food security project. A small group of Indigenous peoples, who had recently migrated to an area near where the project was taking place, expressed an interest in what the team was doing to address food security. Everyone agreed that an Indigenous person involved with the centre should be one of the members to meet with this group.

My intention in meeting with the group of Indigenous people in interior Brazil was to learn how food (e.g., traditional foods and their meanings, access and choices, past and present practices) is connected to identity. I had no idea that my visit would become a spiritual journey.

With the arrival of European people in Brazil over 500 years ago, much of the Indigenous people's land was taken over by ranchers and industrial projects. Indigenous people were forced onto pieces of land similar to reserve communities in Canada, and poverty levels are high (Baskin, 2008). Languages, cultures, and livelihoods have also been negatively impacted, and the exploitation of Indigenous people threatens traditional knowledges and practices (Baskin, 2008). All of these impacts have affected the Pankararu and Pataxo people whom I visited. They have been dislocated at least twice and have had to start a whole new community in an arid area.

World views between these two tribes in Brazil had much in common with my own world views in Canada. As one of the community members explained:

We have a vision about what we want our community to be like based on working with nature around us. In our vision, everything is connected and has a purpose.... We feel we are solution-focused and believe we can help heal the land that has been almost destroyed by White ranchers, miners and the government. The whole principle is to work responsibly with the earth, take care, nourish and restore what is there, and do as less harm as possible to Her. (Baskin, 2008 p. 8)

All of the people gathered to spend time with me when I visited their territory. Most of the discussions were initiated by the community's Elder and a young political leader. The Elder took on the role of escorting me around the village, explaining things, and offering teachings. He stated that even though he is only middle-aged, he is the oldest one in the community. He clearly feels a huge responsibility in his role as Elder, as he humbly stated, "I have a lot to learn in order to be the people's Elder." He, like all the other people present, was welcoming, open, and generous. Their openness and generosity was expressed through their sharing of information and allowing photographs to be taken.

The Indigenous Brazilian people were interested in learning as much as they could about Indigenous peoples in Canada. They were especially interested in learning about the different Nations, life today, commonalities between us and them, traditional foods, and representation in government. They also wanted to know about me, my family, and my community. Through a translator and by drawing diagrams in the dirt with a stick, I explained as best I could. Afterwards, the Elder announced, "All Indigenous peoples are related. You are our relative."

When I first arrived in the community, the people were dressed in shorts and skirts, but later they changed into their traditional regalia. They wanted to conduct a ceremony for me. They formed a circle and danced while singing. Then they called out, asking, "Where is our relative?" They brought me into the circle to dance with them and sang an honour song. The Elder explained the meaning of the song: "Your strength comes to us and our strength goes to you. Your clan is the fish and the fish from where our original territory is will protect you and give you strength always." This was only the first time I cried because I was feeling spiritually overwhelmed. They asked for a song and, of course, I sang one of thanks. When it was time to leave, the families presented gifts of jewellery which they had created from gifts of the Earth such as seeds and dye from plants. The Elder gave me one of his shakers and a bow with three arrows. I cried again. We joked and laughed for a bit before my departure. Four years have passed, but these memories remain vivid. I was fundamentally changed by this visit to the interior of Brazil in ways that are impossible to articulate (Baskin, 2008).

I remain in touch with my Pankararu and Pataxo relatives. Three of these relatives travelled to Toronto a few years ago as part of my food security research project. Besides that visit, we have continued to exchange letters and gifts from time to time. These people have many positive messages for the world. One message comes from one of the young women in the community. When I mentioned how inspired I was by the people of her village who have so little materially and yet are so generous and glowing with happiness, she responded:

> We need money for certain things, so we can be comfortable, but that's all. We don't need or want many materialistic things. We don't want to accumulate a lot of things, but rather share amongst ourselves. We are a group of people who want to be together and enjoy doing things together. We love to live. We like each other. We like ourselves. We want to live free. (Baskin, 2008, p. 9)

TAKING A STAND

We are living in a time when we all need to strive for wellness and balance. In the Lakota philosophy, the phrase "mitakuye oyasin" emphasizes that we are all related. The well-being of one group of people necessarily influences the well-being of others. The Medicine Wheel of the Anishnawbe teaches us that all people from the four directions are needed in order to maintain a world that is in balance. Hopi teachings say that their people must continue their cere-monies or the world will end. They pray for the well-being of all of us. While Indigenous peoples see themselves as members of their own communities and citizens of their own Nations, they also see themselves as members of the world community.

Taking a stand to promote Indigenous world views can happen in many ways and in many spaces, from the social work classroom, to demanding the return of cultural objects to their original communities, to adopting Indigen-ous helping practices and learning about oneself. Social work and the world at large need a movement toward a global dialogue in which all world views have an equal place, but this will not happen as long as we stay centred on theoretical models and analysis. Moving into action requires a revolutionary transformation in how we teach and practise social work and other forms of helping. Educators in the helping professions, in particular, have the power and privilege to be inclusive of all world views. And it is educators who change the practice of our professions in communities. This change process can be seen in the social work field as a move toward anti-oppressive practice. Furthermore, it is educators who prepare learners to work in the field, so we have endless opportunities to create spaces where inclusiveness is honoured.

Learners need to be encouraged to challenge educators about what they are teaching. Learners need to safely take the risk of challenging educators if they do not see the world views of their communities reflected in their education. If educators are open to listening, and if learners know they can contribute to the education process through respectful challenges, then genuine conversations can occur that can potentially lead to action and transformation.

I am reminded of the recent movements of Doctors without Borders and Dentists without Borders and "a beyond boundaries approach ... using multiple perspectives and practices ... to work with those who walk between worlds" (Marais & Marais, 2007, p. 819). I would say that not only Indigenous peoples, but also many populations across the planet walk between worlds. Thus, how well social work and other helping professions do in the future may well depend on the ability of service providers to walk between worlds.

Both Indigenous and non-Indigenous peoples can also take an action-oriented stand when it comes to land claims, Indigenous peoples' rights, and the reclamation of cultural objects that do not belong in museums. It can be incredibly painful for Indigenous peoples to see their sacred, spiritual, and cultural objects such as eagle staffs, pipes, and scrolls displayed in museums. What is particularly difficult about this situation is that White people and tourists have access to these objects, but Indigenous peoples do not. Referred to as "artifacts" by the West, Indigenous cultural objects are collected and housed in museums in order "to preserve Native heritages" (West, 1995, p. 284). Although some anthropologists advocate that Indigenous peoples should be involved in the extraction and review of their own cultural objects, others continue to insist that these objects should not be returned to Indigenous peoples unless the rightful owners have the proper facilities to keep them safe (West, 1995). According to one source, "returning collections to communities that have no resources or commitment to care for them, for the sake of political appeasement, is unacceptable" (Janes & Arnoldas as cited in West, 1995, p. 284).

Such statements are not only insulting, they are illogical. How can it be that archaeologists and museologists acknowledge a need to be educated by Indigenous peoples in the practice of their professions, but still insist that cultural objects that belong to Indigenous peoples must remain within the formal structures of these professions? I call this exploitation and, of course, a misuse of power. Indigenous and non-Indigenous peoples are called upon to question this present-day form of colonization and work toward its eradication. If, for example, communities do not have the resources to safely care for their cultural objects, then the money spent on caring for these objects in museums can be transferred to those communities. I encourage readers to have this discussion.

All of us can also take a stand when it comes to poisoning the Earth and the people who live on her. As Derek Rasmussen (2001), who is a non-Indigenous policy adviser to Nunavut Tunnagavick Inc., which is a land claims organization, writes, "Nunavut's and the US's communities are tied together by the US's invisible exhalation of death. The US breathes out, Inuit die" (p. 113). According to Rasmussen (2001), dioxin from incinerators and iron-smelting plants rise with warm air, but fall with cold temperatures when they reach the far North. Since it is too cold for them to evaporate, they settle and are absorbed by lichen, which are eaten by caribou, which, in turn, are then eaten by Inuit.

Rasmussen (2001) has a humorous yet serious suggestion on what can be done to learn about these situations first-hand:

> Go on a field trip to Alpena, Michigan or Hartford, Illinois. Figure out how to clean it up, slow it down, stop it. It's the Euro-American way of life that needs to be put under the microscope, not intriguing tribes in faraway lands. Instead of exotic slide shows on the Arctic, how about US Schools exotic field trips to the municipal incinerators in Bethlehem Steel and US Steel's iron-smelting plants in Chesterton and Gary, Indiana? (p. 113)

The message to the U.S. is clear: learn about the self and about what is happening around you, which includes learning about those of us who are living just to the North, in Canada. Then take action in the form of teachings, such as those offered through Buddhism, which have existed for about 2,500 years: "First, cease to do evil; then learn to do good" (Rasmussen, 2001, p. 113). North America uses 80 percent of the world's resources and takes resources from many other parts of the world with little regard for the people who are often forced to give up these resources. Since a North American way of life is the cause of the majority of the world's problems, North Americans need to address this life of excess and move toward change (Rasmussen, 2001). As sociologist Robert R. Paine wrote in 1977 in what he considered his most important message to White people, drop the illusion that you are "in the Arctic to teach the Inuit" and instead focus on "learning about white behaviour" (p. xii as cited in Rasmussen, 2001, p.113).

Rasmussen (2001) builds on Paine's suggestion, by stating that for those who want to live harmoniously with others on the planet, it is necessary to become deeply aware of what has formed one's present-day culture. This author advises people living in North America to let go of their belief in cultural superiority, to stop forcing their values and lifestyles on every civilization in the name of progress, and to stop the delusion that materialism and individualism equal happiness (Rasmussen, 2001). In coming to understand themselves, North Americans "must cease to do evil. Only then, with full awareness of the assumptions and values that we carry with us as Euro-Americans, can we have the clarity, wisdom, and insight to learn to do good" (Rasmussen, 2001, p. 114).

CONCLUSION

This chapter has shown how Indigenous peoples across the globe are connected through their world views, their history of colonization, and their hopes for the future. Throughout the world, Indigenous peoples and their allies are taking political and cultural stands, as well as building social movements. There are now some allies who are publishing strong messages that Indigenous world views and rights need to be privileged in order to begin healing the Earth. Others write about the urgent need for non-Indigenous peoples to closely examine their values and lifestyles to learn how to do good in the world.

All of these messages are particularly significant for those involved in the social work profession. We are now learning how not to perpetuate evil, as evidenced in the rise in anti-oppression education and practice and the rise of values of self-determination and social justice. The question still remains: How exactly will we implement these values to do good in the world? There are endless possibilities and opportunities awaiting us if we listen and become informed by Indigenous knowledges, which is the overall message of this book.

REFERENCES

Baskin, C. (2008). Indigenous youth exploring identities through food security in Canada and Brazil. *Maori and Indigenous Peoples Review, 3*(5), 1–11. Retrieved from http://ojs.review.mai.ac.nz

Battiste, M. (2000). *Reclaiming Indigenous voice and vision.* Vancouver: UBC Press.

Davis, A.Y. (1974). *With my mind on freedom: An autobiography.* New York: Bantam.

Dei, G.J.S. (2000). African development: The relevance and implications of "Indigenousness." In G. Dei, B. Hall & D. Rosenburg (Eds.), *Indigenous knowledges in global contexts: Multiple readings of our world* (pp. 70–86). Toronto: University of Toronto Press.

Ernst, J. (2001). Culture and child welfare: Insights from New Zealand. *International Social Work, 44*(2), 163–178. doi: 10.1177/002087280104400203

Fitznor, L. (1998). The circle of life: Affirming Aboriginal philosophies in everyday living. In G. Dei, B.L. Hall & D. Rosenberg (Eds.), *Life ethics in world religions* (pp. 21–40). Toronto: Canadian Scholars' Press Inc.

Garrett, M., Brubaker, M., Torres-Rivera, E., West-Olatunji, C. & Conwill, W.L. (2008). The medicine of coming to center: Use of the Native American centering technique—Ayeli—to promote wellness and healing in group work. *The Journal for Specialists in Group Work, 33*(2), 179–198. doi:10.1080/01933920801977322

Gray, M., Coates, J. & Hetherington, T. (2007). Hearing Indigenous voices in mainstream social work. *Families in Society, 88*(1), 55–66. doi: 10.1606/1044-3894.3592

Hart, M. A. (2002). Seeking mino-pimatisiwin: An Aboriginal approach to helping. Halifax: Fernwood Publishing

Hicks, C.J.B. & Somby, A. (2005). Sami responses to poverty in the Nordic countries. In R. Eversole, J. McNeish & A.D. Cimadamore (Eds.), *Indigenous peoples and poverty: An international perspective* (pp. 275–289). London: Zed Books Ltd.

Holmes, L. (2000). Heart knowledge, blood memory, and the voice of the land: Implications of research among Hawaiian Elders. In G. Dei, B. Hall & D. Rosenburg (Eds.), *Indigenous knowledges in global contexts: Multiple readings of our world* (pp. 37–53). Toronto: University of Toronto Press.

hooks, b. (1984). *From margin to centre.* Boston: South End Press.

Kabat-Zinn, J. (2005). *Full catastrophe living: Using the wisdom of your body and mind to face stress, pain, and illness.* New York: Bantam Dell.

Ling, H.K. (2003). Drawing lessons from locally designated helpers to develop culturally appropriate social work practice. *Asia Pacific Journal of Social Work, 13*(2), 26–45.

Marais, L. & Marais, L.C. (2007). Walking between worlds: An exploration of the interface between Indigenous and first-world industrialized culture. *International Social Work, 50*(6), 809–820. doi: 10.1177/0020872807081920

Mazama, M.A. (2002). Afrocentricity and African spirituality. *Journal of Black Studies, 33*(2), 218–234. Retrieved from http://www.jstor.org

Nagpaul, H. (1993). Analysis of social work teaching materials in India: The need for Indigenous foundations. *International Social Work, 36*, 207–220 doi:10.1177/002087289303600303

Odora Hoppers, C.A. (2002) Indigenous knowledge and the integration of knowledge systems: Towards a conceptual and methodological framework. In C.A. Odora Hoppers (Ed.), *Indigenous knowledge and the integration of knowledge systems: Towards a philosophy of articulation* (pp. 2–22). Claremont: New Africa Books.

Palmer, D., Watson, J., Watson, A., Ljubic, P., Wallace-Smith, H. & Johnson, M. (2006). "Going back to country with bosses": The Yiriman project, youth participation, and walking along with Elders. *Children, Youth, and Environments, 16*(2), 316–337.

Porsanger, J. (2004). *An essay about Indigenous methodology.* Retrieved from http://www.ub.uit.no

Rasmussen, D. (2001). Qallunology: A pedagogy for the oppressor. *Canadian Journal of Native Education, 25*(2), 105–116.

Schaefer, C. (2006). *Grandmothers counsel the world: Women Elders offer their vision for our planet.* Boston: Trumpeter Books.

Schiff, J.W. & Moore, K. (2006). The impact of the sweat lodge ceremony on dimensions of well-being. *American Indian and Alaska Native Mental Health Research: The Journal of the National Centre, 13*(3), 48–69.

Steinhauer, E. (2002). Thoughts on an Indigenous methodology. *Canadian Journal of Native Education, 26*(2), 69–81.

Stiegelbauer, S.M. (1996). What is an Elder? What do Elders do?: First Nation Elders as teachers in culture-based urban organizations. *The Canadian Journal of Native Studies, 16*(1), 37–66.

Wane, N.N. (2000). Indigenous knowledge: Lessons from the Elders—a Kenyan case study. In G. Dei, B. Hall & D. Rosenburg (Eds.), *Indigenous knowledges in global contexts: Multiple readings of our world* (pp. 54–69). Toronto: University of Toronto Press.

West, D.A. (1995). Epistemological dependency and Native peoples: An essay on the future of Native/non-Native relations in Canada. *The Canadian Journal of Native Studies, 15*, 279–291.

Chapter 14
The End of the World as We Know It

INTRODUCTION

As I began the final chapter of this book, I found myself thinking that writing this book was much more like a beginning than an ending. My hope is that some readers will see the messages in these pages as a beginning, a way to begin incorporating Indigenous world views into their work and lives in ways that lead to action. I've learned so much in the writing of this book, thanks to all the brilliant scholars who have published their work and the gifted people who shared their stories with me. I stand firm in the knowledge that Indigenous peoples around the globe can make our world a much better place, not only in social work, but in other helping work as well. I encourage all the magnificent academic warriors who are coming up to continue the journey that has been started. I pass the teachings on to you with the wish that you make these teachings stronger and pass them on to as many of the world's people as possible. I just have a few more things to say.

STAYING CURRENT

What I have written about in this book is not new knowledge, although I'm certain that some readers will receive it as such. However, most of what is written in this book is ancient knowledge that can be applied to our current time. Consider medicines as an example. Many of the early colonists benefited from and survived diseases due to the generosity of Indigenous peoples who shared their medicines with them (Mancini, 2004 as cited in Portman & Garrett, 2006). Clearly, these healing practices were successful in treating people during this time.

Subsequently, Indigenous medicines were shunned as inferior to those of European medicines. However, due to socio-economic necessity near the beginning of the 19th century, Indigenous medicines were taken up again. A significant example of this phenomenon was during the Revolutionary War and the War of 1812 between England and what became the United States. During these wars, it became very difficult to access European medicines and doctors as ships were limited in their ability to transport goods and people to Turtle Island (Mancini, 2004 as cited in Portman & Garrett, 2006). Hence, attitudes toward Indigenous medicines and helpers shifted again. Mancini (2004, as cited in Portman & Garrett, 2006) reported

... documentation of Indigenous medicines over a 200-year time period in three Indigenous communities in the United States shows that Indigenous healing practices that implemented the same medicinal plants prevailed over time, thereby "leaving a healing thread across two centuries" (Portman & Garrett, 2006, p. 454). It is no wonder, then, that Indigenous medicines have greatly influenced current medical and naturopathic medicine, and that some people believe that "cures" for modern illnesses may be found within Indigenous healing practices. Thus, staying current means remembering the past, acknowledging where knowledges originated, and listening to Indigenous peoples as they may have the key to saving Westerners once again.

Another area in which social work education and practice can stay current is how we view oppression. It seems as though social work sees two groups of people: those who dominate (the oppressors) and those who are dominated (the oppressed or victims). But these are not the only two possible roles that people can have. There is a continuum of power and privileges at one end of the spectrum and of oppressions at the other end. The majority of us live somewhere along that continuum. Power is neither good nor bad, and there are many kinds of power. Social work might want to consider assisting both learners and practitioners to tap into their own personal power and use it to make positive change. As much as awareness is necessary, I don't think it is either healthy or helpful to stay stuck in critiques of the system without assisting those in our classrooms to take action in initiating change and healing. It is time for us to stop merely talking about what's wrong and start doing something to make it right. As educators in particular, we need to constantly keep in mind that academic discourse on its own will do little to improve the well-being of the families and communities that we seek to assist and are supposed to be accountable to.

A POST-COLONIAL OR ANTI-COLONIAL LENS

One of the ways in which social work education can stay current is by incorporating post-colonial theory into its curriculum. According to Innu social work educator Gail Baikie (2009), "post colonial thought ... raises the possibility of creatively drawing upon the knowledge from diverse cultures (including the diversity of Indigenous cultures) or creating new Indigenous knowledge applicable to contemporary social challenges" (p. 56). Although I would refer to "world views" rather than "cultures," I agree that post-colonial theory offers the potential for creativity with regard to putting Indigenous knowledges into practice for the benefit of all.

First, I must be clear that the term "post-colonial" is not meant to refer to a time period that is after colonization since many forms of colonization continue today. Rather, post-colonial theory offers a framework whereby those who have been colonized have a theoretical base for their discourses and knowledge (Ashcraft, 2001). Despite the perception that post-colonial theory is a relatively new framework, it has, in fact, been in existence since colonization began. This is because Indigenous peoples around the world have always resisted colonization and have also survived (Ashcraft, 2001). Post-colonial theory provides a language and ideas that help to explain the common experiences of Indigenous peoples globally (Ashcroft, 2001; Battiste, 2004; Gandhi, 1998; Loomba, 1998).

One of the ways in which post-colonial theory is promising is that it counters what Western authors have written about Indigenous peoples, and examines the relationships between those who are colonized and those who are the colonizers (Ashcroft, 2001; Battiste, 2004; Gandhi, 1998; Loomba, 1998). A focus on relationships is critical if we are to make positive changes between the present-day descendants of the colonized and the colonizers. Positive changes equal decolonization, which, in large part, must focus on relationships. Within social work education, post-colonial theory is a way in which Indigenous authors can be brought out from the margins into the centre of academic discourses. However, proponents of Eurocentric theories are cautioned not to co-opt a post-colonial lens in order to claim it as their own. This would simply be another form of appropriation.

An Indigenous post-colonial lens offers a way in which social work academia can examine its curriculum and suggests ways in which Indigenous world views can inform current social work discourses. This lens also offers an analysis of what is not included in social work curriculum. A groundbreaking thesis dissertation by Andrea Tamburro (2010), of the Piqua Shawnee Tribe, examines the Canadian Association for Social Work Education policy (CASWE) on Indigenous content in social work curriculum. Tamburro (2010) not only discussed what is included in this policy, but also shines a light on what is missing:

> A post-colonial examination of the CASWE policy on Aboriginal content shows that the policy did not include several themes that were included in the literature. These themes include history from Aboriginal perspectives, Indigenous worldviews, and current issues foregrounding the effects of colonization. This ahistorical approach to Aboriginal content is an important omission from the CASWE Accreditation Standard SB 5.10.13. Omitted from the policy was the need to decolonize social work practice with Indigenous-centric content and a post-colonial theoretical or anti-colonial approach. (p. 276)

Tamburro's work offers clear directions on how the CASWE can increase its relevance when it comes to addressing Indigenous content in social work education. Dr. Tamburro (2010) also raises the important issue of decolonization, which can only be achieved if Indigenous and non-Indigenous peoples work together:

> In order to create a Canadian society that is equitable, fair, and just, the Indigenous people of this land, the colonizers and their descendents, must work together to find solutions to decolonize society and to address the inequities that were created by colonization. Post-colonial writers provide useful insights on how to create social justice because they also struggle with these issues. They ask questions useful to Aboriginal peoples in Canada. For example, what is the importance of identity and nationhood in global awareness of our world? Post-colonial writers also explore ways that people who have been colonized re-member their history and reclaim their self-determination. They also explore how decolonization happens within communities. Post-colonial writers also explore ways in which cultures recover and re-form after being colonized. ... Post-colonial theory addresses the transformation of the people who have been colonized and also provides insights into ending oppression for those who were or are oppressive, calling into question those who have a privileged place in society today (Gandhi, 1998; Loomba, 1998; Moore-Gilbert, 1997, pp. 77–78).

Thus, post-colonial writers examine the issues of colonization, exploitation, resistance, healing, and transformation, all of which are critical to the work of decolonization.

Tamburro (2010) discusses how post-colonial theory can assist non-Indigenous social workers through the teaching of values, knowledge, and skills, so that they can become allies and develop partnerships with Indigenous communities. Post-colonial writers identify strategies for decolonization, while Indigenous social workers can provide leadership and guidance in this area. Post-colonial writers emphasize the significance of Indigenous peoples remembering and speaking about their histories and present-day situations, and of the importance of non-Indigenous peoples listening to these stories. Also important is that post-colonial theory urges social workers to support Indigenous peoples' self-determination and self-governance, and that Indigenous peoples must be able to determine their own solutions and processes of decolonization and healing. Of course, as Tamburro (2010) reminds us, solutions will vary based on the history, current issues, and specific circumstances of each individual community.

Tamburro's (2010) work also provides concrete ways in which social work educators can examine their curriculum for what is and is not included with regard to Indigenous content. Tamburro (2010) suggests that educators first consult with Indigenous communities, organizations, and agencies to define which topics are relevant to cover in their curriculum. Next, educators can review their course outlines to identify how the topics are addressed and if the resources that are used are current and accurate. Program documents, such as mission statements, program descriptions, and goals, can also be reviewed based on the identified topics.

Educators can compare their program's course outlines to reveal which courses address which topics, and decide where expansion and clarity are needed. Through this process, they can also identify which topics are missing and decide which courses would be best to take up those topics. Educators may need to conduct literature reviews in order to locate relevant writing by Indigenous peoples that can be included in their courses. Educators can also look to videos and guest speakers as resources for topics. However, they must ensure that guest speakers are compensated for sharing their knowledge. As Tamburro (2010) states, "this process provides an excellent opportunity for faculty to engage in this meaningful analysis of their curriculum" (p. 322).

By incorporating curriculum that includes Indigenous content, educators can better prepare learners to join with Indigenous peoples in co-creating effective and relevant social services for both Indigenous and non-Indigenous communities and agencies that centre decolonization and healing. From a post-colonial standpoint, this process can encourage educators to see beyond critical theory, and take in a much broader picture that focuses on Indigenous peoples' resistance and strengths (Tamburro, 2010). Hence, identifying a social work program's strengths and gaps provides the potential for further inclusion of Indigenous world views along with local, national, and international community-based content within social work curriculum (Tamburro, 2010).

OUR MOTHER IS COUNTING ON US

It would appear that some of us Indigenous scholars think alike. Anishnawbe scholar Deborah McGregor (2009) recently shared her wisdom in an interview for *First Nations House Magazine* called "Can Indigenous Education Save the World?" McGregor recounts that Indigenous peoples have been making their position known about the interconnectedness of all creation for many years. She notes, for example, that the National Indian Brotherhood (now the Assembly of First Nations) wrote in 1972 that the survival of our Earth in the 20th century means that people must live in harmony with nature in order to preserve the balance between people and the environment (McGregor, 2009).

McGregor (2009) emphasizes the importance of finding appropriate ways to share Indigenous world views with all peoples across the globe. She asks: "Given that such sharing is already beginning to take place, what might Indigenous education mean in relation to the environmental crisis facing the planet [today]?" (p. 17).

In answering this question, McGregor (2009) reminds us that Indigenous creation stories provide instructions about how to live harmoniously with all beings, and that such teachings were passed on for generations from the beginning of time to the present day. McGregor (2009) also points out that the responsibilities that come through Indigenous education are necessary in order to ensure that creation continues. Today, these teachings are referred to as "traditional knowledge" (TK) and are becoming important to what environmentalists and scientists are now calling "sustainability." According to McGregor (2009), there is an interest throughout the world in learning more about traditional knowledges in order to use them to address the planet's current environmental crisis.

McGregor (2009) beautifully connects some of the teachings of the Anishnawbe creation story to our current environmental challenges:

> Key principles that emerge from the Anishinawbe Re-Creation Story for example, are that: "everything is important," "all beings in Creation have a role," " cooperation and co-existence will lead to survival," "everything is connected to everything else," and "all life must be respected." Principles such as these, adhered to not only in ceremony but in everyday living, ensured that Indigenous peoples lived harmoniously and in balance with the rest of Creation. Today these principles can also be thought of as vital principles in ecological science. For example, we now know that industrial activities in one part of the world affect people and the environment in another—climate change being the currently most well-known example. One can't help but feel that today's world might have been a "greener" place

had colonial societies paid heed to at least some of these Aboriginal examples of ecological thinking. Given that we are where we are, however, it seems that now more than ever the principles and values that inform traditional knowledge are needed. (p. 18)

I could not agree more.

Two questions arise out of McGregor's interview: What are appropriate ways to share traditional knowledges? How do we ensure that such knowledges are used in the ways that they were intended? To answer such questions, I turn to the Elders and Traditional Teachers who shared their wisdom with me for this book.

Dan Smoke (Seneca Nation) and Mary Lou Smoke (Anishnawbe Nation) have been a couple since the 1970s. Today, they share their teachings and conduct ceremonies in Canada and the United States. They also teach courses in the Department of Journalism at the University of Western Ontario in London, Ontario. Mary Lou explains how she and Dan share their knowledge:

We teach Aboriginal and non-Aboriginal students. This provides opportunities for all students to gain an appreciation of what we have been taught. Students can believe or not, accept or not. Our approach is non-threatening, not intended to evoke guilt in students.

We believe it is important for us to share Aboriginal world views as we see that all people can be a part of these. We believe that we are to teach the foundations of Aboriginal world views to all people because we know that these foundations are similar for all peoples of the world.

We believe that Aboriginal ways can help others to heal. We put non-Aboriginal people in touch with Elders and Traditional Teachers who include non-Aboriginal people in their circles and ceremonies.

We stress that Aboriginal people are meant to share the gifts that have been given to us by the Creator. Aboriginal people have always shared what they had, which is what they did when non-Aboriginal people first came to Turtle Island.

Students tell us that prior to taking classes with us, they were searching so much for instant gratification, but afterwards they feel more human, they have been changed. (M.L. Smoke, personal communication, February 20, 2009)

Dan added:

> People from all over the world and their knowledge need to come together
> in order for there to be the best of anything. Many people are looking for
> serenity and they do not want to be negative, so they are drawn to Abo-
> riginal world views. However, it is important for everyone to understand
> that this place—Turtle Island—is the Mother of the original peoples who
> were placed here by the Creator. People of European and other descent
> have their own Mother in their places of origin. Their journey is to go
> look for their roots, beliefs and cultures. This will help to ensure that
> appropriation of Aboriginal teachings does not happen. (D. Smoke, per-
> sonal communication, February 20, 2009)

Mary Lou agrees with Dan about appropriation, stating:

> We as Aboriginal peoples need to decide what to share and what not to
> share based on our intuition or what spirit shows or tells us to share.
> I share knowledge with others for their personal growth, but I caution
> them "I don't want to see a sign on your front lawn saying 'ceremonies for
> sale.'" (M. L. Smoke, personal communication, February 20, 2009)

Grafton Antone is Oneida from Oneida of the Thames First Nation. He is
the Elder in Residence at the University of Toronto's First Nations House and
teaches the Oneida language in this university's Aboriginal Studies Program.
Both he and his partner, Eileen, who first appeared in Chapter 7, are respected
Elders who conduct teachings and ceremonies and sit on many committees in
the Toronto area.

Grafton has encouraging words about sharing Indigenous knowledges:

> We as Aboriginal people are Indigenizing the country. We need to teach
> and coach others. They need to listen as we speak out. We're at the [table
> of the] United Nations now, so our problems have been heard, but now
> we need to state our positions, say what we value, talk to others about
> worldviews. People need to stand with their hands open to receive our
> teachings. They may be ready now. (G. Antone, personal communica-
> tion, July 10, 2009)

Eileen offers words of grounding and simplicity for sharing knowledges:

> All my relations means that everything and everyone is included. In an individualistic society, people don't talk about being related to other people and everything else around them, but they are. It can be difficult for Aboriginal peoples to put into language what all these relationships mean. Modern language as expressed in English makes it seem like it's new information, but none of it is. It's ancient knowledge, not new concepts or ideas. (E. Antone, personal communication, July 10, 2009)

Joanne Dallaire, who also appeared earlier, also has words of encouragement that fit perfectly with what the other Elders shared with me:

> A holistic approach is for all people: how can anyone not acknowledge all aspects of a person? These are human issues as everyone knows what it is to feel pain, for example. Creator gave teachings and medicines to all people of the world—just not exactly the same ones. It is no mistake that North America is a place made up of people from everywhere. All people came from living on the land that is now North America. This is a continent built on survivors as all of them came from persecution of some sort.
>
> It's healthy to come together to learn from each other, educate ourselves about other peoples' experiences. Coming together is not a compromise of self, but rather about a common humanity and finding common ground. (J. Dallaire, personal communication, July 23, 2009)

Jacqui Lavalley is very direct about her understanding of the teachings she has been given in terms of the spirit, which exists in all of us. She states:

> It doesn't matter to the spirits about the colour of one's skin. [When we pray or conduct ceremonies], we call out to wise old ones who sit in the four directions, asking them to enter our minds, bodies and hearts. (J. Lavalley, personal communication, June 22, 2009)

Jacqui's statement relates to some of the teachings from Elders that talk about the four directions. Carol Schaefer (2006) has published a beautiful collection of female Elders' teachings about how Indigenous knowledges can heal the world. Thirteen Grandmothers from the Arctic, North, South and

Central America, Africa, Tibet, and Nepal came together to speak about "ways of bringing about sustainability, sovereignty, and a united alliance among all the Earth's people" (Schaefer, 2006, p. 8). These Grandmothers are following a Hopi prophecy that states that people from the four directions must come together before there can be peace on the Earth. They are fulfilling this prophecy by coming together with their teachings and healing methods for the first time in history, in order to find ways of creating a better world (Schaefer, 2006). These Grandmothers have also met with Western women Elders as they know this connection is vital for the future of the Earth. Their humility, generosity, and love for all of humanity is expressed by Schaefer (2006), who writes: "prophecy revealed to each one that they must now share even their most secret and sacred ways with the very people who have been their oppressors, as the survival of humanity, if not the entire planet, is at stake" (p. 4).

The 13 Grandmothers know that the world as we know it is coming to an end. The Mayan people have told us that 2012 will mark the beginning of this end. However, dire prophesies are fulfilled only when people refuse to make changes. We still have choices. Many Indigenous Nations of the world have had prophecies about environmental changes such as global warming, changes in the weather, disease, and the hole in the ozone layer, which the Hopi call "the hole in our lodging" (Schaefer, 2006, p. 119). These are prophesies that have all been realized. Why would we not believe that this latest one that speaks of the destruction of the Earth will not happen as well?

Omyene Grandmother Bernadette Rebienot, of Gabon, Africa, explains why the Earth is in such turmoil. She states that because male energies across the world are in control, power cannot be balanced because women's power is undermined and women's wisdom and access to feminine energy are often cut off (Schaefer, 2006). Everything in the world, including politics and consciousness, is connected. The Grandmothers are certain that women will show us a different way of being in this world.

This group of women Elders encourages all of us to do our personal healing as this is a necessary first step to healing the world. These Elders emphasize that people need to resolve the conflicts they have within themselves in order to see how we unconsciously create damage to our world. Healing and resolving conflicts are a part of what social work does, so we can see how we—as social work educators, learners, and practitioners—can act on the teachings of these Elders.

The Grandmothers also speak about forgiveness, releasing the past, and letting go of judgments. Yupik Elder Rita Pitka Blumenstien, of Alaska, tells us that when we do this, "we give ourselves permission to define ourselves, rather than being defined by others or past events. We are free to become who we are" (as cited in Schaefer, 2006, p. 142). Release such as this is part of the healing process that social workers can be a part of.

The Grandmothers tell us that it is women's wisdom that will save the world. Women need to build alliances and share their wisdom. When women come together in circles, they can awaken the wisdom in each other's hearts and spirits. This hope is expressed by Grandmother Agnes Baker Pilgrim, of the Takelma Siletz Nation in Oregon:

> It is my hope that the Grandmothers' Council will have a mushroom effect throughout the world. That women will start circling up, come together, and bond together, to help one another to be better and stand tall with their voices, to say they've had enough of oppression. It is my hope that they will form matriarchal bridges with each other and be a voice again for our Mother Earth and Her children. (Schaefer, 2006, p. 143)

WHAT IF ...

... there had been a partnership rather than colonization between Indigenous peoples and settler societies? Some of my Haudenosaunee Elders and friends tell me there was a partnership at one time between their ancestors and the settlers. This partnership is represented by the Two-Row Wampum, which still exists today (Antone, 2005; J. Bomberry, personal communication, April 6, 2009; A. Jock, personal communication, August 7, 1986). Historically, wampum belts were used to communicate and seal agreements or treaties. Those historical wampum belts continue to represent such agreements. In addition, today these belts are teaching tools used to pass on history and traditional teachings.

The Two-Row Wampum has two rows of purple shells or beads that run along the two edges of a belt. There is a white row of shells that separates the two purple rows. One purple row represents the Haudenosaunee, while the other represents the settlers. The row between the two represents the river that divides them. The Two-Row Wampum represented the agreement between the two groups that they would both live on Turtle Island, but would be separate from one another. Each would retain its own world views, languages, and processes of government and not interfere with the other. Needless to say, the settler society did not live up to its part of the agreement. But what if they had?

When I envision a partnership between the Indigenous peoples of Turtle Island and the settler society, it is somewhat different from the one depicted in the Two-Row Wampum. I wholeheartedly support the idea of non-interference, meaning that there should be no religious or any other interference on the part of the settlers. But it saddens me to think that both groups are supposed to live separately forever. I picture more of an interconnected relationship, a sharing of knowledges, a discovering of commonalities, and a desire to reach consensus when it came to differences. Each group could take up whatever they saw as valuable from each other's values and ways of doing things, and be able to blend what might be equally beneficial for all.

I envision the newcomers as settlers and not colonists, people who did not see themselves as superior to anyone or anything else, and who are ever appreciative of the generosity of the original peoples of Turtle Island. Out of both respect and common sense, the newcomers would have relied on the teachings of the Indigenous peoples, not only to survive in the harsh environmental conditions in this part of the world, but they would also have learned how to live in harmony with the environment.

Since the settlers left their original territories in search of a better life for themselves and their families, I picture them doing just that, leaving behind the systems and beliefs that oppressed them and listening to the teachings of the Indigenous peoples. These teachings would include values based on egalitarianism, sharing, respect for all life, and an understanding that all people are valuable and have much to offer. Now imagine what such a place might look like today.

Over the years that I have been privileged to learn about traditional knowledges and teachings from many Elders and Traditional Teachers, there have been a few times when I've been briefly told about a future prophecy. This future prophecy is an extension of the Seven Fires Prophecies, which tell about the time of creation, European contact, colonization and its impacts, and present-day healing, which is the time of the Seventh Fire (E. Benton-Banai, personal communication, 1982; J. Dumont, personal communication, 1983; G. Kidd, personal communication, 1982; E. Manitowabi, personal communication, 1984).

According to the Elders who speak of an Eighth Fire, this Eighth Fire will occur at an unknown time in the future once the healing of Indigenous peoples is complete. This Eighth Fire will occur when the non-Indigenous peoples of the world turn to Indigenous peoples for help and healing (E. Benton-Banai, personal communication, 1982; J. Dumont, personal communication, 1982; G. Kidd, personal communication, 1982; E. Manitowabi, personal communication, 1984). I sometimes catch glimpses of this future time in the present as seen throughout this book. In addition, Elder Jacqui Lavalley spoke to me about her interpretations of the teachings of the prophecies of the Eighth Fire:

> Within Anishnawbe teachings, there are prophesies which are explained as fires, which were brought to the people by certain grandfathers and grandmothers a long time ago. Up until 10 years ago, I was always told by my teachers that there were teachings that were to be kept to ourselves as Aboriginal people. Yet, I was raised to share everything so I always wondered about this, and so struggled with what to share and not to share.
>
> More recently, some of the old people have told me that we are in the eighth fire and we don't need to worry about others abusing our knowledges any longer. Rather we need to share our knowledges with others. We need to give the teachings over to others. Some of our foundational principles within our world views tell us not to be judgemental and to understand that everyone has the right to learn about Indigenous world views.
>
> I believe strongly that we're in the eighth fire now and I no longer struggle with what to share and not to share. (J. Lavalley, personal communication, June, 29, 2009)

To me, this seems like the final piece of an entire journey around the circle of history. The future will be a return to the past, to the first contact with Indigenous and European peoples, when the latter required the assistance of the former to survive. At the time, my ancestors chose to help the European peoples, but will the future generation of Indigenous peoples make the same choice?

I suspect the pleas for help will likely focus on the survival of our planet. I cannot say for sure, but I do know that our Mother is watching and counting on us. I also know for sure that another, better world is possible if we all choose to transform it together.

CONCLUSION

As I finish writing this book, I am reminded of Elder Grafton Antone's words to me when I first told him what I was writing about. He said I was "creating a new song for the people" (G. Antone, personal communication, July 10, 2009). Writing this book has certainly been a creative endeavour. But as I think back over the experience, it feels more like a meditation or a prayer for the world. However, singing, meditating, and praying are all connected, as each is a spiritual activity.

I feel both humbled and affirmed by what I was able to learn while writing this book. I was humbled by the messages that I need to put aside ego and begin to forgive. I was affirmed in that I believe I am on the right journey in my desire to teach social work in the ways that I do. I know that my work of bringing Indigenous and non-Indigenous learners together and sharing the teachings that have been passed on to me is the absolute right thing to do.

The profession of social work has great potential for helping and healing the world and for being a positive force in helping to create change for the better. It is my hope that all of us will be able to come together to share our knowledges and experiences, and that Indigenous world views and teachings will no longer be left out of the world's discourses. Social work educators, learners, and practitioners can, like the Council of the 13 Grandmothers, change the world.

All my relations.

Thank you for listening.

Now, connect with your inner self and go out into the world and do some good, please!

REFERENCES

Antone, E. (2005). *Reconciling Aboriginal and non-Aboriginal perspectives in Aboriginal literacy practice*. Retrieved from http://www.cst.ed.ac.uk

Ashcroft, B. (2001). *Post-colonial transformations*. London: Routledge.

Baikie, G. (2009). Indigenous-centred social work: Theorizing a social work way-of-being. In R. Sinclair, M.A. Hart & G. Bruyere (Eds.), *Wicihitowin: Aboriginal social work in Canada* (pp. 42–61). Winnipeg: Fernwood Publishing.

Battiste, M. (2004). *Animating site of post-colonial education: Indigenous knowledge and the humanities*. Paper presented at the Canadian Society for Studies in Education, Winnipeg, Manitoba. Retrieved from http://www.usask.ca/education

Gandhi, L. (1998). *Postcolonial theory: A critical introduction*. New York: Columbia University Press.

Gosine, K. (2000). Essentialism versus complexity: Conceptions of racial identity construction in education scholarship. *Canadian Journal of Education, 27*(1), 81–99. Retrieved from http://www.jstor.org

Hall, S. (1989). Cultural identity and cinematic representation. *Framework, 36*, 69–81.

Loomba, A. (1998). *Colonialism/Postcolonialism*. New York: Routledge.

McGregor, D. (2009). Can Indigenous education save the world? *First Nations House Magazine, 1*, 17–19.

Portman, T.A.A. & Garrett, M.T. (2006). Native American healing traditions. *International Journal of Disability, Development, and Education, 53*(4), 453–469. doi: 10.1080/10349120601008647.

Schaefer, C. (2006). *Grandmothers counsel the world: Women Elders offer their wisdom for our planet*. Boston: Trumpeter Books.

Tamburro, A. (2010). *A framework and tool for assessing Indigenous content in Canadian social work curricula*. Unpublished doctoral dissertation, Simon Fraser University, Surrey, B.C.

Weber-Pillwax, C. (2001). What is Indigenous research? *Canadian Journal of Native Education, 25*(2), 166–174.

Yon, D. (2000). *Elusive culture: Schooling, race, and identity in global times*. New York: State University of New York Press.